Creative Projects for Rust Programmers

Build exciting projects on domains such as web apps,
WebAssembly, games, and parsing

Carlo Milanesi

BIRMINGHAM - MUMBAI

Creative Projects for Rust Programmers

Commissioning Editor: Richa Tripathi
Acquisition Editor: Denim Pinto
Content Development Editor: Ruvika Rao
Senior Editor: Afshaan Khan
Technical Editor: Pradeep Sahu
Copy Editor: Safis Editing
Project Coordinator: Francy Puthiry
Proofreader: Safis Editing
Indexer: Manju Arasan
Production Designer: Nilesh Mohite

First published: June 2020

Production reference: 1180620

Published by Packt Publishing Ltd.
Livery Place
35 Livery Street
Birmingham
B3 2PB, UK.

ISBN 978-1-78934-622-0

www.packt.com

To my mother, Anna Mazza, and to the memory of my father, Pietro,
for their sacrifices and for exemplifying the power of determination

`Packt.com`

Subscribe to our online digital library for full access to over 7,000 books and videos, as well as industry leading tools to help you plan your personal development and advance your career. For more information, please visit our website.

Why subscribe?

- Spend less time learning and more time coding with practical eBooks and Videos from over 4,000 industry professionals

- Improve your learning with Skill Plans built especially for you

- Get a free eBook or video every month

- Fully searchable for easy access to vital information

- Copy and paste, print, and bookmark content

Did you know that Packt offers eBook versions of every book published, with PDF and ePub files available? You can upgrade to the eBook version at `www.packt.com` and as a print book customer, you are entitled to a discount on the eBook copy. Get in touch with us at `customercare@packtpub.com` for more details.

At `www.packt.com`, you can also read a collection of free technical articles, sign up for a range of free newsletters, and receive exclusive discounts and offers on Packt books and eBooks.

Contributors

About the author

Carlo Milanesi has a computer science degree from the State University of Milan, and lives in Bergamo, Italy. He is a software engineer with decades of experience in teaching and developing software for desktop and the web on Windows or Linux, using C, C++, Smalltalk, Delphi, Visual Basic, C#, Java, JavaScript, and Rust.

He loves writing tests and documentation and has experience in the domains of banking, portfolio management, construction engineering, CAD systems for milling machines, human-machine interface systems for machine tools, and websites and web applications for enterprises and for public administration management. He has written a book on Rust entitled, *Beginning Rust: From Novice to Professional*.

About the reviewer

Daniel Durante has been both an author and a technical reviewer for Packt publishing. He is a consultant and strategist for Fortune 100 companies and a full stack developer from the age of 12. His code exists in infrastructures such as Hubcash, Stripe, and Walmart.

He has worked on text-based browser games that have reached over 1,000,000 active players. He has created bin-packing software for CNC machines, embedded programming with cortex-m and PIC circuits, high-frequency trading applications. He has also helped and contributed to maintain one of the oldest ORMs of Node.js (SequelizeJS).

I would like to thank my parents, my brother, my mentors, and friends who have all put up with my insanity sitting in front of a computer day in and day out. I would not be here today if it wasn't for their patience, guidance, and love.

Packt is searching for authors like you

If you're interested in becoming an author for Packt, please visit authors.packtpub.com and apply today. We have worked with thousands of developers and tech professionals, just like you, to help them share their insight with the global tech community. You can make a general application, apply for a specific hot topic that we are recruiting an author for, or submit your own idea.

Table of Contents

Preface

This book is a presentation of the most interesting and useful libraries and frameworks that are freely available for Rust programmers to use in building interesting and useful projects, such as frontend and backend web applications, games, interpreters, compilers, computer emulators, and Linux-loadable modules.

Who this book is for

This book is for developers who have already learned the Rust programming language and are eager to put it to work to build useful software, whether for businesses or for a hobby project. The book addresses diverse needs, such as building a web application, a computer game, an interpreter, a compiler, an emulator, or a device driver.

Some knowledge of SQL is required to understand the chapter on databases, and knowledge of the C programming language and Linux tools is required to understand the chapter on Linux modules.

What this book covers

Chapter 1, *Rust 2018 – Productivity*, describes recent innovations in the Rust language and its ecosystem of tools and libraries. In particular, it shows you how to use some utility libraries that are in widespread usage.

Chapter 2, *Storing and Retrieving Data*, describes how to read and write some of the most popular text file formats in the Rust world: TOML, JSON, and XML. It also describes how to access some of the most popular database engines in the Rust world, such as SQLite, PostgreSQL, and Redis.

Chapter 3, *Creating a REST Web Service*, describes how to use the Actix framework to develop a REST service that can be used as a backend for any kind of client application, particularly web applications.

Chapter 4, *Creating a Full Server-Side Web App*, describes how to use the Tera template engine to replace placeholders in a text file, and how to use the Actix framework to create a full server-side web application.

Chapter 5, *Creating a Client-Side WebAssembly App Using Yew*, describes how to use the Yew framework, which exploits the WebAssembly technology, to create the frontend of a web application.

Chapter 6, *Creating a WebAssembly Game Using Quicksilver*, describes how to use the Quicksilver framework to create graphical 2D games that can be run in a web browser, exploiting the WebAssembly technology, or as a desktop application.

Chapter 7, *Creating a Desktop Two-Dimensional Game Using ggez*, describes how to use the ggez framework to create graphical 2D games for desktop, including the coverage of widgets.

Chapter 8, *Using a Parser Combinator for Interpreting and Compiling*, describes how to use the Nom parser combinator to create parsers of formal languages and then build syntax checkers, interpreters, and compilers.

Chapter 9, *Creating a Computer Emulator Using Nom*, describes how to use the Nom library to parse binary data and interpret a machine language program, which is the first step in building a computer emulator.

Chapter 10, *Creating a Linux Kernel Module*, describes how to build Linux loadable modules using Rust, focusing on the Mint distribution; specifically, a character device driver will be built.

Chapter 11, *The Future of Rust*, describes the innovations that are probably going to appear in the next few years in the Rust ecosystem. In particular, the new asynchronous programming technique is briefly shown.

To get the most out of this book

Software/hardware covered in the book	OS requirements
You will need version 1.31 of Rust (from December 2018) or a newer version installed on your computer.	The content of this book was tested on 64-bit Linux Mint and 32-bit Windows 10 systems. Most examples should work on any system supporting Rust. Chapter 5, *Creating a Client-Side WebAssembly App Using Yew*, and Chapter 6, *Creating a WebAssembly Game Using Quicksilver*, require a web browser that supports WebAssembly, such as Chrome or Firefox. Chapter 6, *Creating a WebAssembly Game Using Quicksilver*, and Chapter 7, *Creating a Desktop Two-Dimensional Game Using ggez*, require support for OpenGL. Chapter 10, *Creating a Linux Kernel Module*, works only on Linux Mint.

If you are using the digital version of this book, we advise you to type the code yourself or access the code via the GitHub repository (link available in the next section). Doing so will help you avoid any potential errors related to the copying and pasting of code.

Download the example code files

You can download the example code files for this book from your account at www.packt.com. If you purchased this book elsewhere, you can visit www.packtpub.com/support and register to have the files emailed directly to you.

You can download the code files by following these steps:

1. Log in or register at www.packt.com.
2. Select the **Support** tab.
3. Click on **Code Downloads**.
4. Enter the name of the book in the **Search** box and follow the onscreen instructions.

Once the file is downloaded, please make sure that you unzip or extract the folder using the latest version of:

- WinRAR/7-Zip for Windows
- Zipeg/iZip/UnRarX for Mac
- 7-Zip/PeaZip for Linux

The code bundle for the book is also hosted on GitHub at https://github.com/PacktPublishing/Creative-Projects-for-Rust-Programmers. In case there's an update to the code, it will be updated on the existing GitHub repository.

We also have other code bundles from our rich catalog of books and videos available at https://github.com/PacktPublishing/. Check them out!

Download the color images

We also provide a PDF file that has color images of the screenshots/diagrams used in this book. You can download it here: https://static.packt-cdn.com/downloads/9781789346220_ColorImages.pdf.

Conventions used

There are a number of text conventions used throughout this book.

CodeInText: Indicates code words in text, database table names, folder names, filenames, file extensions, pathnames, dummy URLs, user input, and Twitter handles. Here is an example: "The pos variable is the position of the current digit in the digits array."

A block of code is set as follows:

```
{
    for pos in pos..5 {
        print!("{}", digits[pos] as u8 as char);
    }
}
```

Any command-line input or output is written as follows:

```
curl -X GET http://localhost:8080/datafile.txt
```

Bold: Indicates a new term, an important word, or words that you see onscreen. For example, words in menus or dialog boxes appear in the text like this. Here is an example: "The **Name portion** edit box and the **Filter** button to its right are for filtering the table below it, in a similar way to the list project."

 Warnings or important notes appear like this.

 Tips and tricks appear like this.

Get in touch

Feedback from our readers is always welcome.

General feedback: If you have questions about any aspect of this book, mention the book title in the subject of your message and email us at customercare@packtpub.com.

Errata: Although we have taken every care to ensure the accuracy of our content, mistakes do happen. If you have found a mistake in this book, we would be grateful if you would report this to us. Please visit www.packtpub.com/support/errata, selecting your book, clicking on the Errata Submission Form link, and entering the details.

Piracy: If you come across any illegal copies of our works in any form on the Internet, we would be grateful if you would provide us with the location address or website name. Please contact us at copyright@packt.com with a link to the material.

If you are interested in becoming an author: If there is a topic that you have expertise in, and you are interested in either writing or contributing to a book, please visit authors.packtpub.com.

Reviews

Please leave a review. Once you have read and used this book, why not leave a review on the site that you purchased it from? Potential readers can then see and use your unbiased opinion to make purchase decisions, we at Packt can understand what you think about our products, and our authors can see your feedback on their book. Thank you!

For more information about Packt, please visit packt.com.

Rust 2018: Productivity

The Rust Standard Library and tooling have improved a lot over the years. Since February 2018, the Rust ecosystem has become quite wide and multifaceted. Four domain working groups have been created, each covering one of the main application areas. These areas were already fairly mature, but this development allowed them to improve even further. In the coming years, we will see the introduction of other domain working groups as well.

It's not an easy task to develop a high-quality and cost-effective application, even after learning a language as a developer. To avoid reinventing the (presumably low-quality) wheel, you as a developer should use a high-quality framework or some high-quality libraries that cover the kind of application you are going to develop.

The purpose of this book is to guide you as a developer to choose the best open source Rust libraries available for developing software. This book covers several typical domains, each using different libraries. Because some non-standard libraries are useful in a number of different domains, it would be quite limiting to present them as confined to a single domain.

In this chapter, you will learn about the following topics:

- Understanding the different editions of Rust
- Understanding the most important recent improvements made to Rust
- Understanding domain working groups
- Understanding the kind of projects that we will cover in this book
- An introduction to some useful Rust libraries

Technical requirements

To follow this book, you will need to have access to a computer on which a recent Rust system is installed. Any release since version 1.31 is okay. Some optional libraries will be listed for some specific projects later on.

Any cited source code and additional examples can (and should) be downloaded from the repository: `https://github.com/PacktPublishing/Creative-Projects-for-Rust-Programmers`.

Understanding the different editions of Rust

On December 6, 2018, a very important version of the Rust language, its compiler, and its standard library was released: stable version **1.31**. This version has been defined as the **2018 edition**, meaning it is a milestone that will be used as a reference for the years to come.

Before this, there was another version, 1.0, which was defined as the 2015 edition. This edition was characterized by the word *stability*. Up until version 1.0, every version of the compiler applied breaking changes to the language or to the standard library, forcing the developers to apply sweeping changes to their code base. From version 1.0, efforts have been made to ensure that any future version of the compiler can correctly compile any code written for version 1.0 or successive versions. This is called **backward compatibility**.

However, many features were applied to the language and to the standard library before the release of the 2018 edition. Many new libraries used these new features, meaning that these libraries could not be used by older compilers. For this reason, there was a need to tag a specific version of Rust as aimed at being used with newer libraries. This was the main reason for the 2018 edition.

Some of the features added to the language are marked as for the 2015 edition, while others are marked as for the 2018 edition. The features for the 2015 edition are just small improvements, while the features for the 2018 edition are more in-depth changes. Developers must mark their crates as for the 2018 edition in order to use the features that are specific to the 2018 edition.

In addition, although the 2015 edition marked a stable milestone for the language and the standard library, the command-line tools were not actually stabilized; they were still quite immature. In the three and a half years from May 2015 to December 2018, the main official command-line tools have matured, and the language has also been improved to allow more efficient coding. The 2018 edition can be characterized by the word *productivity*.

The following table shows a timeline of the features stabilized in the language, the standard library, and the tooling:

2015	**May:** 2015 edition	**August:** Parallel compilation on multi-core CPUs				
2016	**April:** Microsoft C compiler format supported	**May:** Ability to capture panics	**September:** Improved compiler error messages	**November:** The ? operator	**December:** The `rustup` command	
2017	**February:** Custom derive attributes	**March:** The cargo check command	**July:** The `union` keyword	**August:** Associated constants	**November:** The ? operator with Option	
2018	**February:** • The formation of four Domain Working Groups. • The `rustfmt` program	**May:** • The Rust Programming Language Second Edition. • The `impl` Trait language feature. • `main` can return a Result. • Inclusive ranges with `..=` • The *i128* and *u128* native types. • Improved patterns for `match`	**June:** • The SIMD library feature • The `dyn` Trait language feature	**August:** Custom global allocator	**September:** • The `cargo fix` command • The `cargo clippy` command	**October:** • Procedural macros • Changes to the module system and the `use` statement • Raw identifiers • `no_std` applications	**December:** • The 2018 edition • Non-lexical lifetimes • The `const fn` language feature • The new `https://www.rust-lang.org/` website • `try`, `async`, and `await` are reserved words

Many improvements have been applied since the 2015 edition. More information can be found in the official documentation (`https://blog.rust-lang.org/2018/12/06/Rust-1.31-and-rust-2018.html`). The most important improvements are listed as follows:

- A new official tutorial book, available free online (`https://doc.rust-lang.org/book/`), or printed on paper (*The Rust Programming Language* by Steve Klabnik and Carol Nichols).
- A revamped official website.

- The formation of four domain working groups, which are open committees to design the future of the ecosystem in four key areas:
  - **Networking**: Designing the new asynchronous paradigm around a concept of delayed computation, named *future*, as it is already done in other languages, such as C++, C#, and JavaScript (with *promises*).
  - **Command-line applications**: Designing some standard libraries to support any non-graphical, non-embedded applications.
  - **WebAssembly**: Designing tools and libraries to build applications to be run inside web browsers.
  - **Embedded software**: Designing tools and libraries to build applications to be run on bare-metal systems or on strictly constrained hardware.
- We witnessed some good improvements to the language:
  - Non-lexical lifetimes; any bindings that are no longer used are considered *dead*. For example, now this program is allowed:

```
fn main() {
    let mut _a = 7;
    let _ref_to_a = &_a;
    _a = 9;
}
```

In this code, the object bound to the variable _a is borrowed by the variable _ref_to_a in the second statement. Prior to the introduction of non-lexical lifetimes, such bindings would last till the end of the scope, and so the last statement would have been illegal because it tries to change that object through binding _a when it is still borrowed to variable _ref_to_a. Now, because variable _ref_to_a is no longer used, its lifetime ceases in the same line it is declared, and so, in the last statement, variable _a is again free to change its own object.

- The Impl Trait feature, which allows functions to return unspecified types, such as **closures**.
- The i128 and u128 native types.
- Some other reserved keywords such as try, async, and await.

- The `?` operator, usable even in the `main` function, because now it can return `Result`. The following program is an example of the `main` function returning a `Result`:

```
fn main() -> Result<(), String> {
    Err("Hi".to_string())
}
```

It can succeed, by returning the usual empty tuple or fail by returning the type you specify. In this case, it was `String`. The following program is an example using the `?` operator used in the `main` function:

```
fn main() -> Result<(), usize> {
    let array = [12, 19, 27];
    let found = array.binary_search(&19)?;
    println!("Found {}", found);
    let found = array.binary_search(&20)?;
    println!("Found {}", found);
    Ok(())
}
```

This program will print `Found 1` on the standard output stream, meaning that the number `19` has been found at position `1`, and it will print `Error: 2` on the standard error stream, meaning that the number `20` hasn't been found, but that it should be inserted at position `2`.

- Procedural macros, which allow a kind of meta-programming, manipulating source code to generate Rust code at compile time.
- More powerful and more ergonomic pattern matching in `match` expressions.
- And also some improvements to the standard tooling:
  - The `rustup` program, which allows users to easily choose the default compiler target or to update the toolchain.
  - The `rustfix` program, which converts a 2015 edition project to a 2018 edition project.

- The Clippy program, which checks for non-idiomatic syntax, and suggests changes to code for better maintainability.
- Faster compilation speed, in particular, if just a syntax check is required.
- The **Rust Language Server (RLS)** program, which is currently still unstable, but which allows IDEs and programmable editors to spot syntax errors, and to suggest allowed operations.

Rust is still evolving as a language, like any other programming language. The following areas are still left to be improved:

- The IDE tools, including a language interpreter (REPL) and a graphical debugger
- Libraries and tools to support bare-metal and real-time software development
- Application-level frameworks and libraries for the main application areas

This book will focus primarily on the third point on this list.

The projects

When we write a real-world application, the Rust language and its standard library are not sufficient. Application frameworks are needed for particular kinds of applications, such as GUI apps, web apps, or games.

Of course, if you use a good-quality and comprehensive library, you can reduce the number of lines of code that you need to write. Using a library also offers the following two advantages:

- The overall design is improved, particularly if you are using a framework (since it imposes an architecture on your app) as it will be created by knowledgeable engineers and time-tested by a number of users.
- The number of bugs will be reduced because it will have undergone more thorough testing than that which you are likely to be able to apply.

There are actually many Rust libraries, also known as **crates**, but most are low-quality or quite narrow in their range of applications. This book will look at the best quality and most complete libraries for some typical application areas of the Rust language.

The application areas are as follows:

- **Web apps**: There are various popular technologies, including the following:
  - The REST web service (backend only)
  - An event-driven web client (frontend only)
  - A full web app (full-stack)
  - A web game (frontend only)

- **Games**: When I say *games*, I'm not referring to anything that is entertaining. I am referring to a graphical application where a continuous animation is shown, as opposed to event-driven graphical applications that do nothing until an event occurs, such as the user pressing a key, moving the mouse, or some data arriving from a connection. As well as games for the web browser, there are also games for desktop and laptop computers, for video game consoles, and for mobile devices. However, video game consoles and mobile devices are not yet that well supported by Rust, so we will only be looking at games for desktop and laptop computers in this book.

- **Language interpreters**: There are two kinds of languages that can be interpreted. Both are covered in this book:
  - **Text**: Like a programming language, a markup language, or a machine command language
  - **Binary**: Like the machine language of a computer to be emulated, or the intermediate bytecode of a programming language.

- **C-language-callable libraries**: This is an important use case of Rust: to develop a library to be invoked by another application, typically written in a higher-level language. Rust cannot assume that other languages can invoke the Rust code, but it can assume that they can invoke the C-language code. We will look at how to build a library that can be invoked as if it were written in C. One particularly challenging case is to build a module for the Linux operating system, which notoriously has to be written in C.

Most applications read and write data to and from a file, or a communication channel, or a database. In the next chapter, we will be looking at various different techniques that will be useful for all the other projects.

Other application areas have not been listed here as they are either not used much in Rust, they are still immature, or they are still in a state of flux. The libraries available for these immature areas will be completely different in a couple of years. These areas include software for micro-controllers, or other real-time or low-resource systems, and also software for mobile or wearable systems.

Working through the examples in this book

To follow the examples in the book, you should download all the examples from the online repository: https://github.com/PacktPublishing/Creative-Projects-for-Rust-Programmers. This repository contains a sub-folder for each chapter of the book and a sub-sub-folder for any project in a chapter.

For example, to run the use_rand project in this chapter, you should go to the Chapter01/use_rand folder and type cargo run. Notice that the most important files of any project are cargo.toml and src/main.rs, so you should always take a look at them first.

Exploring some utility crates

Before moving on to looking at how to use the most complex crates, let's take a look at some basic Rust crates. These are not a part of the standard library, but they are useful in many different kinds of projects. They should be known by all Rust developers since they are of general applicability.

Pseudo-random number generators – the rand crate

The ability to generate pseudo-random numbers is needed for several kinds of applications, especially for games. The rand crate is rather complex, but its basic usage is shown in the following example (named use_rand):

```
// Declare basic functions for pseudo-random number generators.
use rand::prelude::*;

fn main() {
    // Create a pseudo-Random Number Generator for the current thread
    let mut rng = thread_rng();

    // Print an integer number
    // between 0 (included) and 20 (excluded).
    println!("{}", rng.gen_range(0, 20));

    // Print a floating-point number
    // between 0 (included) and 1 (excluded).
    println!("{}", rng.gen::<f64>());
```

```
    // Generate a Boolean.
    println!("{}", if rng.gen() { "Heads" } else { "Tails" });
}
```

First, you create a pseudo-random number generator object. Then, you call several methods on this object. Any generator must be **mutable** because any generation modifies the state of the generator.

The `gen_range` method generates an integer number in a right-open range. The `gen` generic method generates a number of the specified type. Sometimes, this type can be inferred, like in the last statement, where a Boolean is expected. If the generated type is a floating-point number, it is between 0 and 1, with 1 excluded.

Logging – the log crate

For any kind of software, in particular for servers, the ability to emit logging messages is essential. The logging architecture has two components:

- **API**: Defined by the `log` crate
- **Implementation**: Defined by several possible crates

Here, an example using the popular `env_logger` crate is shown. If you want to emit logging messages from a library, you should only add the API crate as a dependency, as it is the responsibility of the application to define the logging implementation crate.

In the following example (named `use_env_logger`), we are showing an application (not a library), and so we need both crates:

```
#[macro_use]
extern crate log;

fn main() {
    env_logger::init();
    error!("Error message");
    warn!("Warning message");
    info!("Information message");
    debug!("Debugging message");
}
```

In a Unix-like console, after having run `cargo build`, execute the following command:

```
RUST_LOG=debug ./target/debug/use_env_logger
```

It will print something like the following:

```
[2020-01-11T15:43:44Z ERROR logging] Error message
[2020-01-11T15:43:44Z WARN logging] Warning message
[2020-01-11T15:43:44Z INFO logging] Information message
[2020-01-11T15:43:44Z DEBUG logging] Debugging message
```

By typing `RUST_LOG=debug` at the beginning of the command, you defined the temporary environment variable `RUST_LOG`, with `debug` as its value. The `debug` level is the highest, and hence all logging statements are performed. Instead, if you execute the following command, only the first three lines will be printed, as the `info` level is not detailed enough to print debug messages:

```
RUST_LOG=info ./target/debug/use_env_logger
```

Similarly, if you execute the following command, only the first two lines will be printed, as the `warn` level is not detailed enough to print either the `debug` or the `info` messages:

```
RUST_LOG=warn ./target/debug/use_env_logger
```

If you execute one or the other of the following commands, only the first line will be printed, as the default logging level is `error`:

- `RUST_LOG=error ./target/debug/use_env_logger`
- `./target/debug/use_env_logger`

Initializing static variables at runtime – the lazy_static crate

It's well known that Rust does not allow *mutable static variables in safe code*. Immutable static variables are allowed in safe code, but they must be initialized by constant expressions, possibly by invoking `const fn` functions. However, the compiler must be able to evaluate the initialization expression of any static variable.

Sometimes, however, there is a need to initialize a static variable at runtime, because the initial value depends on an input, such as a command-line argument or a configuration option. In addition, if the initialization of a variable takes a long time, instead of initializing it at the start of the program, it may be better to initialize it only the first time the variable is used. This technique is called **lazy initialization**.

There is a small crate, named `lazy_static`, that contains only one macro, which has the same name as the crate. This can be used to solve the issue mentioned previously. Its use is shown in the following project (named `use_lazy_static`):

```rust
use lazy_static::lazy_static;
use std::collections::HashMap;

lazy_static! {
    static ref DICTIONARY: HashMap<u32, &'static str> = {
        let mut m = HashMap::new();
        m.insert(11, "foo");
        m.insert(12, "bar");
        println!("Initialized");
        m
    };
}

fn main() {
    println!("Started");
    println!("DICTIONARY contains {:?}", *DICTIONARY);
    println!("DICTIONARY contains {:?}", *DICTIONARY);
}
```

This will print the following output:

```
Started
Initialized
DICTIONARY contains {12: "bar", 11: "foo"}
DICTIONARY contains {12: "bar", 11: "foo"}
```

As you can see, the `main` function starts first. Then, it tries to access the `DICTIONARY` static variable, and that access causes the initialization of variables. The initialized value, which is a reference, is then dereferenced and printed.

The last statement, which is identical to the previous one, does not perform the initialization again, as you can see by the fact that the `Initialized` text is not printed again.

Parsing the command line – the structopt crate

The command-line arguments of any program are easily accessible through the `std::env::args()` iterator. However, the code that parses these arguments is actually rather cumbersome. To get more maintainable code, the `structopt` crate can be used, as shown in the following project (named `use_structopt`):

```
use std::path::PathBuf;
use structopt::StructOpt;

#[derive(StructOpt, Debug)]
struct Opt {
    /// Activate verbose mode
    #[structopt(short = "v", long = "verbose")]
    verbose: bool,

    /// File to generate
    #[structopt(short = "r", long = "result", parse(from_os_str))]
    result_file: PathBuf,

    /// Files to process
    #[structopt(name = "FILE", parse(from_os_str))]
    files: Vec<PathBuf>,
}

fn main() {
    println!("{:#?}", Opt::from_args());
}
```

If you execute the `cargo run input1.txt input2.txt -v --result res.xyz` command, you should get the following output:

```
Opt {
    verbose: true,
    result_file: "res.txt",
    files: [
        "input1.tx",
        "input2.txt"
    ]
}
```

As you can see, the filenames `input1.txt` and `input2.txt` have been loaded into the `files` field of the structure. The `--result res.xyz` argument caused the `result_file` field to be filled, and the `-v` argument caused the `verbose` field to be set to `true`, instead of the default `false`.

Summary

In this chapter, we introduced the new Rust 2018 edition. We learned about the kind of projects that are going to be described in this book. We then took a quick look at four useful crates which you can apply in your Rust code.

In the next chapter, we will learn how to store or retrieve data to and from a file, a database, or another application.

Questions

1. Is there an official printed book to learn the Rust language?
2. How long was the longest primitive Rust integer in 2015, and how long was it at the end of 2018?
3. Which are the four domain working groups at the end of 2018?
4. What is the purpose of the Clippy utility?
5. What is the purpose of the `rustfix` utility?
6. Write a program that generates 10 pseudo-random `f32` numbers between 100 and 400.
7. Write a program that generates 10 pseudo-random `i32` numbers between 100 and 400 (without truncating or rounding the numbers generated by the previous exercise).
8. Write a program that creates a static vector containing all squared integers between 1 and 200.
9. Write a program that emits a warning message and an info message, and then run it so that only the warning message appears.
10. Try to parse a command-line argument that contains a value from 1 to 20, emitting an error message if the value is out of range. The short option should be `-l`, and the long option should be `--level`.

Storing and Retrieving Data

2

A typical need of any software application is to input/output data by reading/writing data files or data streams or by querying/manipulating a database. Regarding files and streams, unstructured data, or even binary data, is hard to manipulate, and so they are not recommended.

Also, proprietary data formats are not recommended because of the vendor lock-in risk, and so only standard data formats should be used. Fortunately, there are free Rust libraries that come to the rescue in these situations. There are Rust crates available to manipulate some of the most popular file formats, such as TOML, JSON, and XML.

In terms of databases, there are Rust crates to manipulate data using some of the most popular databases, such as SQLite, PostgreSQL, and Redis.

In this chapter, you will learn about the following:

- How to read configuration data from a TOML file
- How to read or write a JSON data file
- How to read an XML data file
- How to query or manipulate data in a SQLite database
- How to query or manipulate data in a PostgreSQL database
- How to query or manipulate data in a Redis database

Technical requirements

It is required for you to install the SQLite runtime library when you're running the SQLite code. However, it is also useful (although not required) to install a SQLite interactive manager. You can download the precompiled binaries of SQLite tools from `https://www.sqlite.org/download.html`. However, version 3.11 or higher would be ideal.

Please note that if you're using Debian-derived Linux distribution, the `libsqlite3-dev` package should be installed.

It is also required for you to install and run the PostgreSQL **Database Management System (DBMS)** when you're running the PostgreSQL code. As with SQLite, it is useful but not required to install a PostgreSQL interactive manager. You can download the precompiled binary of PostgreSQL DBMS from `https://www.postgresql.org/download/`. However, version 7.4 or higher would be acceptable.

Installing and running the Redis server is necessary when you're running the Redis code. You can download it from `https://redis.io/download`.

The complete source code for this chapter can be found in the `Chapter02` folder of the repository at `https://github.com/PacktPublishing/Creative-Projects-for-Rust-Programmers`. In this folder, there is a sub-folder for every project, plus a folder named `data`, which contains the data that we'll use as input for the projects.

Project overview

In this chapter, we'll look at how to build a program that loads a JSON file and an XML file into three databases: a SQLite database, a PostgreSQL database, and a Redis key-value store. To avoid hardwiring the names and positions of the files and the database credentials into the program, we are going to load them from a TOML configuration file.

The final project is named `transformer`, but we'll explain this through several preliminary small projects:

- `toml_dynamic` and `toml_static`: These read a TOML file in two different ways.
- `json_dynamic` and `json_static`: These read a JSON file in two different ways.
- `xml_example`: This reads an XML file.
- `sqlite_example`: This creates two tables in a SQLite database, inserts records into them, and queries them.
- `postgresql_example`: This creates two tables in a PostgreSQL database, inserts records into them, and queries them.
- `redis_example`: This adds some data to a key-value store and queries it.

Reading a TOML file

One simple and maintainable way to store information in a filesystem is to use a text file. This is also very efficient for data spanning no more than 100 KB. However, there are several competing standards for storing information in text files, such as INI, CSV, JSON, XML, YAML, and others.

The one used by Cargo is TOML. This is a really powerful format that is used by many Rust developers to store the configuration data of their apps. It is designed to be written by hand, using a text editor, but it can also be written by an application very easily.

The `toml_dynamic` and `toml_static` projects (using the `toml` crate) load data from a TOML file. Reading a TOML file is useful when configuring a software application, and this is what we'll do. We will use the `data/config.toml` file, which contains all of the parameters for the projects of this chapter.

You can also create or modify a TOML file by using code, but we are not going to do that. Being able to modify a TOML file can be useful in some scenarios, such as to save user preferences.

It is important to consider that when a TOML file is changed by a program, it undergoes dramatic restructuring:

- It acquires specific formatting, which you may dislike.
- It loses all of its comments.
- Its items are sorted alphabetically.

So, if you want to use the TOML format both for manually edited parameters and for program-saved data, you would be better off using two distinct files:

- One edited only by humans
- One edited primarily by your software, but occasionally also by humans

This chapter describes two projects in which a TOML file is read using different techniques. These techniques are to be used in two different cases:

- In a situation where we are not sure which fields are contained in the file, and so we want to explore it. In this case, we use the `toml_dynamic` program.
- In another situation where, in our program, we describe exactly which fields should be contained in the file and we don't accept a different format. In this case, we use the `toml_static` program.

Using toml_dynamic

The purpose of this section is to read the `config.toml` file, located in the `data` folder, when we want to explore the content of that file. The first three lines of this file are as follows:

```
[input]
xml_file = "../data/sales.xml"
json_file = "../data/sales.json"
```

After these lines, the file contains other sections. Among them is the `[postgresql]` section, which contains the following line:

```
database = "Rust2018"
```

To run this project, enter the `toml_dynamic` folder and type in `cargo run ../data/config.toml`. A long output should be printed. It will begin with the following lines:

```
Original: Table(
    {
        "input": Table(
            {
                "json_file": String(
                    "../data/sales.json",
                ),
                "xml_file": String(
                    "../data/sales.xml",
                ),
            },
        ),
```

Notice that this is just a verbose representation of the first three lines of the `config.toml` file. This output proceeds with emitting a similar representation for the rest of the file. After having printed the whole data structure representing the file that is read, the following line is added to the output:

```
[Postgresql].Database: Rust2018
```

This is the result of a specific query on the data structure loaded when the file is read.

Let's look at the code of the `toml_dynamic` program:

1. Declare a variable that will contain a description of the whole file. This variable is initialized in the next three statements:

    ```
    let config_const_values =
    ```

2. We add the pathname of the file from the first argument in the command line to `config_path`. Then, we load the contents of this file into the `config_text` string and we parse this string into a `toml::Value` structure. This is a recursive structure because it can have a `Value` property among its fields:

    ```
    {
        let config_path = std::env::args().nth(1).unwrap();
        let config_text =
         std::fs::read_to_string(&config_path).unwrap();
        config_text.parse::<toml::Value>().unwrap()
    };
    ```

3. This structure is then printed using the debug structured formatting (`:#?`), and a value is retrieved from it:

    ```
    println!("Original: {:#?}", config_const_values);
    println!("[Postgresql].Database: {}",
        config_const_values.get("postgresql").unwrap()
        .get("database").unwrap()
        .as_str().unwrap());
    ```

Notice that to get the value of the `"database"` item contained the `"postgresql"` section, a lot of code is required. The `get` function needs to look for a string, which may fail. That is the price of uncertainty.

Using toml_static

On the other hand, if we are quite sure of the organization of our TOML file, we should use another technique shown in the project, `toml_static`.

To run it, open the `toml_static` folder and type in `cargo run ../data/config.toml`. The program will only print the following line:

```
[postgresql].database: Rust2018
```

This project uses two additional crates:

- serde: This enables the use of the basic serialization/deserialization operations.
- serde_derive: This provides a powerful additional feature known as the **custom-derive** feature, which allows you to serialize/deserialize using a struct.

serde is the standard serialization/deserialization library. **Serialization** is the process of converting data structures of the program into a string (or a stream). **Deserialization** is the reverse process; it is the process of converting a string (or a stream) into some data structures of the program.

To read a TOML file, we need to use deserialization.

In these two projects, we don't need to use serialization as we are not going to write a TOML file.

In the code, first, a struct is defined for any section contained in the data/config.toml file. That file contains the Input, Redis, Sqlite, and Postgresql sections, and so we declare as many Rust structs as the sections of the file we want to read; then, the Config struct is defined to represent the whole file, having these sections as members.

For example, this is the structure for the Input section:

```
#[allow(unused)]
#[derive(Deserialize)]
struct Input {
    xml_file: String,
    json_file: String,
}
```

Notice that the preceding declaration is preceded by two attributes.

The allow(unused) attribute is used to prevent the compiler from warning us about unused fields in the following structure. It is convenient for us to avoid these noisy warnings. The derive(Deserialize) attribute is used to activate the automatic deserialization initiated by serde for the following structure.

After these declarations, it is possible to write the following line of code:

```
toml::from_str(&config_text).unwrap()
```

This invokes the `from_str` function, which parses the text of the file into a struct. The type of that struct is not specified in this expression, but its value is assigned to the variable declared in the first line of the `main` function:

```
let config_const_values: Config =
```

So, its type is `Config`.

Any discrepancies between the file's contents and the struct type will be considered an error in this operation. So, if this operation is successful, any other operation on the structure cannot fail.

While the previous program (`toml_dynamic`) had a kind of dynamic typing, such as that of Python or JavaScript, this program has a kind of static typing, similar to Rust or C++.

The advantage of static typing appears in the last statement, where the same behavior as the long statement of the previous project is obtained by simply writing `config_const_values.postgresql.database`.

Reading and writing a JSON file

For storing data that is more complex than that which is stored in a configuration file, JSON format is more appropriate. This format is quite popular, particularly among those who use the JavaScript language.

We are going to read and parse the `data/sales.json` file. This file contains a single anonymous object, which contains two arrays—"`products`" and "`sales`".

The "`products`" array contains two objects, each one having three fields:

```
"products": [
  {
    "id": 591,
    "category": "fruit",
    "name": "orange"
  },
  {
    "id": 190,
    "category": "furniture",
    "name": "chair"
  }
],
```

The "`sales`" array contains three objects, each one containing five fields:

```
"sales": [
    {
      "id": "2020-7110",
      "product_id": 190,
      "date": 1234527890,
      "quantity": 2.0,
      "unit": "u."
    },
    {
      "id": "2020-2871",
      "product_id": 591,
      "date": 1234567590,
      "quantity": 2.14,
      "unit": "Kg"
    },
    {
      "id": "2020-2583",
      "product_id": 190,
      "date": 1234563890,
      "quantity": 4.0,
      "unit": "u."
    }
  ]
```

The information in the arrays is about some products to sell and some sale transactions associated with those products. Notice that the second field of each sale ("`product_id`") is a reference to a product, and so it should be processed after the corresponding product object has been created.

We will see a pair of programs with the same behavior. They read the JSON file, increment the quantity of the second sale object by `1.5`, and then save the whole updated structure into another JSON file.

Similarly to the TOML format case, there can also be a dynamic parsing technique used for JSON files, where the existence and type of any data field is checked by the application code, and a static parsing technique, where it uses the deserialization library to check the existence and type of any field.

So, we have two projects: `json_dynamic` and `json_static`. To run each of them, open its folder and type in `cargo run ../data/sales.json ../data/sales2.json`. The program will not print anything, but it will read the first file specified in the command line and create the second file that is specified.

The created file is similar to the read file, but with the following differences:

- The fields of the file created by `json_dynamic` are sorted in alphabetical order, while the fields of the file created by `json_static` are sorted in the same order as in the Rust data structure.
- The quantity of the second sale is incremented from `2.14` to `3.64`.
- The final empty line is removed in both created files.

Now, we can see the implementations of the two techniques of serialization and deserialization.

The json_dynamic project

Let's look at the source code of the project:

1. This project gets the pathnames of two files from the command line—the existing JSON file (`"input_path"`) to read into a memory structure and a JSON file to create (`"output_path"`) by saving the loaded structure, after having modified it a bit.
2. Then, the input file is loaded into the string named `sales_and_products_text` and the generic `serde_json::from_str::<Value>` function is used to parse the string into a dynamically typed structure representing the JSON file. This structure is stored in the `sales_and_products` local variable.

Imagine that we want to change the quantity sold by the second sale transaction, incrementing it by `1.5` kilograms:

1. First, we must get to this value using the following expression:

```
sales_and_products["sales"][1]["quantity"]
```

2. This retrieves the `"sales"` sub-object of the general object. It is an array containing three objects.

3. Then, this expression gets the second item (starting from zero (`[1]`)) of this array. This is an object representing a single sale transaction.

4. After this, it gets the `"quantity"` sub-object of the sale transaction object.

5. The value we have reached has a dynamic type that we think should be `serde_json::Value::Number`, and so we make a pattern matching with this type, specifying the `if let Value::Number(n)` clause.

6. If all is good, the matching succeeds and we get a variable named n—containing a number, or something that can be converted into a Rust floating-point number by using the `as_f64` function. Lastly, we can increment the Rust number and then create a JSON number from it using the `from_f64` function. We can then assign this object to the JSON structure using the same expression we used to get it:

```
sales_and_products["sales"][1]["quantity"]
    = Value::Number(Number::from_f64(
        n.as_f64().unwrap() + 1.5).unwrap());
```

7. The last statement of the program saves the JSON structure to a file. Here, the `serde_json::to_string_pretty` function is used. As the name suggests, this function adds formatting whitespace (blanks and new lines) to make the resulting JSON file more human-readable. There is also the `serde_json::to_string` function, which creates a more compact version of the same information. It is much harder for people to read, but it is somewhat quicker to process for a computer:

```
std::fs::write(
    output path,
    serde_json::to_string_pretty(&sales_and_products).unwrap(),
).unwrap();
```

The json_static project

If, for our program, we are sure that we know the structure of the JSON file, a statically typed technique can and should be used instead. It is shown in the `json_static` project. The situation here is similar to that of the projects processing the TOML file.

The source code of the static version first declares three structs—one for every object type contained in the JSON file we are going to process. Each struct is preceded by the following attribute:

```
#[derive(Deserialize, Serialize, Debug)]
```

Let's understand the preceding snippet:

- The `Deserialize` trait is required to parse (that is, read) JSON strings into this struct.
- The `Serialize` trait is required to format (that is, write) this struct into a JSON string.
- The `Debug` trait is just handy for printing this struct on a debug trace.

The JSON string is parsed using the `serde_json::from_str::<SalesAndProducts>` function. Then, the code to increment the quantity of sold oranges becomes quite simple:

```
sales_and_products.sales[1].quantity += 1.5
```

The rest of the program is unchanged.

Reading an XML file

Another very popular text format is XML. Unfortunately, there is no stable serialization/deserialization library to manage XML format. However, this is not necessarily a shortcoming. In actual fact, XML format is often used to store large datasets; so large, in fact, that it would be inefficient to load them all before we start converting the data into an internal format. In these cases, it may be more efficient to scan the file or incoming stream and process it as long as it is read.

The `xml_example` project is a rather convoluted program that scans the XML file specified on the command line and, in a procedural fashion, loads information from the file into a Rust data structure. It is meant to read the `../data/sales.xml` file. This file has a structure corresponding to the JSON file we sought in the previous section. The following lines show an excerpt of that file:

```
<?xml version="1.0" encoding="utf-8"?>
<sales-and-products>
    <product>
        <id>862</id>
    </product>
    <sale>
        <id>2020-3987</id>
    </sale>
</sales-and-products>
```

All XML files have a header in the first line and then one root element; in this case, the root element it is named `sales-and-products`. This element contains two kinds of elements—`product` and `sale`. Both kinds of elements have specific sub-elements, which are the fields of the corresponding data. In this example, only the `id` fields are shown.

To run the project, open its folder and type in `cargo run ../data/sales.xml`. Some lines will be printed on the console. The first four of them should be as follows:

```
Got product.id: 862.
Got product.category: fruit.
Got product.name: cherry.
  Exit product: Product { id: 862, category: "fruit", name: "cherry" }
```

These describe the contents of the specified XML file. In particular, the program found a product with ID `862`, then it detected that it is a fruit, then that it is a cherry, and then, when the whole product had been read, the whole struct representing the product was printed. A similar output will appear for sales.

The parsing is performed using only the `xml-rs` crate. This crate enables a mechanism of parsing, shown in the following code excerpt:

```
let file = std::fs::File::open(pathname).unwrap();
let file = std::io::BufReader::new(file);
let parser = EventReader::new(file);
for event in parser {
    match &location_item {
        LocationItem::Other => ...
        LocationItem::InProduct => ...
        LocationItem::InSale => ...
    }
}
```

An object of the `EventReader` type scans the buffered file and it generates an event whenever a step is performed in the parsing. The application code handles these kinds of events according to their needs.

The word **event** is used by this crate, but the word **transition** would probably be a better description of the data extracted by the parser.

A complex language is hard to parse, but for languages as simple as our data, the situation during the parsing can be modeled by a state machine. To that purpose, three enum variables are declared in the source code: `location_item`, with the `LocationItem` type; `location_product`, with the `LocationProduct` type; and `location_sale`, with the `LocationSale` type.

The first one indicates the current position of the parsing in general. We can be inside a product (`InProduct`), inside a sale (`InSale`), or outside of both (`Other`). If we are inside a product, the `LocationProduct` enum indicates the current position of parsing inside the current product. This can be within any of the allowed fields or outside of all of them. Similar states happen for sales.

The iteration encounters several kinds of events. The main ones are the following:

- `XmlEvent::StartElement`: Signals that an XML element is beginning. It is decorated by the name of the beginning element and the possible attributes of that element.
- `XmlEvent::EndElement`: Signals that an XML element is ending. It is decorated by the name of the ending element.
- `XmlEvent::Characters`: Signals that the textual contents of an element is available. It is decorated by that available text.

The program declares a mutable `product` struct, with the `Product` type, and a mutable `sale` struct, with the `Sale` type. They are initialized with default values. Whenever there are some characters available, they are stored in the corresponding field of the current struct.

For example, consider a situation where the value of `location_item` is `LocationItem::InProduct` and the value of `location_product` is `LocationProduct::InCategory`—that is, we are in a category of a product. In this situation, there can be the name of the category or the end of the category. To get the name of the category, the code contains this pattern of a `match` statement:

```
Ok(XmlEvent::Characters(characters)) => {
    product.category = characters.clone();
    println!("Got product.category: {}.", characters);
}
```

In this statement, the `characters` variable gets the name of the category and a clone of it is assigned to the `product.category` field. Then, the name is printed to the console.

Accessing databases

Text files are good when they are small and when they don't need to be changed often. Actually, the only way that a text file can be changed is if you append something to the end of it or rewrite it completely. If you want to change the information in a large dataset quickly, the only way to do so is to use a database manager. In this section, we are going to learn how to manipulate a SQLite database with a simple example.

But first, let's look at three popular, broad categories of database managers:

- **Single-user databases**: These store all of the databases in a single file, which must be accessible by the application code. The database code is linked into the application (it may be a static-link library or a dynamic-link library). Only one user at a time is allowed to access it, and all users have administrative privileges. To move the database anywhere, you simply move the file. The most popular choices in this category are SQLite and Microsoft Access.
- **DBMS**: This is a process that has to be started as a service. Multiple clients can connect to it at the same time, and they can also apply changes at the same time without any data corruption. It requires more storage space, more memory, and much more start up time (for the server). There are several popular choices in this category, such as Oracle, Microsoft SQL Server, IBM DB2, MySQL, and PostgreSQL.
- **Key-value stores**: This is a process that has to be started as a service. Multiple clients can connect to it at the same time and apply changes at the same time. It is essentially a large memory hash map that can be queried by other processes and that can optionally store its data in a file and reload it when it is restarted. This category is less popular than the other two, but it is gaining ground as the backend of high-performance websites. One of the most popular choices is Redis.

In the following sections, we are going to show you how to access SQLite single-user databases (in the `sqlite_example` project), PostgreSQL DBMSes (in the `postgreSQL_example` project), and Redis key-value stores (in the `redis_example` project). Then, in the `transformer` project, all three kinds of databases will be used together.

Accessing a SQLite database

The source code for this section is found in the `sqlite_example` project. To run it, open its folder and type in `cargo run`.

This will create the `sales.db` file in the current folder. This file contains a SQLite database. Then, it will create the `Products` and `Sales` tables in this database, it will insert a row into each of these tables, and it will perform a query on the database. The query asks for all the sales, joining each of them with its associated product. For each extracted row, a line will be printed onto the console, showing the timestamp of the sale, the weight of the sale, and the name of the associated product. As there is only one sale in the database, you will see just the following line printed:

```
At instant 1234567890, 7.439 Kg of pears were sold.
```

This project only uses the `rusqlite` crate. Its name is a contraction of **Rust SQLite**. To use this crate, the `Cargo.toml` file must contain the following line:

```
rusqlite = "0.23"
```

Implementing the project

Let's look at how the code for the `sqlite_example` project works. The `main` function is quite simple:

```
fn main() -> Result<()> {
    let conn = create_db()?;
    populate_db(&conn)?;
    print_db(&conn)?;
    Ok(())
}
```

It invokes `create_db` to open or create a database with its empty tables, and to open and return a connection to this database.

Then, it invokes `populate_db` to insert rows into the tables of the database referred to by that connection.

Then, it invokes `print_db` to execute a query on this database and prints the data extracted by that query.

The `create_db` function is long but easy to understand:

```
fn create_db() -> Result<Connection> {
    let database_file = "sales.db";
    let conn = Connection::open(database_file)?;
    let _ = conn.execute("DROP TABLE Sales", params![]);
    let _ = conn.execute("DROP TABLE Products", params![]);
    conn.execute(
```

```
                    "CREATE TABLE Products (
                        id INTEGER PRIMARY KEY,
                        category TEXT NOT NULL,
                        name TEXT NOT NULL UNIQUE)",
                    params![],
                )?;
                conn.execute(
                    "CREATE TABLE Sales (
                        id TEXT PRIMARY KEY,
                        product_id INTEGER NOT NULL REFERENCES Products,
                        sale_date BIGINT NOT NULL,
                        quantity DOUBLE PRECISION NOT NULL,
                        unit TEXT NOT NULL)",
                    params![],
                )?;
                Ok(conn)
            }
```

The `Connection::open` function simply uses a path to a SQLite database file to open a connection. If this file does not exist, it will be created. As you can see, the created `sales.db` file is very small. Typically, empty databases of DBMSes are 1,000 times larger.

To perform a data manipulation command, the `execute` method of the connection is called. Its first argument is a SQL statement, possibly containing some parameters, specified as $1, $2, $3, and so on. The second argument of the function is a reference to a slice of values that are used to replace such parameters.

Of course, if there are no parameters, the parameter values list must be empty. The first parameter value, which has an index of 0, replaces the $1 parameter, the second one replaces the $2 parameter, and so on.

Notice that the arguments of a parameterized SQL statement can be of different data types (numeric, alpha-numeric, BLOBs, and so on), but Rust collections can only contain objects of the same data type. Therefore, the `params!` macro is used to perform a bit of magic. The data type of the second argument of the `execute` method must be that of a collection that can be iterated over and whose items implement the `ToSql` trait. The objects implementing this trait, as its name implies, can be used as parameters of a SQL statement. The `rusqlite` crate contains an implementation of this trait for many Rust basic types, such as numbers and strings.

So, for example, the `params!(34, "abc")` expression generates a collection that can be iterated over. The first item of this iteration can be converted into an object containing the number `34`, and that number can be used to replace a SQL parameter of a numeric type. The second item of this iteration can be converted into an object containing the `"abc"` string, and that string can be used to replace a SQL parameter of an alpha-numeric type.

Now, let's look at the `populate_db` function. It contains statements to insert rows into the database. Here is one of those statements:

```
conn.execute(
    "INSERT INTO Products (
        id, category, name
        ) VALUES ($1, $2, $3)",
    params![1, "fruit", "pears"],
)?;
```

As explained before, this statement will have the effect of executing the following SQL statement:

```
INSERT INTO Products (
        id, category, name
        ) VALUES (1, 'fruit', 'pears')
```

At last, we see the whole `print_db` function, which is more complex than the others:

```
fn print_db(conn: &Connection) -> Result<()> {
    let mut command = conn.prepare(
        "SELECT p.name, s.unit, s.quantity, s.sale_date
        FROM Sales s
        LEFT JOIN Products p
        ON p.id = s.product_id
        ORDER BY s.sale_date",    -> Statement
    )?;
    for sale_with_product in command.query_map(params![], |row| {
        Ok(SaleWithProduct {
            category: "".to_string(),
            name: row.get(0)?,
            quantity: row.get(2)?,
            unit: row.get(1)?,
            date: row.get(3)?,
        })
    })? {
        if let Ok(item) = sale_with_product {
            println!(
                "At instant {}, {} {} of {} were sold.",
                item.date, item.quantity, item.unit, item.name
```

```
                    );
                }
            }
        Ok((())
    }
```

To perform a SQL query, first, the `SELECT` SQL statement must be prepared by calling the `prepare` method of the connection, to convert it into an efficient internal format, with the `Statement` data type. This object is assigned to the `command` variable. A prepared statement must be mutable to allow the following replacement of parameters. In this case, however, we don't have any parameters.

A query can generate several rows, and we want to process one at a time, so we must create an iterator from this command. It is performed by calling the `query_map` method of the command. This method receives two arguments—a slice of parameter values and a closure—and it returns an iterator. The `query_map` function performs two jobs—first, it replaces the specified parameters, and then it uses the closure to map (or transform) each extracted row into a more handy structure. But in our case, we have no parameters to replace, and so we just create a specific structure with the `SaleWithProduct` type. To extract the fields from a row, the `get` method is used. It has a zero-based index on the fields specified in the `SELECT` query. This structure is the object returned by the iterator for any row extracted by the query, and it is assigned to the iteration variable named `sale_with_product`.

Now that we have learned how to access a SQLite database, let's check the PostgreSQL database management system.

Accessing a PostgreSQL database

What we did in the SQLite database is similar to what we will be doing in the PostgreSQL database. This is because they are both based on the SQL language, but mostly because SQLite is designed to be similar to PostgreSQL. It may be harder to convert an application from PostgreSQL into SQLite because the former has many advanced features that are not available in the latter.

In this section, we are going to convert the example from the previous section so that it works with a PostgreSQL database instead of SQLite. So, we'll explain the differences.

The source code for this section can be found in the `postgresql_example` folder. To run it, open its folder and type in `cargo run`. This will carry out essentially the same operations that we saw for `sqlite_example`, and so after creating and populating the database, it will print the following:

```
At instant 1234567890, 7.439 Kg of pears were sold.
```

Implementation of the project

This project only uses the crate named `postgres`. Its name is a popular contraction of the `postgresql` name.

Creating a connection to a PostgreSQL database is very different from creating a connection to a SQLite database. As the latter is only a file, you do so in a similar way to opening a file, and you should write `Connection::open(<pathname of the db file>)`. Instead, to connect to a PostgreSQL database, you need access to a computer where a server is running, then access to the TCP port where that server is listening, and then you need to specify your credentials on this server (your username and password). Optionally, you can then specify which of the databases managed by this server you want to use.

So, the general form of the call is `Connection::connect(<URL>, <TlsMode>)`, where the URL can be, for example, `postgres://postgres:post@localhost:5432/Rust2018`. The general form of the URL is `postgres://username[:password]@host[:port][/database]`, where the password, the port, and the database parts are optional. The `TlsMode` argument specifies whether the connection must be encrypted.

The port is optional because it has a value of `5432` by default. Another difference is that this crate does not use the `params!` macro. Instead, it allows us to specify a reference to a slice. In this case, it is an empty slice (`&[]`) because we don't need to specify parameters.

The table creation and population process is similar to the way it was done for `sqlite_example`. The query is different, however. This is the body of the `print_db` function:

```
for row in &conn.query(
    "SELECT p.name, s.unit, s.quantity, s.sale_date
    FROM Sales s
    LEFT JOIN Products p
    ON p.id = s.product_id
    ORDER BY s.sale_date",
    &[],
```

```
)? {
    let sale_with_product = SaleWithProduct {
        category: "".to_string(),
        name: row.get(0),
        quantity: row.get(2),
        unit: row.get(1),
        date: row.get(3),
    };
    println!(
        "At instant {}, {} {} of {} were sold.",
        sale_with_product.date,
        sale_with_product.quantity,
        sale_with_product.unit,
        sale_with_product.name
    );
}
```

With PostgreSQL, the `query` method of the connection class carries out parameter substitution, similarly to the `execute` method, but it does not map the row to a structure. Instead, it returns an iterator, which can be immediately used in a `for` statement. Then, in the body of the loop, the `row` variable can be used (as it is in the example) to fill a struct.

As we now know how to access data in the SQLite and PostgreSQL databases, let's see how to store and retrieve data from a Redis store.

Storing and retrieving data from a Redis store

Some applications need a very fast response time for certain kinds of data; faster than what a DBMS can offer. Usually, a DBMS dedicated to one user would be fast enough, but for some applications (typically large-scale web applications) there are hundreds of concurrent queries and many concurrent updates. You can use many computers, but the data must be kept coherent among them, and keeping coherence can cause a bottleneck of performance.

A solution to this problem is to use a key-value store, which is a very simple database that can be replicated across a network. This keeps the data in memory to maximize the speed, but it also supports the option to save the data in a file. This avoids losing information if the server is stopped.

A key-value store is similar to the `HashMap` collection of the Rust standard library, but it is managed by a server process, which could possibly be running on a different computer. A query is a message exchanged between the client and a server. Redis is one of the most used key-value stores.

The source code for this project is found in the `redis_example` folder. To run it, open the folder and type in `cargo run`. This will print the following:

```
a string, 4567, 12345, Err(Response was of incompatible type: "Response
type not string compatible." (response was nil)), false.
```

This simply creates a data store in the current computer and stores in it the following three key-value pairs:

- `"aKey"`, associated with `"a string"`
- `"anotherKey"`, associated with `4567`
- `45`, associated with `12345`

Then, it queries the store for the following keys:

- `"aKey"`, which obtains an `"a string"` value
- `"anotherKey"`, which obtains a `4567` value
- `45`, which obtains a `12345` value
- `40`, which obtains an error

Then, it queries whether the `40` key exists in the store, which obtains `false`.

Implementing the project

Only the `redis` crate is used in this project.

The code is quite short and simple. Let's look at how it works:

```
fn main() -> redis::RedisResult<()> {
    let client = redis::Client::open("redis://localhost/")?;
    let mut conn = client.get_connection()?;
```

First, a client must be obtained. The call to `redis::Client::open` receives a URL and just checks whether this URL is valid. If the URL is valid, a `redis::Client` object is returned, which has no open connections. Then, the `get_connection` method of the client tries to connect, and if it is successful, it returns an open connection.

Any connection essentially has three important methods:

- `set`: This tries to store a key-value pair.
- `get`: This tries to retrieve the value associated with the specified key.
- `exists`: This tries to detect whether the specified key is present in the store, without retrieving its associated value.

Then, `set` is invoked three times, with different types for the key and value:

```
conn.set("aKey", "a string")?;
conn.set("anotherKey", 4567)?;
conn.set(45, 12345)?;
```

At last, `get` is invoked four times and `exists` is invoked once. The first three calls get the stored value. The fourth call specifies a non-existent value, so a null value is returned, which cannot be converted into `String`, as is required, and so an error is generated:

```
conn.get::<_, String>("aKey")?,
conn.get::<_, u64>("anotherKey")?,
conn.get::<_, u16>(45)?,
conn.get::<_, String>(40),
conn.exists::<_, bool>(40)?);
```

You can always check the error to find out whether your key is present, but a cleaner solution is to call the exists method, which returns a Boolean value specifying whether the key is present.

With this, we now know how Rust crates are used to access, store, and retrieve data using the most popular databases.

Putting it all together

You should now know enough to build an example that does what we described at the beginning of the chapter. We have learned the following:

- How to read a TOML file to parameterize the program
- How to load the data regarding products and sales into memory, specified in a JSON file and in an XML file
- How to store all of this data in three places: a SQLite DB file, a PostgreSQL database, and a Redis key-value store

The source code of the complete example is found in the `transformer` project. To run it, open its folder and type in `cargo run ../data/config.toml`. If everything is successful, it will recreate and populate the SQLite database contained in the `data/sales.db` file, the PostgreSQL database, which can be accessed from `localhost` on port `5432` and is named `Rust2018`, and the Redis store, which can be accessed from `localhost`. Then, it will query the SQLite and PostgreSQL databases for the number of rows in their tables, and it will print the following:

```
SQLite #Products=4.
SQLite #Sales=5.
PostgreSQL #Products=4.
PostgreSQL #Sales=5.
```

So, we have now seen a rather broad example of data manipulation.

Summary

In this chapter, we looked at some basic techniques to access data in popular text formats (TOML, JSON, and XML) or data managed by popular database managers (SQLite, PostgreSQL, and Redis). Of course, many other file formats and database managers exist, and there is still a lot to be learned about these formats and these database managers. Nevertheless, you should now have a grasp of what they do. These techniques are useful for many kinds of applications.

In the next chapter, we will learn how to build a web backend service using the REST architecture. To keep that chapter self-contained, we will only use a framework to receive and respond to web requests, and not use a database. Of course, that is quite unrealistic; but by combining those web techniques with the ones introduced in this chapter, you can build a real-world web service.

Questions

1. Why is it not a good idea to change programmatically a TOML file edited by a user?
2. When is it better to use a dynamically typed parsing of TOML or JSON files and when is it better to use statically typed parsing?
3. When is it required to derive a structure from the `Serialize` and the `Deserialize` trait?

4. What is a pretty generation of a JSON string?
5. Why could it be better to use a stream parser, rather than a single-call parser?
6. When is SQLite a better choice and when is it better to use PostgreSQL?
7. Which is the type of the parameters passed with a SQL command to a SQLite database manager?
8. What does the `query` method do on a PostgreSQL database?
9. What are the names of the functions to read and write values in a Redis key-value store?
10. Can you try to write a program that gets an ID from the command line, queries SQLite, PostgreSQL, or the Redis database for the ID, and prints some information regarding the data found?

Creating a REST Web Service

3

Historically, a lot of technologies have been developed and used to create a client-server system. In recent decades, though, all client-server architectures tend to be web-based—that is, based on the **HyperText Transfer Protocol** (**HTTP**). HTTP is based on the **Transfer Control Protocol** (**TCP**) and the **Internet Protocol** (**IP**). In particular, two web-based architectures have become popular—the **Simple Object Access Protocol** (**SOAP**) and **Representational State Transfer** (**REST**).

While SOAP is an actual protocol, REST is only a collection of *principles*. The web services adhering to the REST principles are said to be RESTful. In this chapter, we'll see how to build RESTful services using the popular Actix web framework.

Any web service (REST web services included) can be used by any web client—that is, any program that can send HTTP requests over a TCP/IP network. The most typical web clients are web pages running in a web browser, and containing JavaScript code. Any program written in any programming language and running in any operating system implementing the TCP/IP protocols can act as a web client.

The web servers are also known as the **backend**, while the web client is known as the **frontend**.

The following topics will be covered in this chapter:

- The REST architecture
- Building a stub of a web service using the Actix web framework and implementing the REST principles
- Building a complete web service capable of uploading files, downloading files, and deleting files on client request
- Handling an inner state as a memory database or a pool of connections to a database
- Using **JavaScript Object Notation** (**JSON**) format to send data to clients

Technical requirements

To easily understand this chapter, you should have beginner knowledge of HTTP. The required concepts are as follows:

- **Uniform Resource Identifiers (URIs)**
- Methods (such as GET)
- Headers
- Body
- Content type (such as plain/text)
- Status code (such as Not Found=404)

Before starting the projects in this chapter, a generic HTTP client should be installed on your computer. The tool used in the examples is the command-line tool curl freely available for many operating systems. The official download page is https://curl.haxx.se/download.html. In particular, the page for Microsoft Windows is https://curl.haxx.se/windows/.

Alternatively, you can use one of the several good, free web-browser utilities, such as Advanced REST Client for Chrome, or RESTED and RESTer for Firefox.

The complete source code for this chapter is in the Chapter03 folder of the repository, located at https://github.com/PacktPublishing/Creative-Projects-for-Rust-Programmers.

The REST architecture

The REST architecture is strongly based on the HTTP protocol but does not require any specific kind of data format, and so it can transmit data in several formats such as plain text, JSON, **Extensible Markup Language** (**XML**), or binary (encoded as Base64).

Many web resources describe what the REST architectural paradigm is. One such can be found at https://en.wikipedia.org/wiki/Representational_state_transfer.

However, the concept of the REST architecture is quite simple. It is the purest extension of the ideas behind the **World Wide Web** (**WWW**) project.

The WWW project was born in 1989 as a global library of **hypertexts**. A hypertext is a document that contains links to other documents so that, by clicking repeatedly on the links, you can see many documents by using only your mouse. Such documents are scattered over the internet and are identified by a unique description, the **Uniform Resource Locator** (**URL**). The protocol to share such documents is HTTP, and the documents are written in **HyperText Markup Language** (**HTML**). A document can embed images, referenced by URL addresses too.

The HTTP protocol allows you to download pages to your document viewer (the web browser), but also to upload new documents to be shared with other people. You can also replace existing documents with a new version, or delete existing documents.

If the concept of a *document* or *file* is replaced by that of *named data*, or a *resource*, you get the concept of REST. Any interaction with a RESTful server is a manipulation of a piece of data, referencing it by its name. Of course, such data can be a disk file, but it can also be a set of records in a database that is identified by a query, or even a variable kept in memory.

A peculiar aspect of RESTful servers is the absence of server-side client sessions. As with any hypertext server, RESTful servers do not store the fact that a client has logged in. If there is some data associated with a session, such as the current user or the previously visited pages, that data belongs only to the client side. As a consequence, any time the client needs access to privileged services, or to user-specific data, the request must contain the credentials of the user.

To improve performance, the server can store session information in a cache, but that should be transparent. The server (except for its performance) should behave as if it doesn't keep any session information.

Project overview

We are going to build several projects, introducing new features in every project. Let's look at each one, as follows:

- The first project will build a stub of a service that should allow any client to upload, download, or delete files from the server. This project shows how to create a REST **application programming interface** (**API**), but it does no useful work.
- The second project will implement the API described in the previous project. It will build a service that actually allows any client to upload, download, or delete files from the server filesystem.

- The third project will build a service that allows clients to add key-value records to a memory database residing in the server process, and to recall some predefined queries built into the server. The result of such queries will be sent back to the client in plain text format.
- The fourth project will be similar to the third one, but the results will be encoded in JSON format.

Our source code is small, but it includes the Actix web crate, which in turn includes around 200 crates, and so the first build of any project will take around 10 minutes. Following any changes to the application code, a build will take from 12 to 30 seconds.

The Actix web crate has been chosen as it is the most feature-full, reliable, high-performance, and well-documented server-side web application framework for Rust.

This framework is not limited to RESTful services, as it can be used to build different kinds of server-side web software. It is an extension of the Actix net framework, which is a framework designed to implement different kinds of network services.

Essential background theory and context

Previously, we said that a RESTful service is based on the HTTP protocol. This is a rather complex protocol, but its most important parts are quite simple. Here is a simplified version of it.

The protocol is based on a pair of messages. First, the client sends a request to the server, and after the server receives this request, it replies by sending a response to the client. Both messages are in **American Standard Code for Information Interchange (ASCII)** text, and so they are easily manipulated.

The HTTP protocol is usually based on the TCP/IP protocol, which guarantees that these messages arrive at the addressed process.

Let's see a typical HTTP request message, as follows:

```
GET /users/susan/index.html HTTP/1.1
Host: www.acme.com
Accept: image/png, image/jpeg, */*
Accept-Language: en-us
User-Agent: Mozilla/5.0
```

This message contains six lines because there is an empty line at the end.

The first line begins with the word GET. This word is the *method* that specifies which operation is requested. Then, there is a Unix-style *path* of a resource, and then the version of the protocol (here, it is 1.1).

Then, there are four lines containing rather simple attributes. These attributes are name **headers**. There are many possible optional headers.

What follows the first empty line is the *body*. Here, the body is empty. The body is used to send raw data—even a lot of data.

So, any request from the HTTP protocol sends a command name (the method) to a specific server, followed by an identifier of a resource (the path). Then, there are a few attributes (one per line), then an empty line, and, finally, the possible raw data (the body).

The most important methods are detailed as follows:

- GET: This requests a resource to be downloaded from the server (typically an HTML file or an image file, but also any data). The path specifies where the resource should be read.
- POST: This sends some data to the server that the server should consider as new. The path specifies where to add this data. If the path identifies any existing data, the server should return an error code. The contents of the data to post are in the body section.
- PUT: This is similar to the POST command, but it is meant to replace existing data.
- DELETE: This requests the resource to be removed specified by the path. It has an empty body.

Here is a typical HTTP response message:

```
HTTP/1.1 200 OK
Date: Wed, 15 Apr 2020 14:03:39 GMT
Server: Apache/2.2.14
Accept-Ranges: bytes
Content-Length: 42
Connection: close
Content-Type: text/html

<html><body><p>Some text</p></body></html>
```

The first line of any response message begins with the protocol version, followed by the status code both in text format and in numeric format. Success is represented by 200 OK.

Then, there are several headers—six, in this example—then an empty line, and then the body, which may be empty. In this case, the body contains some HTML code.

You can find more information regarding the HTTP protocol at: `https://en.wikipedia.org/wiki/Hypertext_Transfer_Protocol`.

Building a stub of a REST web service

The typical example of a REST service is a web service designed for uploading and downloading text files. As it would be too complex to understand, first we will look at a simpler project, the `file_transfer_stub` project, which mimics this service without actually doing anything on the filesystem.

You will see how an API of a RESTless web service is structured, without being overwhelmed by the details regarding the implementation of the commands.

In the next section, this example will be completed with the needed implementation, to obtain a working file-managing web app.

Running and testing the service

To run this service, it is enough to type the command `cargo run` in a console. After building the program, it will print `Listening at address 127.0.0.1:8080 ...`, and it will remain listening for incoming requests.

To test it, we need a web client. You can use a browser extension if you prefer, but in this chapter, the curl command-line utility will be used.

The `file_transfer_stub` service and the `file_transfer` service (we'll see them in the next section) have the same API, containing the following four commands:

1. Download a file with a specified name.
2. Upload a file with a specified name and specified contents.
3. Upload a file with a specified name prefix and specified contents, obtaining the complete name as a response.
4. Delete a file with a specified name.

Getting a resource using the GET method

To download a resource in the REST architecture, the GET method should be used. For these commands, the URL should specify the name of the file to download. No additional data should be passed, and the response should contain the contents of the file and the status code, which can be 200, 404, or 500:

1. Type the following command into a console:

   ```
   curl -X GET http://localhost:8080/datafile.txt
   ```

2. In that console, the following mock line should be printed, and then the prompt should appear immediately:

   ```
   Contents of the file.
   ```

3. Meanwhile, on the other console, the following line should be printed:

   ```
   Downloading file "datafile.txt" ... Downloaded file "datafile.txt"
   ```

   This command mimics the request to download the datafile.txt file from the filesystem of the server.

4. The GET method is the default one for curl, and hence you can simply type the following:

   ```
   curl http://localhost:8080/datafile.txt
   ```

5. In addition, you can redirect the output to any file by typing the following:

   ```
   curl http://localhost:8080/datafile.txt >localfile.txt
   ```

So, we have now seen how our web service can be used by curl to download a remote file, to print it on the console, or to save it in a local file.

Sending a named resource to the server using the PUT method

To upload a resource in the REST architecture, either the PUT or POST methods should be used. The PUT method is used when the client knows *where* the resource should be stored, in essence, what will be its *identifying key*. If there is already a resource that has this key, that resource will be replaced by the newly uploaded resource:

1. Type the following command into a console:

```
curl -X PUT http://localhost:8080/datafile.txt -d "File contents."
```

2. In that console, the prompt should appear immediately. Meanwhile, on the other console, the following line should be printed:

```
Uploading file "datafile.txt" ... Uploaded file "datafile.txt"
```

This command mimics the request to send a file to the server, with the client specifying the name of that resource, so that if a resource with that name already exists, it is overwritten.

3. You can use *curl* to send the data contained in a specified local file in the following way:

```
curl -X PUT http://localhost:8080/datafile.txt -d @localfile.txt
```

Here, the curl command has an additional argument, -d, which allows us to specify the data we want to send to the server. If it is followed by an @ symbol, the text following this symbol is used as the path of the uploaded file.

For these commands, the URI should specify the name of the file to upload and also the contents of the file, and the response should contain only the status code, which can be 200, 201 (Created), or 500. The difference between 200 and 201 is that in the first case, an existing file is overwritten, and in the second case, a new file is created.

So, we have now learned how our web service can be used by curl to upload a string into a remote file, while also specifying the name of the file.

Sending a new resource to the server using the POST method

In the REST architecture, the POST method is the one to use when it is the responsibility of the service to generate an identifier key for the new resource. Thus, the request does not have to specify it. The client can specify a pattern or prefix for the identifier, though. As the key is automatically generated and unique, there cannot be another resource that has the same key. The generated key should be returned to the client, though, because otherwise, it cannot reference that resource afterward:

1. To upload a file with an unknown name, type the following command into the console:

   ```
   curl -X POST http://localhost:8080/data -d "File contents."
   ```

2. In that console, the text data17.txt should be printed, and then the prompt should appear. This text is the simulated name of the file, received from the server. Meanwhile, on the other console, the following line should be printed:

   ```
   Uploading file "data*.txt" ... Uploaded file "data17.txt"
   ```

This command represents the request to send a file to the server, with the server specifying a new unique name for that resource so that no other resource will be overwritten.

For this command, the URI should not specify the full name of the file to upload, but only a prefix; of course, the request should also contain the contents of the file. The response should contain the complete name of the newly created file and the status code. In this case, the status code can only be 201 or 500, because the possibility of a file already existing is ruled out.

We have now learned how our web service can be used by curl to upload a string into a new remote file, leaving the task of inventing a new name for that file to the server. We have also seen that the generated filename is sent back as a response.

Deleting a resource using the DELETE method

In the REST architecture, to delete a resource, the DELETE method should be used:

1. Type the following command into a console (don't worry—no file will be deleted!):

   ```
   curl -X DELETE http://localhost:8080/datafile.txt
   ```

2. After typing that command, the prompt should appear immediately. Meanwhile, in the server console, the following line should be printed:

```
Deleting file "datafile.txt" ... Deleted file "datafile.txt"
```

This command represents the request to delete a file from the filesystem of the server. For such a command, the URL should specify the name of the file to delete. No additional data needs to be passed, and the only response is the status code, which can be 200, 404, or 500. So, we have seen how our web service can be used by *curl* to delete a remote file.

As a summary, the possible status codes of this service are as follows:

- 200: OK
- 201: Created
- 404: Not Found
- 500: Internal Server Error

Also, the four commands of our API are as follows:

Method	URI	Request data format	Response data format	Status codes
GET	/{filename}	---	text/plain	200, 404, 500
PUT	/{filename}	text/plain	---	200, 201, 500
POST	/{filename prefix}	text/plain	text/plain	201, 500
DELETE	/{filename}	---	---	200, 404, 500

Sending an invalid command

Let's see the behavior of the server when an invalid command is received:

1. Type the following command into a console:

```
curl -X GET http://localhost:8080/a/b
```

2. In that console, the prompt should appear immediately. Meanwhile, in the other console, the following line should be printed:

```
Invalid URI: "/a/b"
```

This command represents the request to get the /a/b resource from the server, but, as our API does not permit this method of specifying a resource, the service rejects the request.

Examining the code

The `main` function contains the following statements:

```
HttpServer::new(|| ... )
.bind(server_address)?
.run()
```

The first line creates an instance of an HTTP server. Here, the body of the closure is omitted.

The second line binds the server to an IP endpoint, which is a pair composed of an IP address and an IP port, and returns an error if such a binding fails.

The third line puts the current thread in listening mode on that endpoint. It blocks the thread, waiting for incoming TCP connection requests.

The argument of the `HttpServer::new` call is a closure, shown here:

```
App::new()
    .service(
        web::resource("/{filename}")
            .route(web::delete().to(delete_file))
            .route(web::get().to(download_file))
            .route(web::put().to(upload_specified_file))
            .route(web::post().to(upload_new_file)),
    )
    .default_service(web::route().to(invalid_resource))
```

In this closure, a new web app is created, and then one call to the `service` function is applied to it. Such a function contains a call to the `resource` function, which returns an object on which four calls to the `route` function are applied. Lastly, a call to the `default_service` function is applied to the application object.

This complex statement implements a mechanism to decide which function to call based on the path and method of the HTTP request. In web programming parlance, such a kind of mechanism is named **routing**.

The request routing first performs pattern matching between the address URI and one or several patterns. In this case, there is only one pattern, `/{filename}`, which describes a URI that has an initial slash and then a word. The word is associated with the `filename` name.

The four calls to the `route` method proceed with the routing, based on the HTTP method (`DELETE`, `GET`, `PUT`, `POST`). There is a specific function for every possible HTTP method, followed by a call to the `to` function that has a handling function as an argument.

Such calls to `route` mean that the following applies:

- If the request method of the current HTTP command is `DELETE`, then such a request should be handled by going to the `delete_file` function.
- If the request method of the current HTTP command is `GET`, then such a request should be handled by going to the `download_file` function.
- If the request method of the current HTTP command is `PUT`, then such a request should be handled by going to the `upload_specified_file` function.
- If the request method of the current HTTP command is `POST`, then such a request should be handled by going to the `upload_new_file` function.

Such four handling functions, named **handlers**, must of course be implemented in the current scope. In actuality, they are defined, albeit interleaved with `TODO` comments, recalling what is missing to have a working application instead of a stub. Nevertheless, such handlers contain much functionality.

Such a routing mechanism can be read in English, in this way—for example, for a `DELETE` command:

Create a `service` *to manage the* `web::resource` *named* `/{filename}`, *to* `route` *a* `delete` *command to the* `delete_file` *handler.*

After all of the patterns, there is the call to the `default_service` function that represents a catch-all pattern, typically to handle invalid URIs, such as `/a/b` in the previous example.

The argument of the catch-all statement—that is, `web::route().to(invalid_resource)`, causes the routing to the `invalid_resource` function. You can read it as follows:

For this `web` *command,* `route` *it to the* `invalid_resource` *function.*

Now, let's see the handlers, starting with the simplest one, as follows:

```
fn invalid_resource(req: HttpRequest) -> impl Responder {
    println!("Invalid URI: \"{}\"", req.uri());
    HttpResponse::NotFound()
}
```

This function receives an `HttpRequest` object and returns something implementing the `Responder` trait. It means that it processes an HTTP request, and returns something that can be converted to an HTTP response.

This function is quite simple because it does so little. It prints the URI to the console and returns a *Not Found* HTTP status code.

The other four handlers get a different argument, though. It is the following: `info:` `Path<(String,)>`. Such an argument contains a description of the path matched before, with the `filename` argument put into a single-value tuple, inside a `Path` object. This is because such handlers do not need the whole HTTP request, but they need the parsed argument of the path.

Notice that we have one handler receiving an argument of the `HttpRequest` type, and the others receiving an argument of the `Path<(String,)>` type. This syntax is possible because the `to` function, called in the `main` function, expects as an argument a generic function, whose arguments can be of several different types.

All four handlers begin with the following statement:

```
let filename = &info.0;
```

Such a statement extracts a reference to the first (and only) field of the tuple containing the parameters resulting from the pattern matching of the path. This works as long as the path contained exactly one parameter. The `/a/b` path cannot be matched with the pattern, because it has two parameters. Also, the `/` path cannot be matched, because it has no parameters. Such cases end in the *catch-all* pattern.

Now, let's examine the `delete_file` function specifically. It continues with the following lines:

```
print!("Deleting file \"{}\" ... ", filename);
flush_stdout();

// TODO: Delete the file.

println!("Deleted file \"{}\"", filename);
HttpResponse::Ok()
```

It has two informational printing statements, and it ends returning a success value. In the middle, the actual statement to delete the file is still missing. The call to the `flush_stdout` function is needed to emit the text on the console immediately.

The `download_file` function is similar, but, as it has to send back the contents of the file, it has a more complex response, as illustrated in the following code snippet:

```
HttpResponse::Ok().content_type("text/plain").body(contents)
```

The object returned by the call to `Ok()` is decorated, first by calling `content_type` and setting `text/plain` as the type of the returned body, and then by calling `body` and setting the contents of the file as the body of the response.

The `upload_specified_file` function is quite simple, as its two main jobs are missing: getting the text to put in the file from the body of the request, and saving that text into the file, as illustrated in the following code block:

```
print!("Uploading file \"{}\" ... ", filename);
flush_stdout();

// TODO: Get from the client the contents to write into the file.
let _contents = "Contents of the file.\n".to_string();

// TODO: Create the file and write the contents into it.

println!("Uploaded file \"{}\"", filename);
HttpResponse::Ok()
```

The `upload_new_file` function is similar, but it should have another step that is still missing: to generate a unique filename for the file to save, as illustrated in the following code block:

```
print!("Uploading file \"{}*.txt\" ... ", filename_prefix);
flush_stdout();

// TODO: Get from the client the contents to write into the file.
let _contents = "Contents of the file.\n".to_string();

// TODO: Generate new filename and create that file.
let file_id = 17;

let filename = format!("{}{}.txt", filename_prefix, file_id);

// TODO: Write the contents into the file.

println!("Uploaded file \"{}\"", filename);
HttpResponse::Ok().content_type("text/plain").body(filename)
```

So, we have examined all of the Rust code of the stub of the web service. In the next section, we'll look at the complete implementation of this service.

Building a complete web service

The `file_transfer` project completes the `file_transfer_stub` project, by filling in the missing features.

The features were omitted in the previous project for the following reasons:

- To have a very simple service that actually does not really access the filesystem
- To have only synchronous processing
- To ignore any kind of failure, and keep the code simple

Here, these restrictions have been removed. First of all, let's see what happens if you compile and run the `file_transfer` project, and then test it using the same commands as in the previous section.

Downloading a file

Let's try the following steps on how to download a file:

1. Type the following command into the console:

   ```
   curl -X GET http://localhost:8080/datafile.txt
   ```

2. If the download is successful, the server prints the following line to the console:

   ```
   Downloading file "datafile.txt" ... Downloaded file "datafile.txt"
   ```

   In the console of the client, curl prints the contents of that file.

In the case of an error, the service prints the following:

```
Downloading file "datafile.txt" ... Failed to read file "datafile.txt": No
such file or directory (os error 2)
```

We have now seen how our web service can be used by curl to download a file. In the next sections, we'll learn how our web service can perform other operations on remote files.

Uploading a string to a specified file

Here is the command to upload a string into a remote file with a specified name:

```
curl -X PUT http://localhost:8080/datafile.txt -d "File contents."
```

If the upload is successful, the server prints the following to the console:

```
Uploading file "datafile.txt" ... Uploaded file "datafile.txt"
```

If the file already existed, it is overwritten. If it didn't exist, it is created.

In the case of an error, the web service prints the following line:

```
Uploading file "datafile.txt" ... Failed to create file "datafile.txt"
```

Alternatively, it prints the following line:

```
Uploading file "datafile.txt" ... Failed to write file "datafile.txt"
```

This is how our web service can be used by curl to upload a string into a remote file while specifying the name of the file.

Uploading a string to a new file

Here is the command to upload a string into a remote file with a name chosen by the server:

```
curl -X POST http://localhost:8080/data -d "File contents."
```

If the upload is successful, the server prints to the console something similar to the following:

```
Uploading file "data*.txt" ... Uploaded file "data917.txt"
```

This output shows that the name of the file contains a pseudo-random number— for this example, this is 917, but you'll probably see some other number.

In the console of the client, curl prints the name of that new file, as the server has sent it back to the client.

In the case of an error, the server prints the following line:

```
Uploading file "data*.txt" ... Failed to create new file with prefix
"data", after 100 attempts.
```

Alternatively, it prints the following line:

```
Uploading file "data*.txt" ... Failed to write file "data917.txt"
```

This is how our web service can be used by curl to upload a string into a new remote file, leaving the task of inventing a new name for that file to the server. The curl tool receives this new name as a response.

Deleting a file

Here is the command to delete a remote file:

```
curl -X DELETE http://localhost:8080/datafile.txt
```

If the deletion is successful, the server prints the following line to the console:

```
Deleting file "datafile.txt" ... Deleted file "datafile.txt"
```

Otherwise, it prints this:

```
Deleting file "datafile.txt" ... Failed to delete file "datafile.txt": No
such file or directory (os error 2)
```

This is how our web service can be used by curl to delete a remote file.

Examining the code

Let's now examine the differences between this program and the one described in the previous section. The `Cargo.toml` file contains two new dependencies, as illustrated in the following code snippet:

```
futures = "0.1"
rand = "0.6"
```

The `futures` crate is needed for asynchronous operations, and the `rand` crate is needed for randomly generating the unique names of the uploaded files.

Many new data types have been imported from the external crates, as can be seen in the following code block:

```
use actix_web::Error;
use futures::{
    future::{ok, Future},
    Stream,
```

```
};
use rand::prelude::*;
use std::fs::{File, OpenOptions};
```

The main function has just two changes, as follows:

```
.route(web::put().to_async(upload_specified_file))
.route(web::post().to_async(upload_new_file)),
```

Here, two calls to the `to` function have been replaced by calls to the `to_async` function. While the `to` function is *synchronous* (that is, it keeps the current thread busy until that function is completed), the `to_async` function is *asynchronous* (that is, it can be postponed until the expected events have happened).

This change was required by the nature of upload requests. Such requests can send large files (several megabytes), and the TCP/IP protocol sends such files split into small packets. If the server, when it receives the first packet, just waits for the arrival of all the packets, it can waste a lot of time. Even with multithreading, if many users upload files concurrently, the system will dedicate as many threads as possible to handle such uploads, and this is rather inefficient. A more performant solution is asynchronous processing.

The `to_async` function, though, cannot receive as an argument a synchronous handler. It must receive a function that returns a value having the `impl Future<Item = HttpResponse, Error = Error>` type, instead of the `impl Responder` type, returned by synchronous handlers. This is actually the type returned by the two upload handlers: `upload_specified_file` and `upload_new_file`.

The object returned is of an abstract type, but it must implement the `Future` trait. The concept of a *future*, used also in C++ since 2011, is similar to JavaScript *promises*. It represents a value that will be available in the future, and in the meantime, the current thread can handle some other events.

Futures are implemented as asynchronous closures, meaning that these closures are put in a queue in an internal futures list, and not run immediately. When no other task is running in the current thread, the future at the top of the queue is removed from the queue and executed.

If two futures are chained, the failure of the first chain causes the second future to be destroyed. Otherwise, if the first future of the chain succeeds, the second future has the opportunity to run.

Going back to the two upload functions, another change for their signature is the fact that they now get two arguments. In addition to the argument of the `Path<(String,)>` type, containing the filename, there is an argument of the `Payload` type. Remember that the contents can arrive piece-wise, and so such a `Payload` argument does not contain the text of the file, but it is an object to get the contents of the uploaded file asynchronously.

Its use is somewhat complex.

First, for both upload handlers, there is the following code:

```
payload
    .map_err(Error::from)
    .fold(web::BytesMut::new(), move |mut body, chunk| {
        body.extend_from_slice(&chunk);
        Ok::<_, Error>(body)
    })
    .and_then(move |contents| {
```

The call to `map_err` is required to convert the error type.

The call to `fold` receives from the network one chunk of data at a time and uses it to extend an object of the `BytesMut` type. Such a type implements a kind of extensible buffer.

The call to `and_then` chains another future to the current one. It receives a closure that will be called when the processing of `fold` will be finished. Such a closure receives all the uploaded contents as an argument. This is a way to chain two futures—any closure invoked in this way is executed asynchronously, after the previous one is finished.

The contents of the closure simply write the received contents into a file with the specified name. This operation is synchronous.

The last line of the closure is `ok(HttpResponse::Ok().finish())`. This is the way to return from a future. Notice the lowercase `ok`.

The `upload_new_file` function is similar to the previous one, in terms of the web programming concepts. It is more complex, just because of the following:

- Instead of having a complete filename, only a prefix is provided, and the rest must be generated as a pseudo-random number.
- The resulting filename must be sent to the client.

The algorithm to generate a unique filename is the following:

1. A three-digit pseudo-random number is generated, and it is concatenated to the prefix.
2. The name obtained is used to create a file; this avoids overwriting an existing file with that name.
3. If a collision happens, another number is generated until a new file is created, or until 100 failed attempts have been tried.

Of course, this assumes that the number of uploaded files will always be significantly less than 1,000.

Other changes have been made to consider the chance of failure.

The final part of the `delete_file` function now looks like this:

```
match std::fs::remove_file(&filename) {
    Ok(_) => {
        println!("Deleted file \"{}\"", filename);
        HttpResponse::Ok()
    }
    Err(error) => {
        println!("Failed to delete file \"{}\": {}", filename, error);
        HttpResponse::NotFound()
    }
}
```

This code handles the case of a failure in the deletion of the file. Notice that in the case of an error, instead of returning the success status code `HttpResponse::Ok()` representing the number `200`, a `HttpResponse::NotFound()` failure code is returned, representing the number `404`.

The `download_file` function now contains a local function to read the whole contents of a file into a string, as follows:

```
fn read_file_contents(filename: &str) -> std::io::Result<String> {
    use std::io::Read;
    let mut contents = String::new();
    File::open(filename)?.read_to_string(&mut contents)?;
    Ok(contents)
}
```

The function ends with some code to handle the possible failure of the function, as follows:

```
match read_file_contents(&filename) {
    Ok(contents) => {
        println!("Downloaded file \"{}\"", filename);
        HttpResponse::Ok().content_type("text/plain").body(contents)
    }
    Err(error) => {
        println!("Failed to read file \"{}\": {}", filename, error);
        HttpResponse::NotFound().finish()
    }
}
```

Building a stateful server

The web app of the `file_transfer_stub` project was completely stateless, meaning that every operation had the same behavior independently of the previous operations. Other ways to explain this are that no data was kept from one command to the next, or that it computed pure functions only.

The web app of the `file_transfer` project had a state, but that state was confined to the filesystem. Such a state was the content of the data files. Nevertheless, the application itself was still stateless. No variable survived from one request handling to another request handling.

The REST principles are usually interpreted as prescribing that any API *must be stateless*. That is a misnomer because REST services can have a state, but they *must behave as if they were stateless*. To be stateless means that, except for the filesystem and the database, no information survives in the server from one request handling to another request handling. To behave as if stateless means that any sequence of requests should obtain the same results even if the server is terminated and restarted between one request and a successive one.

Clearly, if the server is terminated, its state is lost. So, to behave as stateless means that the behavior should be the same even if the state is reset. So, what is the purpose of the possible server state? It is to store information that can be obtained again with any request, but that would be costly to do so. This is the concept of caching.

Usually, any REST web server has an internal state. The typical information stored in this state is a pool of connections to the database. A pool is initially empty, and when the first handler must connect to the database, it searches the pool for an available connection. If it finds one, it uses it. Otherwise, a new connection is created and added to the pool. A pool is a shared state that must be passed to any request handler.

In the projects of the previous sections, the request handlers were pure functions; they had no possibility of sharing a common state. In the `memory_db` project, we'll see how we can have a shared state in the Actix web framework that is passed to any request handler.

This web app represents access to a very simple database. Instead of performing actual access to a database, which would require further installations in your computer, it simply invokes some functions exported by the `data_access` module, defined in the `src/data_access.rs` file, that keep the database in memory.

A memory database is a state that is shared by all the request handlers. In a more realistic app, a state would contain only one or more connections to an external database.

How to have a stateful server

To have a state in an Actix service, a struct must be declared, and any data that should be part of the state should be a field of that struct.

At the beginning of the `main.rs` file, there is the following code:

```
struct AppState {
    db: db_access::DbConnection,
}
```

In the state of our web app, we need only one field, but other fields can be added.

The `DbConnection` type declared in the `db_access` module represents the state of our web app. In the `main` function, just before creating the server, there is the following statement that instantiates the `AppState`, and then properly encapsulates it:

```
let db_conn = web::Data::new(Mutex::new(AppState {
    db: db_access::DbConnection::new(),
}));
```

The state is shared by all the requests, and the Actix web framework uses several threads to handle the requests, and so the state must be thread-safe. The typical way of declaring a thread-safe object in Rust is to encapsulate it in a `Mutex` object. This object is then encapsulated in a `Data` object.

To ensure that such a state is passed to any handler, the following line must be added before calling the `service` functions:

```
.register_data(db_conn.clone())
```

Here, the `db_conn` object is cloned (cheaply, as it is a smart pointer), and it is registered into the app.

The effect of this registration is that it is now possible to add another type of argument to the request handlers (both synchronous and asynchronous), as follows:

```
state: web::Data<Mutex<AppState>>
```

Such an argument can be used in statements like this:

```
let db_conn = &mut state.lock().unwrap().db
```

Here, the state is locked to prevent concurrent access by other requests, and its `db` field is accessed.

The API of this service

The rest of the code in this app is not particularly surprising. The API is clear from the names used in the `main` function, as illustrated in the following code block:

```
.service(
    web::resource("/persons/ids")
        .route(web::get().to(get_all_persons_ids)))
.service(
    web::resource("/person/name_by_id/{id}")
        .route(web::get().to(get_person_name_by_id)),
)
.service(
    web::resource("/persons")
        .route(web::get().to(get_persons)))
.service(
    web::resource("/person/{name}")
        .route(web::post().to(insert_person)))
.default_service(
    web::route().to(invalid_resource))
```

Notice that the first three patterns use the GET method, and so they *query* the database. The last one uses the POST method, and so it inserts new records into the database.

Notice also the following lexical conventions.

The path of the URI for the first and third patterns begins with the plural word `persons`, which means that zero, one, or several items will be managed by this request and that any such item represents a person. Instead, the path of the URI for the second and fourth patterns begins with the singular word `person`, and this means that no more than one item will be managed by this request.

The first pattern ends with the plural word `ids`, and so several items regarding the `id` will be handled. It has no condition, and so all the IDs are requested. The second pattern contains the word `name_by_id`, followed by an `id` parameter, and so it is a request of the `name` database column for all the records for which the `id` column has the value specified.

Even in the case of any doubt, the name of the handling functions or comments should make the behavior of the service clear, without having to read the code of the handlers. When looking at the implementation of the handlers, notice that they either return nothing at all or simple text.

Testing the service

Let's test the service with some curl operations.

First of all, we should populate the database that is initially empty. Remember that, being only in memory, it is empty any time you start the service.

After starting the program, type the following commands:

```
curl -X POST http://localhost:8080/person/John
curl -X POST http://localhost:8080/person/Jonathan
curl -X POST http://localhost:8080/person/Mary%20Jane
```

After the first command, a number 1 should be printed to the console. After the second command, 2 should be printed, and after the third command, 3 should be printed. They are the IDs of the inserted names of people.

Now, type the following command:

```
curl -X GET http://localhost:8080/persons/ids
```

It should print the following: 1, 2, 3. This is the set of all the IDs in the database.

Now, type the following command:

```
curl -X GET http://localhost:8080/person/name_by_id/3
```

It should print the following: Mary Jane. This is the name of the unique person for which the id is equal to 3. Notice that the input sequence %20 has been decoded into a blank.

Now, type the following command:

```
curl -X GET http://localhost:8080/persons?partial_name=an
```

It should print the following: 2: Jonathan; 3: Mary Jane. This is the set of all the people for which the name column contains the an substring.

Implementing the database

The whole database implementation is kept in the db_access.rs source file.

The implementation of the database is quite simple. It is a DbConnection type, containing Vec<Person>, where Person is a struct of two fields—id and name.

The methods of DbConnection are described as follows:

- new: This creates a new database.
- get_all_persons_ids(&self) -> impl Iterator<Item = u32> + '_: This returns an iterator that provides all the IDs contained in the database. The lifetime of such an iterator must be no more than that of the database itself.
- get_person_name_by_id(&self, id: u32) -> Option<String>: This returns the name of the unique person having the specified ID if there is one, or zero if there isn't one.
- get_persons_id_and_name_by_partial_name<'a>(&'a self, subname: &'a str) -> impl Iterator<Item = (u32, String)> + 'a: This returns an iterator that provides the ID and the name of all the people whose name contains the specified string. The lifetime of such an iterator must be no more than that of the database itself, and also no more than that of the specified string.
- insert_person(&mut self, name: &str) -> u32: This adds a record to the database, containing a generated ID and the specified name. This returns the generated ID.

Handling queries

The request handlers, contained in the `main.rs` file, get arguments of several types, as follows:

- `web::Data<Mutex<AppState>>`: As described previously, this is used to access the shared app state.
- `Path<(String,)>`: As described in the previous sections, this is used to access the path of the request.
- `HttpRequest`: As described in the previous sections, this is used to access general request information.

> But also, the request handlers get the `web::Query<Filter>` argument to access the optional arguments of the request.

The `get_persons` handler has a query argument—it is a generic argument, whose parameter is the `Filter` type. Such a type is defined as follows:

```
#[derive(Deserialize)]
pub struct Filter {
    partial_name: Option<String>,
}
```

This definition allows requests such as
`http://localhost:8080/persons?partial_name=an`. In this request, the path is just
`/persons`, while `?partial_name=an` is the so-called query. In this case, it contains just
one argument whose key is `partial_name`, and whose value is `an`. It is a string and it is
optional. This is exactly what is described by the `Filter` struct.

In addition, such a type is deserializable, as such an object must be read by the request through serialization.

The `get_persons` function accesses the query through the following expression:

```
&query.partial_name.clone().unwrap_or_else(|| "".to_string()),
```

The `partial_name` field is cloned to get a string. If it is nonexistent, it is taken as an empty string.

Returning JSON data

The previous section returned data in plain text. This is unusual in a web service and rarely satisfactory. Usually, web services return data in JSON, XML, or another structured format. The `json_db` project is identical to the `memory_db` project, except for its returning data in the JSON format.

First of all, let's see what happens when the same curl commands from the previous section are executed on it, as follows:

- The insertions have the same behavior because they just printed a number.
- The first query should print the following: `[1,2,3]`. The three numbers are in an array, and so they are enclosed in brackets.
- The second query should print the following: `"Mary Jane"`. The name is a string, and so it is enclosed in quotation marks.
- The third query should print the following: `[[2,"Jonathan"],[3,"Mary Jane"]]`. The sequence of persons is an array of two records, and each of them is an array of two values, which are a number and a string.

Now, let's see the differences in the code of this project with respect to the previous one.

In the `Cargo.toml` file, one dependency has been added, as follows:

```
serde_json = "1.0"
```

This is needed to serialize the data in JSON format.

In the `main.rs` file, the `get_all_persons_ids` function (instead of returning simply a string) has the following code:

```
HttpResponse::Ok()
    .content_type("application/json")
    .body(
        json!(db_conn.get_all_persons_ids().collect::<Vec<_>>())
        .to_string())
```

First, a response with a status code `Ok` is created; then, its content type is set to `application/json`, to let the client know how to interpret the data it will receive; and lastly, its body is set, using the `json` macro taken from the `serde_json` crate. This macro takes an expression—in this case, with type, `Vec<Person>`—and returns a `serde_json::Value` value. Now, we need a string, and so `to_string()` is called. Notice that the `json!` macro requires its argument to implement the `Serialize` trait or to be convertible into a string.

The `get_person_name_by_id`, `get_persons`, and `insert_person` functions have similar changes. The `main` function has no changes. The `db_access.rs` files are identical.

Summary

We have learned about a few features of the Actix web framework. It is a really complex framework that covers most needs of the backend web developer, and it is still in active development.

Particularly, in the `file_transfer_stub` project, we learned how to create an API of a RESTful service. In the `file_transfer` project, we discussed how to implement the operations of our web service. In the `memory_db` project, we went through how to manage an inner state, in particular, one containing a database connection. In the `json_db` project, we have seen how to send a response in JSON format.

In the next chapter, we will be learning how to create a full server-side web application.

Questions

1. According to the REST principles, what are the meanings of the GET, PUT, POST, and DELETE HTTP methods?
2. Which command-line tool can be used to test a web service?
3. How can a request handler retrieve the value of URI parameters?
4. How can the content type of an HTTP response be specified?
5. How can a unique file name be generated?
6. Why do services that have a stateless API need to manage a state?
7. Why must the state of a service be encapsulated in a `Data` and a `Mutex` object?
8. Why may asynchronous processing be useful in a web service?
9. What is the purpose of the `and_then` function of futures?
10. Which crates are useful to compose an HTTP response in JSON format?

Further reading

To learn more about the Actix framework, view the official documentation at `https://actix.rs/docs/`, and view official examples at `https://github.com/actix/examples/`.

4
Creating a Full Server-Side Web App

In the previous chapter, we saw how to build a REST web service using the Actix web framework. A REST web service must be used by a client app in order for it to be useful to us.

In this chapter, we'll see how to build a very small but complete web app using the Actix web framework. We will use HTML code to be formatted in a web browser, JavaScript code to be executed in the same web browser, and the Tera crate to perform HTML templating. This is useful for embedding dynamic data inside HTML pages.

The following topics will be covered in this chapter:

- Understanding what a classical web app is and what its HTML templates are
- Using the Tera template engine with Rust and Actix web
- Using Actix web to handle requests of web pages
- Handling authentication and authorization in web pages

Technical requirements

To best understand this chapter, you will need to have read the previous chapter. In addition, basic knowledge of HTML and JavaScript is assumed.

The complete source code for this chapter can be found in the `Chapter04` folder of the repository at `https://github.com/PacktPublishing/Rust-2018-Projects`.

Definition of a web app

Everyone knows what a web page or a website is, and everyone knows that some web pages are quite static, while others have more dynamic behavior. The definition of a web app, however, is more subtle and controversial.

We will start with an operational definition of a web app; that is, looking at the appearance and behavior of web apps.

For our purposes, a web app is a website that has the following behavior:

- It appears as one or more web pages in a web browser. On these pages, the user can interact with the page by pressing keys on a keyboard, clicking with a mouse, tapping on a touchscreen, or using another input device. For some user interactions, these web pages send requests to a server and receive data from that site as a response.
- In the case of a *static* web page, the data received is always the same for the same request; but for a web app, the data received depends on the current state of the server, which can change with time. Upon receipt of the data, the web page shows other HTML code, either as a new full page or as a portion of the current page.
- Classic web apps receive HTML code from the server only, so all the browser must do is display the HTML code when it arrives. Modern apps more often receive raw data from the server and use JavaScript code within the browser to create the HTML code that displays the data.

Here, we are going to develop a rather classical web app, as our app receives mainly HTML code from the server. Some JavaScript code will be used to improve the structure of the app.

Understanding the behavior of a web app

When a user navigates to a website by using the address bar of the browser or by clicking on a link in a page, the browser sends an HTTP GET request, with the URI specified in the address field or in the link element, such as `http://hostname.domainname:8080/dir/file?arg1=value1&arg2=value2`.

This address is commonly named **Uniform Resource Locator (URL)** or **Uniform Resource Identifier (URI)**. The difference between these two acronyms is that a URI is something that uniquely identifies a resource without necessarily specifying *where* it can be found; a URL, however, specifies exactly *where* a resource can be found. In doing this, it also identifies the resource because there can be only one resource in a single place.

So, every URL is also a URI, but an address can be a URI without being a URL. For example, an address that specifies the pathname of a file is a URL (and also a URI) because it specifies the path to the file. However, an address specifying a filter condition on files is a URI, but not a URL because it does not explicitly specify which file satisfies that condition.

The first part of an address (such as `http://hostname.domainname:8080`), up to the (optional) port number, is needed to route the request to the server process that should handle it. This server must be running on the host computer and it must be waiting for incoming requests addressed at that port; or, as it is usually said, it must be listening on that port.

The subsequent portion of the URI (such as `/dir/file`) is the so-called **path**, which always starts with a slash and ends at the first question mark character or at the end of the URI. The possible subsequent part (such as `?arg1=value1&arg2=value2`) is the so-called **query**, which has one or more fields separated by an ampersand. Any field of the query has a name, followed by an equals sign, followed by a value.

When a request is made, the server should reply by sending an HTTP response, which contains the HTML page to display in the browser as its body.

After the display of the initial page, any further interaction usually happens when the user operates on the page by using the keyboard, the mouse, or other input devices.

Notice that the effect of any user actions on a page can be classified in the following ways:

- **No code**: Some user actions are handled only by the browser, with no invoked application code. For example, when hovering the mouse over a widget, the mouse cursor shape changes; when typing in a text widget, the text inside that widget changes; and when clicking on a checkbox, the box is selected or deselected. Usually, this behavior is not controlled by the application code.

- **Frontend only**: Some user actions (such as the pressing of a key) trigger the execution of the client-side JavaScript code associated with these actions, but no client-server communication is performed and so no server-side code is invoked as a consequence of these user actions. Typically, any push button is associated (using the `onclick` attribute of the button element) to JavaScript code that is executed any time the user clicks that button. This code could, for example, enable or disable other widgets or copy data from a widget to another widget of the same page.

- **Backend only**: Some user actions trigger client-server communication without using any JavaScript code. There are only two examples of these actions:
    - Clicking on a `submit` input element inside an HTML `form` element
    - Clicking on an `a` HTML element, better known as a **link**

- **Full-stack**: Some user actions trigger the execution of the client-side JavaScript code associated with that action. This JavaScript code sends one or more requests to the backend process and receives the responses sent as replies to these requests. The backend process receives the requests and responds properly to them. So, both the client-side application code and server-side application code is run.

Now, let's examine the advantages and disadvantages of these four cases. The *no code* case is the default one. If the basic behavior of the browser is good enough, there is no need to customize it. Some behavior customization can be performed using HTML or CSS.

The *frontend only* and the *full-stack* cases require JavaScript to be supported and enabled in the browser. This was once a problem because some people or platforms couldn't or wouldn't support it. Nowadays, something that wishes to be called a **web app**, and not simply a web page or website, cannot do so without the use of some kind of client-side processing.

The frontend only case does not interact with the server, and so it may be useful and is recommended for any processes that do not need to send data outside of the current computer or do not need to receive data from another computer. For example, a calculator can be implemented in JavaScript with no communication with a server. However, most web apps need this communication.

The backend only case was the original type of web communication available before JavaScript was invented. It is quite limited, though.

The concept of a link is useful for websites that are meant to be hypertext, not apps. Remember that **HT** in HTML and in HTTP stands for **Hypertext**. That was the original purpose of the web, but nowadays, web apps are meant to be general-purpose applications, not just hypertexts.

The concept of a form containing a submit button also limits the interaction to a rigid protocol—some fields are filled in and a button is pressed to send all of the data to the server. The server processes the request and sends back a new page that replaces the current page. In many cases, this can be done, but it is not a very pleasant experience for the user.

The fourth case is called full-stack because, for these apps, there are both application frontend code and application backend code. As the frontend code needs the backend code to work properly, it can be seen as stacked on it.

Notice that *any* web interaction must have some machine code running on the frontend and some machine code running on the backend. On the frontend, there can be the web browser, the `curl` utility, or some other kind of HTTP client. On the backend, there can be a web server, such as **Internet Information Services (IIS)**, Apache, or NGINX, or an application that acts as an HTTP server.

So, for any web app, there is client-server communication using the HTTP protocol.

The term *full-stack* means that, in addition to system software, there is also some application software running on the frontend (acting as an HTTP client) and some application software running on the backend (acting as an HTTP server).

In a typical full-stack application running on a browser, there are no links or forms, just the typical widgets of a GUI. Usually, these widgets are fixed text, editable fields, drop-down lists, check buttons, and push buttons. When the user presses any push button, a request is sent to the server, possibly using the values contained in the widgets, and when the server sends back an HTML page, that page is used to replace the current page or a portion of it.

Project overview

The sample web app that we are going to build has the purpose of managing a list of people contained in a database. It is an extremely simple database as it only has one table with two columns—one for a numeric ID and one for a name. To keep the project simple, the database is actually a vector of struct objects kept in memory; but of course, in a real-world application, it would be stored in a **Database Management System (DBMS)**.

The project will be built in steps, creating four projects that are progressively more complex, that can be downloaded from the GitHub repository linked in the *Technical requirements* section of this chapter:

- The `templ` project is a collection of code snippets that shows how to use the Tera template engine for the projects of this chapter.
- The `list` project is a simple list of records about people that can be filtered by name. These records are actually contained in the database code and cannot be changed by the user.
- The `crud` project contains the features to add, change, and delete people. They are the so-called **Create, Retrieve, Update, and Delete (CRUD)** basic functions.
- The `auth` project adds a login page and ensures that only authorized users can read or change the database. The list of users and their privileges cannot be changed, however.

The `templ` project, which does not use the Actix web framework, can be compiled in 1 to 3 minutes the first time, and in a few seconds after any changes to the code.

Any of the other projects will take around 3 to 9 minutes to compile the first time, then 8 to 20 seconds after any changes.

When you run any of the preceding projects (except the first one), all you will see is `Listening at address 127.0.0.1:8080` printed on the console. To view anything more, you will need a web browser.

Using the Tera template engine

Before starting to develop our web app, we will examine the concept of a **template engine**—in particular, the Tera crate, one of the many template engines available for Rust.

Template engines can have several applications, but they are mostly used for web development.

A typical problem in web development is knowing how to generate HTML code containing some constants parts written by hand and some dynamic parts generated by application code. In general, there are two ways to obtain this kind of effect:

- You have a programming language source file that contains a lot of statements that print strings to create the desired HTML page. These `print` statements mix string literals (that is, strings enclosed in quotation marks) and variables formatted as strings. This is what you'd do in Rust if you didn't have a template engine.
- You write an HTML file containing the desired constant HTML elements and the desired constant text, but it also contains some statements enclosed in specific markers. The evaluation of these statements generates the variable parts of the HTML file. This is what you'd do in PHP, JSP, ASP, and ASP.NET.

However, there is also a compromise, which is to write both application code files and HTML code containing statements to evaluate. You can then choose the best tool for the job. This is the paradigm used by template engines.

Imagine you have some Rust code files and some HTML files that must cooperate with one another. The tool to make the two worlds communicate is a template engine. The HTML files with embedded statements are named **templates** and the Rust application code calls the template engine functions to manipulate these templates.

Now, let's see the code in the `templ` example project. The first statement creates an instance of the engine:

```
let mut tera_engine = tera::Tera::default();
```

The second statement loads one simple template into the engine by calling the `add_raw_template` function:

```
tera_engine.add_raw_template(
    "id_template", "Identifier: {{id}}.").unwrap();
```

The first argument is the name that will be used to refer to this template and the second argument is the template itself. It is a normal reference to a string slice, but it contains the `{{id}}` placeholder. This symbol qualifies it as a **Tera expression**. In particular, this expression contains just a Tera variable, but it could contain a more complex expression.

A constant expression is also allowed, such as `{{3+5}}`, even if there is no point in using constant expressions. A template can contain several expressions or none at all.

Notice that the `add_raw_template` function is fallible, so `unwrap` is called on its result. This function, before adding the template received as an argument, analyzes it to see whether it is well-formed. For example, if it read `"Identifier: {{id}."` (with a missing brace), it would generate an error, and so the call to `unwrap` would panic.

When you have a Tera template, you can **render** it; that is, generate a string that replaces the expressions with some specified strings, in a similar way to how a macro processor does.

To evaluate an expression, the Tera engine has to first replace all of the variables used in it with their current value. To do that, a collection of Tera variables—each one associated with its current value—must be created. This collection is named a context. A context is created and populated by the following two statements:

```
let mut numeric_id = tera::Context::new();
numeric_id.insert("id", &7362);
```

The first one creates a mutable context and the second one inserts a key-value association into it. Here, the value is a reference to a number, but other types are also allowed as values.

Of course, in a real-world example, the value would be a Rust variable, not a constant.

Now, we can render it:

```
println!("id_template with numeric_id: [{}]",
    tera_engine.render("id_template", &numeric_id).unwrap());
```

println!

The `render` method gets a template named `"id_template"` in the `tera_engine` object and applies the substitutions specified by the `numeric_id` context.

This can fail if the specified template is not found, if variables in the template have not been substituted, or if an evaluation has failed for some other reason. If the result is okay, `unwrap` gets the string. Therefore, it should print the following:

```
id_template with numeric_id: [Identifier: 7362.]
```

The next three Rust statements in the example are as follows:

```
let mut textual_id = tera::Context::new();
textual_id.insert("id", &"ABCD");
println!(
    "id_template with textual_id: [{}]",
    tera_engine.render("id_template", &textual_id).unwrap()
);
```

They do the same thing, but with a literal string, showing that the same template variable can be replaced with both a number and a string. The printed line should be as follows:

```
id_template with textual_id: [Identifier: ABCD.]
```

The next statement is as follows:

```
tera_engine
    .add_raw_template("person_id_template", "Person id: {{person.id}}")
    .unwrap();
```

It adds a new template to the engine containing the `{{person.id}}` expression. This Tera dot notation has the same function as the Rust dot notation—it allows us to access a field of a struct. Of course, it only works if the `person` variable is replaced by an object with an `id` field.

So, a `Person` struct is defined in the following way:

```
#[derive(serde_derive::Serialize)]
struct Person {
    id: u32,
    name: String,
}
```

The struct has an `id` field but also derives the `Serialize` trait. This is a requirement for any object that must be passed to a Tera template.

The statement to define the `person` variable in the context is as follows:

```
one_person.insert(
    "person",
    &Person {
        id: 534,
        name: "Mary".to_string(),
    },
);
```

So, the printed string will be as follows:

```
person_id_template with one_person: [Person id: 534]
```

Now, there is a more complex template:

```
tera_engine
    .add_raw_template(
        "possible_person_id_template",
        "{%if person%}Id: {{person.id}}\
        {%else%}No person\
```

```
        {%endif%}",
    )
    .unwrap();
```

The template is one-line long, but it has been split into three lines in Rust source code.

In addition to the `{{person.id}}` expression, there are three markers of another kind; they are **Tera statements**. Tera statements differ from Tera expressions because they are enclosed by the `{%` and `%}` signs, instead of double braces. While Tera expressions are similar to C preprocessor macros (that is, `#define`), Tera statements are similar to the conditional compilation directives of the C preprocessor (that is, `#if`, `#else`, and `#endif`).

The expression after the `if` statement is evaluated by the `render` function. If the expression is not defined or its value is either `false`, `0`, an empty string, or an empty collection, the expression is considered false. The text part—up to the `{%else%}` statement—is then discarded. Otherwise, the part after that statement, up to the `{%endif%}` statement, is discarded.

This template is rendered with two different contexts—one in which the `person` variable is defined and the other in which no variable is defined. The two printed lines are as follows:

```
possible_person_id_template with one_person: [Id: 534]
possible_person_id_template with empty context: [No person]
```

In the first case, the `id` value of the person is printed; in the second case, the `No person` text is printed.

Then, another complex template is created:

```
tera_engine
    .add_raw_template(
        "multiple_person_id_template",
        "{%for p in persons%}\
        Id: {{p.id}};\n\
        {%endfor%}",
    )
    .unwrap();
```

Here, the template contains two other kinds of statements—`{%for p in persons%}` and `{%endfor%}`. They enclose a loop where the newly created `p` variable iterates over the `persons` collection, which must belong to the context used by `render`.

Then, there is the following code:

```
let mut three_persons = tera::Context::new();
three_persons.insert(
    "persons",
    &vec![
        Person {
            id: 534,
            name: "Mary".to_string(),
        },
        Person {
            id: 298,
            name: "Joe".to_string(),
        },
        Person {
            id: 820,
            name: "Ann".to_string(),
        },
    ],
);
```

This adds a Tera variable named `persons` to the `three_persons` Tera context. This variable is a vector containing three people.

Because the `persons` variable can be iterated, it is possible to evaluate the template, thereby obtaining the following:

```
multiple_person_id_template with three_persons: [Id: 534;
Id: 298;
Id: 820;
]
```

Notice that any `Id` object is in a distinct line because the template contains a new-line character (through the `\n` escape sequence); otherwise, they would have been printed in a single line.

So far, we have used templates in string literals. This becomes difficult for long templates, though. Therefore, templates are usually loaded from separate files. This is advisable because the **Integrated Development Environment** (**IDE**) can help the developer (if it knows which language it is processing) and so it is better to keep HTML code in files with a `.html` suffix, CSS code in files with a `.css` suffix, and so on.

The next statement loads a Tera template from a file:

```
tera_engine
    .add_template_file("templates/templ_id.txt", Some("id_file_template"))
    .unwrap();
```

The first argument of the `add_template_file` function is the path of the template file, relative to the root of the project. It is good practice to put all the template files in a separate folder or in its subfolders.

The second argument allows us to specify the name of the new template. If the value of that argument is `None`, the name of the new template is the first argument.

So, the statement is as follows:

```
println!(
    "id_file_template with numeric_id: [{}]",
    tera_engine
        .render("id_file_template", numeric_id.clone())
        .unwrap()
);
```

This will print the following:

```
id_file_template with numeric_id: [This file contains one id: 7362.]
```

The following code will have similar results:

```
tera_engine
    .add_template_file("templates/templ_id.txt", None)
    .unwrap();

println!(
    "templates/templ_id.txt with numeric_id: [{}]",
    tera_engine
        .render("templates/templ_id.txt", numeric_id)
        .unwrap()
);
```

Lastly, let's talk about a convenient feature that can be used to load all of the templates with a single statement.

Instead of loading the templates one at a time, where they are needed, it is possible to load all of the templates at once and store them in a global dictionary. This makes them available to the entire module. To do so, it is convenient to use the `lazy_static` macro, described in Chapter 1, *Rust 2018 – Productivity!*, to write outside of any function:

```
lazy_static::lazy_static! {
    pub static ref TERA: tera::Tera =
        tera::Tera::new("templates/**/*").unwrap();
}
```

This statement defines the TERA static variable as a global template engine. It will be initialized automatically when some Rust code of your app uses it first. This initialization will search all of the files in the specified subtree of folders and will load them, giving each of them the name of the file itself and omitting the name of its folder.

The last feature of the Tera engine to be presented in this section is the `include` statement. The last line of the `templ_names.txt` file is the following one:

```
{% include "footer.txt" %}
```

It will load the contents of the specified file and will expand it inline, replacing the statement itself. It is similar to the `#include` directive of the C preprocessor.

A simple list of persons

Now, we can examine the `list` project. If you run the server in a console and you access the `localhost:8080` address from a web browser, you will see the following page in the browser:

Persons

Name portion: [   ] [Filter]

Id	Name
2	Hamlet
4	Macbeth
7	Othello

There is a heading, a label, a text field, a push button, and a table containing a list of three people.

The only thing you can do on this page is type something into the text field and then click on the button to apply the typed text as a filter. For example, if you type l (that is, a lowercase *L*), only the **Hamlet** and **Othello** lines will appear as they are the only two people whose name contains this letter. If the filter is x, the result will be the **No persons** text as none of the three people has a name containing this letter. The page will look as in the following screenshot:

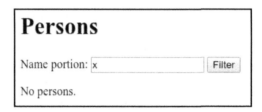

Before explaining how it all works, let's see the dependencies of this project; that is, the external crates used by it. They are as follows:

- actix-web: This is the web framework, also used in Chapter 3, *Creating a REST Web Service*.
- tera: This is the Tera template engine.
- serde and serde_derive: These are the serialization crates used by the Tera engine to pass whole struct objects to a template context.
- lazy_static: This contains the macro to initialize the Tera engine.

Now, let's take a glimpse at the source code. For this project, the src folder contains the following files:

- main.rs: This is the whole server-side application, excluding the database.
- db_access.rs: This is the mock database with some mock data.
- favicon.ico: This is the icon that any website should have as it is automatically downloaded by the browser to display it in the browser tab.

There is also a templates folder, containing the following files:

- main.html: This is the Tera/HTML template of the whole web page with an empty body.
- persons.html: This is the Tera/HTML template of a partial web page, containing only the body of our web app.
- main.js: This is the JavaScript code to be included in the HTML page.

Now, let's examine the mechanics of this web app.

When the user navigates to the `http://localhost:8080/` URI, the browser sends a GET HTTP request (that has only a slash as its path) to our process, with no query and empty body, and it expects an HTML page to be displayed. As described in the previous chapter, the server—using the Actix web framework—can respond to the request if its `main` function contains the following code:

```
let server_address = "127.0.0.1:8080";
println!("Listening at address {}", server_address);
let db_conn = web::Data::new(Mutex::new(AppState {
    db: db_access::DbConnection::new(),
})));
HttpServer::new(move || {
    App::new()
        .register_data(db_conn.clone())
        .service(
            web::resource("/")
                .route(web::get().to(get_main)),
        )
})
.bind(server_address)?
.run()
```

Here, we have a web app whose state is only a shared reference to a database connection (that is actually a mock database). This app accepts only one kind of request—those using the root path (/) and the GET method. These requests are routed to the `get_main` function. The function should return an HTTP response containing the initial HTML page to display.

Here is the body of the `get_main` function:

```
let context = tera::Context::new();
HttpResponse::Ok()
    .content_type("text/html")
    .body(TERA.render("main.html", context).unwrap())
```

This function does not use the request at all because it always returns the same result.

To return a successful response (that is, with status code 200), the `HttpResponse::Ok()` function is called. To specify that the body of the response is HTML code, the `content_type("text/html")` method is called on the response. To specify the content of the body of the response, the `body` method is called on the response.

The argument of the `body` function must be a string containing the HTML code to display. It is possible to write all of that code here, as follows:

```
.body("<!DOCTYPE html><html><body><p>Hello</p></body></html>")
```

However, for more complex pages, it is better to keep all the HTML code in a separate file, with the `.html` filename extension, and to load the contents of this file into a string to pass as an argument to the `body` function. This can be done using the following expression:

```
.body(include_str!("main.html"))
```

This would work well if the `main.html` file was static; that is, it wouldn't need to change at runtime. However, this solution would be too limiting for two reasons:

- We want our initial page to be a *dynamic* page. It should show the list of people that are in the database when the page is opened.
- We want our initial page, and also all of the other possible pages, to be composed of several parts: metadata elements, JavaScript routines, styles, a page header, a page central part, and a page footer. All of these parts, except for the central part, are to be shared by all of the pages to avoid repeating them in source code. So, we need to keep these parts in separate files and then splice them together before the HTML page is sent to the browser. In addition, we want to keep JavaScript code in separate files with the `.js` file extension and style code in separate files with the `.css` file extension so that our IDE recognizes their language.

A solution to these problems is to use the Tera template engine, which we will see in the next section.

The templates folder

It is best to put all deliverable application text files in the `templates` folder (or in some of its subfolders). So, this subtree should contain all the HTML, CSS, and JS files, even if, at the moment, they may contain no Tera statements or expressions.

Instead, non-textual files (such as pictures, audio, video, and many others), user-uploaded files, documents that are to be downloaded explicitly, and databases should be kept elsewhere.

The loading of all template files happens at runtime, but usually only once in the process life. The fact that the loading happens at runtime implies that the `templates` subtree must be deployed and that to deploy a new or changed version of one of those files, a rebuild of the program is not required. The fact that this loading usually happens once in the process life implies that the template engine is quite fast at processing the templates after the first time.

The preceding body statement has the following argument:

```
TERA.render("main.html", context).unwrap()
```

This expression renders the template contained in the main.html file using a Tera context contained in the context Rust variable. This kind of variable has been initialized by the tera::Context::new() expression and so it is an empty context.

The HTML file is very small and it has two noteworthy snippets. The first one is as follows:

```
<script>
{% include "main.js" %}
</script>
```

This uses the include Tera statement to incorporate the JavaScript code into the HTML page. Having it incorporated into the server means that no further HTTP requests will be needed to load it. The second snippet is as follows:

```
<body id="body" onload="getPage('/page/persons')">
```

This causes the invocation of the getPage JavaScript function as soon as the page is loaded. This function is defined in the main.js file and, as its name suggests, it causes the loading of the specified page.

So, when the user navigates to the root of the website, the server prepares an HTML page containing all the required JavaScript code, but almost no HTML code, and sends it to the browser. As soon as the browser has loaded the empty page, it requests another page, which will become the body of the first page.

This may sound complicated, but you can look at it as the page being split into two parts—the metadata, the scripts, the styles, and possibly the page header and footer are the common parts, which do not change during the session. The central part (which here is the body element, but may also be an inner element) is the variable part, which changes with any click from the user.

By reloading only part of the page, the app has better performance and usability.

Let's look at the contents of the main.js file:

```
function getPage(uri) {
    var xhttp = new XMLHttpRequest();
    xhttp.onreadystatechange = function() {
        if (this.readyState == 4 && this.status == 200) {
            document.getElementById('body')
                .innerHTML = xhttp.responseText;
        }
```

```
        };
        xhttp.open('GET', uri, true);
        xhttp.send();
    }
```

This code creates an `XMLHttpRequest` object that, in spite of its name, does not use XML, but it is actually used to send an HTTP request. This object is set to process the response when it arrives by assigning an anonymous function to the `onreadystatechange` field. Then, the specified URI is opened with a `GET` method.

When a response arrives, the code checks whether the message is complete (`readystate == 4`) and valid (`state == 200`). In this case, the text of the response that is assumed to be valid HTML is assigned as the content of the element that has `body` as its unique ID.

The last file in the `templates` folder is the `persons.html` file. It is a partial HTML file—that is, a file containing HTML elements, but without the `<html>` element itself—and so its purpose is to be included in another HTML page. This small app has only one page and so it only has one partial HTML file.

Let's look at some interesting parts of this file. The following is an element to let the user type in some text (a so-called **edit box**):

```
<input id="name_portion" type="text" value="{{partial_name}}"/>
```

Its initial value—that is, the text that is shown to the user when the page is opened—is a **Tera variable**. Rust code should assign a value to the variable.

Then, there is the `Filter` push button:

```
<button onclick="getPage('/page/persons?partial_name='
    + getElementById('name_portion').value)">Filter</button>
```

When the user clicks on it and the preceding edit box contains the word `Ham`, the `'/page/persons?partial_name=Ham'` argument is passed to the JavaScript `getPage` functions. So, the function sends the `GET` request to the backend and replaces the body of the page with whatever is returned by the backend, so long as it is a complete and valid response.

Then, there is the following Tera statement:

```
{% if persons %}
...
{% else %}
    <p>No persons.</p>
{% endif %}
```

Here, the `persons` Tera variable is evaluated. According to the Rust program, the variable can only be a collection. If the variable is a non-empty collection, a table is inserted into the HTML page; if instead the variable is not defined or it is an empty collection, the `No persons.` text will be shown.

Within the HTML code defining the table, there is the following:

```
{% for p in persons %}
    <tr>
        <td>{{p.id}}</td>
        <td>{{p.name}}</td>
    </tr>
{% endfor %}
```

This is an iteration over the items contained in `persons` (which we know is non-empty).

In each iteration, the `p` variable will contain the data of a specific person. This variable is used in two expressions. The first one shows the value of the `id` field of the variable. The second one shows the value of its `name` field.

The other Rust handlers

We have only seen the routing and handling of the root of the site—the `/` path. This happens when the user opens the page.

There are four other requests that can be sent by the browser to this app:

- When the root path is accessed, the page loaded by this request automatically sends—using JavaScript code—another request to load the body of the page.
- When the user presses the **Filter** button, the frontend should send the text contained in the edit box to the backend, and then the backend should respond by sending back the list of the people satisfying this filter.
- The browser automatically requests the `favicon.ico` app icon.
- Any other requests should be treated as errors.

Actually, the first and second of these requests can be handled in the same way, because the initial state can be generated by a filter where an empty string is specified. So, three different kinds of requests remain.

To route these requests, the following code is inserted into the `main` function:

```
.service(
    web::resource("/page/persons")
        .route(web::get().to(get_page_persons)),
)
.service(
    web::resource("/favicon.ico")
        .route(web::get().to(get_favicon)),
)
.default_service(web::route().to(invalid_resource))
```

P89

The first route redirects any GET requests to the /page/persons path to the `get_page_persons` function. These requests come when the user clicks on the **Filter** button, but also indirectly when the / path is requested.

The second route redirects any GET requests to the /favicon.ico path to the `get_favicon` function. These requests come from the browser when it receives a complete HTML page, not a partial page.

The call to `default_resource` redirects any other requests to the `invalid_resource` function. These requests cannot come with proper use of the app, but may come under specific conditions or when the user types an unexpected path into the address bar of the browser. For example, this request occurs if you type in http://127.0.0.1:8080/abc.

Now, let's look at the handler's functions.

The `get_page_persons` function has two arguments:

- `web::Query<Filter>` is used to pass the optional filter condition.
- `web::Data<Mutex<AppState>>` is used to pass the database connection.

The parameter of the `Query` type is defined as follows:

```
#[derive(Deserialize)]
pub struct Filter {
    partial_name: Option<String>,
}
```

This specifies the possible arguments of the *query*, which is the part of the URI following the question mark. Here, there is only one argument and it is optional as it is typical of HTTP queries. A possible query is ?partial_name=Jo, but also an empty string is a valid query in this case.

To be able to receive the `Filter` structure from the request, it must implement the `Deserialize` trait.

The body of the `get_page_persons` function is as follows:

```
let partial_name = &query.partial_name.clone().unwrap_or_else(||
"".to_string());
let db_conn = &state.lock().unwrap().db;
let person_list = db_conn.get_persons_by_partial_name(&partial_name);
let mut context = tera::Context::new();
context.insert("partial_name", &partial_name);
context.insert("persons", &person_list.collect::<Vec<_>>());
HttpResponse::Ok()
    .content_type("text/html")
    .body(TERA.render("persons.html", context).unwrap())
```

The first statement gets the query from the request. If the `partial_name` field is defined, it is extracted; otherwise, an empty string is generated.

The second statement extracts the connection to the database from the shared state.

The third statement uses this connection to get an iterator on the people satisfying the criteria. See the subsection, *Implementing the database* in the section *Building a stateful server* in the previous chapter. See the previous chapter to understand these two lines.

Then, an empty Tera context is created and two Tera variables are added to it:

- `partial_name` is used to keep the typed characters that otherwise would disappear when the page is reloaded in the edit box.
- `persons` is the vector containing the people collected from the database. To make this possible, the `Person` type must implement the `Serialize` trait.

Finally, the Tera engine can render the `persons.html` template using the *context*, because all the variables used in the template have been defined. The result of this rendering is passed as the body of the successful HTTP response. When the JavaScript code inside the browser receives that HTML code, it will use it to replace the contents of the body of the current page.

Now, let's see the body of the `get_favicon` function:

```
HttpResponse::Ok()
    .content_type("image/x-icon")
    .body(include_bytes!("favicon.ico") as &[u8])
```

This is simply a successful HTTP response whose content is of the image HTTP type and the x-icon subtype, and whose body is a slice of bytes containing the icon. This binary object is constructed at compile time from the bytes contained in the favicon.ico file. The content of this file is embedded in the executable program, so it is not required to deploy this file.

Finally, let's look at the body of the invalid_resource function:

```
HttpResponse::NotFound()
    .content_type("text/html")
    .body("<h2>Invalid request.</h2>")
```

This is a failing response (as NotFound generates the 404 status code), which should contain a complete HTML page. For simplicity, a straightforward message has been returned.

We have now looked at a very simple web app. Many of the concepts seen in this section will be used in the following sections, where the database will be modified by user actions.

A CRUD application

The web app shown in the previous section allowed us to view filtered data in a single page. If you now run the project in the crud folder, you will see a much more rich and useful web page:

The **Id** edit box and the **Find** button to its right are used to open a page that allows you to view or edit the data of a person with a specific ID.

The **Name portion** edit box and the **Filter** button to its right are for filtering the table below it, in a similar way as in the `list` project.

Then, there are two buttons—one for deleting data and one for adding data.

Lastly, there is the filtered table of the people. In this app, the initial state of the database is an empty list of people and so no HTML table is shown.

Let's create some people.

Click on the **Add New Person** push button. You will see the following window:

This is the page used to create a person and insert them into the database. The **Id** field is disabled because its value will be generated automatically. To insert a person, type in a name for them—for example, **Juliet**—and click on the **Insert** button. The main page will appear again, but with a small table containing only **Juliet**, preceded by **1** as its ID.

If you repeat these steps, inserting **Romeo** and **Julius**, you'll have the results shown in the following picture:

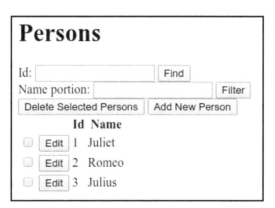

The push buttons near any listed person allow us to open a page related to that person. For example, if the button near **Julius** is clicked, the following page will appear:

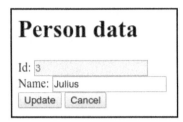

This page is very similar to the page used to insert people, but with the following differences:

- The **Id** field now contains a value.
- The **Name** field now contains an initial value.
- Instead of the **Insert** button, now there is an **Update** button.

If you change the **Julius** value to **Julius Caesar** and click on **Update**, you will see the updated list on the main page.

Another way to open the page relating to a single person is to type the ID of that person into the **Id** field and then click on the **Find** button. If you click on this button when that field is empty or when it contains a value that no person has as its ID, a red error message appears on the page:

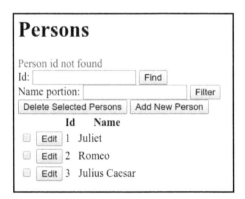

The final feature of this app allows us to delete records. To do that, click on the checkboxes to the left of the lines of the people you want to delete, and then click on the **Delete Selected Persons** button. The list is immediately updated.

Notice that the database is stored in the memory of the backend process. You will see the same list of people if you close the browser and reopen it or if you open another browser. You can even open the page from another computer, as long as you insert the appropriate name or IP address of the computer where the backend process is running. However, if you terminate the backend process by pressing the *Ctrl + C* key combination (or in any other way) and then re-run it, all of the browsers will display no people when the page is reloaded.

The JavaScript code

We are now going to look at what makes this project different from the one described in the previous section.

First of all, the main.js file is much larger because it contains three additional functions:

- sendCommand: This is quite a generic routine used to send HTTP requests to a server and to process the received response asynchronously. It accepts five arguments:
  - method is the HTTP command to use, such as GET, PUT, POST, or DELETE.
  - uri is the path and possible query to send to the server.
  - body is the possible body of the request, used to send data larger than 2 KB.
  - success is a reference to a function that will be called after receiving a successful response (status == 200).
  - failure is a reference to a function that will be called after receiving any failure response (status != 200).

  This function is used to access a REST service as it allows any HTTP method, but it doesn't automatically change the current HTML page. Instead, the getPage function can only use the GET method, but it replaces the current HTML page with the HTML code received.

- delete_selected_persons: This scans the items whose checkboxes are selected and sends a DELETE command to the server with the /persons?id_list= URI followed by a comma-separated list of the IDs of the selected items. The server should delete these records and return a successful state. If the deletion is successful, this JavaScript function reloads the main page with no filter; otherwise, an error message is shown in a message box and the current page is not changed. It should be called when the **Delete Selected Persons** button is clicked.

- `savePerson`: This receives an HTTP method, which can be `POST` (to insert) or `PUT` (to update). It sends a command to the server, using the method received as an argument, and a URI that depends on the method. For a `POST` request, the URI is `/one_person?name=NAME`, while for a `PUT` request, the URI is `/one_person?id=ID&name=NAME`, wherein `ID` and `NAME` are actually the values of the `id` and `name` fields of the record to create or update. This function should be called with a `POST` argument when the **Insert** button is clicked and with a `PUT` argument when the **Update** button is clicked.

Now, let's check the HTML code of the application.

The HTML code

Of course, many HTML elements have been added to the `persons.html` file to create the additional widgets.

First, there is the `<label class="error">{{id_error}}</label>` element, used to display error messages caused by the **Find** button. To correctly process this element, the `id_error` Tera variable needs to be defined in the current Tera context.

Then, there is the following element:

```
<div>
    <label>Id:</label>
    <input id="person_id" type="number">
    <button onclick="getPage(
        '/page/edit_person/' + getElementById('person_id').value)"
        >Find</button>
</div>
```

When the **Find** button is clicked, a page is requested at the `/page/edit_person/` URI, followed by the typed ID.

Then, there are two push buttons:

```
<div>
    <button onclick="delete_selected_persons()">Delete Selected
Persons</button>
    <button onclick="getPage('/page/new_person')">Add New Person</button>
</div>
```

The first one simply delegates all the work to the `delete_selected_persons` function, while the second one gets the page at the `/page/new_person` URI.

Finally, two columns are added to the HTML table containing the list of people. They are found on the left side of the table:

```
<td><input name="selector" id="{{p.id}}" type="checkbox"/></td>
<td><button
onclick="getPage('/page/edit_person/{{p.id}}')">Edit</button></td>
```

The first column is the checkbox to select the record to delete and the second one is the **Edit** button. The value of the HTML `id` attribute of the checkbox element is the `{{p.id}}` Tera expression, which will be replaced by the ID of the record of the current line. So, this attribute can be used to prepare the request to send it to the server to delete the selected items.

The **Edit** button will get the page at the `/page/edit_person/` URI, followed by the ID of the current record.

In addition, there is another HTML partial file, `one_person.html`. This is the page used both to insert a new person and to view/edit an existing person. Its first part is as follows:

```
<h1>Person data</h1>
<div>
    <label>Id:</label>
    <input id="person_id" type="number" value="{{ person_id }}" disabled>
</div>
<div>
    <label>Name:</label>
    <input id="person_name" type="text" value="{{ person_name }}"/>
</div>
```

For both of the `input` elements, the `value` attribute is set to a Tera expression; for the first one, it is the `person_id` Tera variable and for the second, it is the `person_name` Tera variable. When inserting a person, these variables will be empty and when editing a person, these variables will contain the current values of the database fields.

The last part of the file is as follows:

```
{% if inserting %}
    <button onclick="savePerson('POST')">Insert</button>
{% else %}
    <button onclick="savePerson('PUT')">Update</button>
{% endif %}
<button onclick="getPage('/page/persons')">Cancel</button>
```

This page must show the **Insert** button when it has been opened for inserting a person, and the **Update** button when it has been opened for viewing or editing a person. So, the `inserting` Tera variable is used. Its value will be `true` when in insert mode and `false` when in edit mode.

Finally, the **Cancel** button opens the `/page/persons` page, with no filtering.

That's all we need to know about the `templates` folder.

The Rust code

In the `src` folder, both the `db_access.rs` and the `main.rs` files have many changes.

The db_access.rs changes

The `persons` vector is initially empty because users can insert records into it.

The following functions have been added:

- `get_person_by_id`: This searches the vector for a person with a specified ID. It returns the person if found or `None`, otherwise.
- `delete_by_id`: This searches the vector for a person with the specified ID; if found, it is removed from the vector and `true` is returned. Otherwise, `false` is returned.
- `insert_person`: A `Person` object is received as an argument to insert into the database. However, before inserting it into the vector, its `id` field is overwritten by a unique ID value. This value is an integer larger than the largest ID present in the vector if the vector is not empty, or `1`, otherwise.
- `update_person`: This searches the vector for a person that has the specified ID; if found, this person is replaced by the specified person and `true` is returned. Otherwise, `false` is returned.

Nothing web-specific is contained in these functions.

The main.rs changes

For the `main` function, there are many kinds of requests to the route. The new routes are as follows:

```
.service(
    web::resource("/persons")
        .route(web::delete().to(delete_persons)),
)
.service(
    web::resource("/page/new_person")
        .route(web::get().to(get_page_new_person)),
)
.service(
    web::resource("/page/edit_person/{id}")
        .route(web::get().to(get_page_edit_person)),
)
.service(
    web::resource("/one_person")
        .route(web::post().to(insert_person))
        .route(web::put().to(update_person)),
)
```

The first route is used to delete the selected people.

The second route is used to get the page to allow the user to insert a new person—that is, the `one_person.html` page—in insert mode.

The third route is used to get the page to allow the user to view or edit a new person—that is, the `one_person.html` page—in edit mode.

For the fourth resource, there are two possible routes. Actually, this resource can be accessed using the POST method or the PUT method. The first method is used to insert a new record into the database. The second method is used to update the specified record using the specified data.

Now, let's see the handlers. With respect to the previous project, some of them are new, some are old but have been changed, and some are unmodified.

The new handlers are as follows:

Sarwar

D • `delete_persons` is used to delete the selected people.
* • `get_page_new_person` is used to get the page to create a new person.
⌐ • `get_page_edit_person` is used to get the page to edit an existing person.
C • `insert_person` is used to insert a new person into the database.
U • `update_person` is used to update an existing person in the database.

The changed handlers are `get_page_persons` and `invalid_resource`. The unmodified handlers are `get_main` and `get_favicon`.

These handlers can be grouped into three logical kinds:

- The ones whose job it is to generate HTML code to replace part of a web page
- The ones whose job it is to return non-HTML data
- The ones that do some work and then return status information regarding the job that has been done

The HTML-returning functions are `get_main`, `get_page_persons`, `get_page_new_person`, `get_page_edit_person`, and `invalid_resource`. `get_favicon` is the only data-returning function; the other three are data-manipulating functions.

It is logically possible to have a single handler that first does some work and then returns the HTML page to be shown. However, it is better to separate these logically different features into two distinct functions—first, the function that manipulates data is executed, and then the function that returns the HTML code is run. This separation can happen on the backend or on the frontend.

In this project, it is the frontend that does the separation. First, JavaScript code sends a request to manipulate data (for example, to insert a record in the database) and then, if the operation was successful, some other JavaScript code requests the HTML code to show up next in the browser.

An alternative architecture is to have the following sequence of calls:

1. The user performs an action on the web page.
2. That action causes a JavaScript routine to be executed.
3. That routine sends a request from the browser to the server.
4. The server routes that request to a backend handler function.

5. The backend handler first calls a routine to manipulate data and then waits for its completion.
6. If the backend routine is successful, the backend calls another routine to generate and return the next HTML page to the browser. If the backend routine fails, the backend generates and returns another HTML page to the browser, describing the failure.
7. The JavaScript routine receives the HTML page and displays it to the user.

Now, let's look at the body of the get_page_edit_person function one piece at a time.

Remember that the purpose of this routine is to generate the HTML code of a web page to edit the name of a person. The current name of the person to edit is to be found in the database and the constant HTML code is to be found in the one_person.html template.

The first five statements define and initialize as many local variables:

```
let id = &path.0;
let db_conn = &state.lock().unwrap().db;
let mut context = tera::Context::new();
if let Ok(id_n) = id.parse::<u32>() {
    if let Some(person) = db_conn.get_person_by_id(id_n) {
```

The first statement gets the id variable from the path as a string. For this function, the routing was /page/edit_person/{id}, and so the id variable is available to be extracted.

The second statement gets and locks the database connection.

The third statement creates an empty Tera context.

The fourth statement tries to parse the id Rust variable into an integer. If the conversion is successful, the condition of the if statement is satisfied and so the next statement is executed.

The fifth statement searches the database for a person identified by this ID by calling the get_person_by_id method.

Now that the required information is available, the Tera context can be filled in:

```
context.insert("person_id", &id);
context.insert("person_name", &person.name);
context.insert("inserting", &false);
```

Let's see what the purpose of these variables is:

- The `person_id` Tera variable allows us to show the current (disabled) ID of the person on the page.
- The `person_name` Tera variable allows us to show the current (editable) name of the person on the page.
- The `inserting` Tera variable allows us (through a conditional Tera statement) to set the page as an edit page, instead of as an insert page.

Then, we can call the `render` Tera method with this context to get the HTML page and send the resulting page as the HTML body of the response:

```
return HttpResponse::Ok()
    .content_type("text/html")
    .body(TERA.render("one_person.html", context).unwrap());
```

Here, we have considered the cases where every statement was successful. In cases where the typed ID is not a number or it does not exist in the database, the function carries out the following code. This happens when the user types a wrong number in the **Id** field of the main page and then clicks on **Find**:

```
context.insert("id_error", &"Person id not found");
context.insert("partial_name", &"");
let person_list = db_conn.get_persons_by_partial_name(&"");
context.insert("persons", &person_list.collect::<Vec<_>>());
HttpResponse::Ok()
    .content_type("text/html")
    .body(TERA.render("persons.html", context).unwrap())
```

The last line shows that the template we will use is `persons.html`, so we are going to the main page. The Tera variables of that template are `id_error`, `partial_name`, and `persons`. We want a specific error message in the first variable, nothing as the `filter` condition, and a list of all the people. This can be obtained by filtering all the people whose name contains an empty string.

When the user presses the **Update** button, the `update_person` function is called.

This function has the following arguments:

```
state: web::Data<Mutex<AppState>>,
query: web::Query<ToUpdate>,
```

The second is a query using a type defined by the following structure:

```
#[derive(Deserialize)]
struct ToUpdate {
    id: Option<u32>,
    name: Option<String>,
}
```

So, this query allows two optional keywords: `id` and `name`. The first keyword must be an integer number. Here are some valid queries:

- `?id=35&name=Jo`
- `?id=-2`
- `?name=Jo`
- No query

The following are invalid queries for that structure:

- `?id=x&name=Jo`
- `?id=2.4`

Here is the first part of the body of the function:

```
let db_conn = &mut state.lock().unwrap().db;
let mut updated_count = 0;
let id = query.id.unwrap_or(0);
```

The first statement gets and locks the database connection.

A count of the records to update is defined by the second statement. This routine can update only one record, and so this count will be 0 or 1 only.

Then, the `id` variable is extracted from the query, if present and valid, or otherwise, 0 is considered as a substitute.

Notice that because the type of the query variable defines which fields are defined (whether they are optional or required and what is their type), the Actix web framework can perform a strict parsing of the URI query. If the URI query is not valid, the handler is not invoked and the `default_service` routine will be chosen. On the other side, in the handler, we can be sure that the query is valid.

The last part of the body of the function is as follows:

```
let name = query.name.clone().unwrap_or_else(|| "".to_string()).clone();
updated_count += if db_conn.update_person(Person { id, name }) {
    1
} else {
    0
};
updated_count.to_string()
```

First, the `name` variable is extracted from the query, or an empty string is considered if that variable is not contained in the query. This name is cloned as the database operations take ownership of their arguments and we cannot yield the ownership of a field of the query.

Then, the `update_person` method of the database connection is called. This method receives a new `Person` object constructed with the `id` and `name` values that were just extracted. If this method returns `true`, the count of the processed record is set to `1`.

Finally, the count of the processed record is returned as a response.

The other routines are conceptually similar to the one described here.

Handling an application with authentication

All of the features of the previous apps were accessible to everyone that could create an HTTP connection with our server. Usually, a web app should behave differently depending on who is currently using it. Typically, some users are authorized to carry out some important operations, such as adding or updating records, while other users are authorized only to read these records. Sometimes, user-specific data must be recorded.

This opens up the vast world of authentication, authorization, and security.

Let's imagine a simplified scenario. There are two users whose profiles are wired-in to the mock database:

- `joe`, whose password is `xjoe`, can *only read* the database of people.
- `susan`, whose password is `xsusan`, can *read and write* the database of people—that is, she can do what the app in the previous section allowed.

The application starts with a login page. If the user does not insert an existing username and its matching password, they cannot access the other pages. Even if the username and password are valid, the widgets that the user is not authorized for are disabled.

For these situations, some applications create a server-side user session. This may be appropriate to use when there are a limited number of users, but it may overload the server if there are many users. Here, we'll show a solution without server-side sessions.

If you run the `auth` project and access the site from a browser, you will see the following page:

It shows that there is no current users and two fields allow us to type in a username and password. If you type `foo` into the **User name** field and then click on **Log in**, the red **User "foo" not found.** message will appear. If you type in `susan` and then click on **Log in**, the message will be **Invalid password for user "susan"**.

Instead, if you type in the correct password for that user, `xsusan`, the following page will appear:

This is the same main page as the `crud` project, with an added line of widgets: the name of the current user shown in blue and a button to change it. If you click on the **Change User** button, you go back to the login page. Also, the page to view, edit, or insert a person has the same widgets just under the page heading.

If on the login page you insert `joe` as the username and `xjoe` as the password, the following page will appear:

This has the same widgets that appeared for `susan`, but the **Delete Selected Persons** button and the **Add New Person** button now are disabled.

To see how `joe` sees the people, first, you need to log in as `susan`, insert some people, and then change the user to `joe`, because `joe` cannot insert people. If you do this and then you click on the **Edit** button of a person, you will see the following page, where the **Name** field is read-only and the **Update** button is disabled:

Let's start with understanding the nitty-gritty of the application we just did.

The implementation

This project adds some code with respect to the `crud` project.

The first difference is in the `Cargo.toml` file, where the `actix-web-httpauth` = `"0.1"` dependency has been added. This crate handles the encoding of the username and password in the HTTP request.

The HTML code

The `main.html` page, instead of opening the `/page/persons` URI, opens `/page/login` to show the login page, initially. So, this project adds a new TERA template for the login page. This is the `login.html` partial HTML page, shown as follows:

```
<h1>Login to Persons</h1>
<div>
    <span>Current user:</span>
    <span id="current_user" class="current-user"></span>
</div>
<hr/>
<label class="error">{{error_message}}</label>
<div>
    <label>User name:</label>
    <input id="username" type="text">
</div>
<div>
    <label>Password:</label>
    <input id="password" type="password">
</div>
<button onclick="login()">Log in</button>
```

Its noteworthy points are underlined: the `{{error_message}}` Tera variable, the call to `login()` when the **Log in** button is clicked, and three elements whose IDs are `current_user`, `username`, and `password`.

Both the `persons.html` and `one_person.html` templates have the following section just below the heading:

```
<div>
    <span>Current user: </span>
    <span id="current_user" class="current-user"></span>
    <button onclick="getPage('/page/login')">Change User</button>
</div>
<hr/>
```

This will show the current user, or `---`, followed by the **Change User** button. Clicking on this will load the `/page/login` page.

The app contains four buttons that must be disabled for unauthorized users—two in the `persons.html` template and two in the `one_person.html` template. They now contain the following attribute:

```
{% if not can_write %}disabled{% endif %}
```

It assumes that the `can_write` Tera variable is defined as `true`, or any non-null value, if—and only if—the current user has the authorization to modify the content of the database.

There is also an edit box element in the `one_person.html` template that must be made read-only for users that are not authorized to change that data; so, it contains the following attribute:

```
{% if not can_write %}readonly{% endif %}
```

You should be aware that these checks are not an ultimate security guard. The checks of authorization in frontend software can always be bypassed, and so the ultimate security guards are those performed by the DBMS.

However, it is good to always carry out an early check to make that the user experience is more intuitive and the error messages are helpful.

For example, if an attribute of an entity shouldn't be modifiable by the current user, this constraint can be specified in a solid way using the DBMS.

However, if the user interface allows this kind of change, the user could try to change this value and they will be disappointed when they find out that this change is not allowed.

In addition, when a forbidden change is attempted, an error message is issued by the DBMS. The message is probably not internationalized and makes reference to DBMS concepts such as tables, columns, rows, and the names of objects that are unfamiliar to the user. So, this message can be obscure for the user.

The JavaScript code

The `main.js` file has the following additions with respect to the `crud` project.

The `username` and `password` global variables have been added and initialized as empty strings.

The following statement has been added to both the `sendCommand` function and the `getPage` function:

```
xhttp.setRequestHeader("Authorization",
    "Basic " + btoa(username + ":" + password));
```

This sets the `Authorization` header for the HTTP request that is about to be sent. The format of that header is standard HTTP.

In the `getPage` function, after the statement that assigns the HTML code that is received to the current body, the following three lines are inserted:

```
var cur_user = document.getElementById('current_user');
if (cur_user)
    cur_user.innerHTML = username ? username : '---';
```

They set the content of the element whose `id` attribute has `current_user` as its value if the current page contains such an element. This content is the value of the `username` global JavaScript variable if it is defined and not empty, or `---`, otherwise.

Another addition is the definition of the new `login` function. Its body is as follows:

```
username = document.getElementById('username').value;
password = document.getElementById('password').value;
getPage('/page/persons');
```

This gets the values of the `username` and `password` elements of the page and saves them to the global variables with the same names, and then opens the main page. Of course, this should only be called in the `login.html` page as other pages are not likely to have a `password` element.

The mock database code

The mock database has one more table: `users`. So, the type of its elements must be defined:

```
#[derive(Serialize, Clone, Debug)]
pub struct User {
    pub username: String,
    pub password: String,
    pub privileges: Vec<DbPrivilege>,
}
```

Any user has a username, a password, and a set of privileges. A **privilege** has a custom type, which is defined in the same file:

```
#[derive(Serialize, Clone, Copy, PartialEq, Debug)]
pub enum DbPrivilege { CanRead, CanWrite }
```

Here, there are only two possible privileges: to be able to read the database or to be able to write the database. A real-world system would have more granularity.

The `DbConnection` struct now also contains the users field, which is a vector of `Users`. Its content (the records about `joe` and `susan`) is specified inline.

The following function has been added:

```
pub fn get_user_by_username(&self, username: &str) -> Option<&User> {
    if let Some(u) = self.users.iter().find(|u| u.username == username) {
        Some(u)
    }
    else { None }
}
```

This searches the `users` vector for a user with the specified username. If it is found, it is returned; otherwise, `None` is returned.

The main function

The `main` function has just two small changes. The first change is to call `data(Config::default().realm("PersonsApp"))` on the `App` object. This invocation is required to get the authentication context from the HTTP requests. It specifies the context using the `realm` call.

The second change is the addition of the following routing rule:

```
.service(
    web::resource("/page/login")
        .route(web::get().to(get_page_login)),
)
```

This path is used to open the login page. It is used by the main page as the entry point of the app and by the two **Change User** buttons.

The `get_page_login` function is the only new handler. It just calls the `get_page_login_with_message` function, which has a string argument, to be shown as an error message. When this function is called by `get_page_login`, an empty string is specified as an argument because no error has happened yet on this page. However, this function is called in six other places, where various error messages are specified. The purpose of this function is to go to the login page and display the message received as an argument in red.

The login page is obviously accessible to every user, as the favicon resource is, but all of the other handlers have been modified to ensure that only authorized users can access those resources. The bodies of the handlers that manipulate data have the following structure:

```
match check_credentials(auth, &state, DbPrivilege::CanWrite) {
    Ok(_) => {
```

```
        ... manipulate data ...
        HttpResponse::Ok()
            .content_type("text/plain")
            .body(result)
        },
    Err(msg) => get_page_login_with_message(&msg)
}
```

First, the `check_credentials` function checks whether the credentials specified by the `auth` argument identify a user that has the `CanWrite` privilege. Only users allowed to write should manipulate the data. For them, the function returns as `Ok` and so they can change the database and return the result of these changes in a plaintext format.

Users that are not allowed to write are redirected to the login page, which shows the error message returned by `check_credentials`.

Instead, the bodies of the handlers that get HTML pages have the following structure:

```
match check_credentials(auth, &state, DbPrivilege::CanRead) {
    Ok(privileges) => {
        ... get path arguments, query arguments, body ...
        ... get data from the database ...
        let mut context = tera::Context::new();
        context.insert("can_write",
            &privileges.contains(&DbPrivilege::CanWrite));
        ... insert some other variables in the context ...
        return HttpResponse::Ok()
            .content_type("text/html")
            .body(TERA.render("<template_name>.html", context).unwrap());
    },
    Err(msg) => get_page_login_with_message(&msg)
}
```

Here, as is typical, any user that can read the data can also access the web page. In this case, the `check_credentials` function is successful and it returns the complete set of privileges of that user. Matching these results with the `Ok(privileges)` pattern causes the privileges of that user to be used to initialize the `privileges` Rust variable.

If the user has the `CanWrite` privilege, that information is passed to the `can_write` Tera variable as a `true` value and to `false`, otherwise. In this way, the page can enable or disable the HTML widgets in accordance with the user's privileges.

Finally, let's look at the `check_credentials` function.

Among its arguments, there is auth: BasicAuth. Thanks to the actix_web_httpauth crate and to the call to data in the main function, this argument allows access to the authorization HTTP header for basic authentication. The objects of the BasicAuth type have the user_id and password methods, which return the optional credential specified by the HTTP client.

These methods are invoked with the following snippet:

```
if let Some(user) = db_conn.get_user_by_username(auth.user_id()) {
    if auth.password().is_some() && &user.password ==
auth.password().unwrap() {
```

This code gets the user from the database through their username and checks that the stored password matches the password coming from the browser.

This is quite basic. A real-world system would store an encrypted password; it would encrypt the specified password using the same one-way encryption and it would compare the encrypted strings.

Then, the routine discriminates between the different kinds of errors:

- The HTTP request does not contain credentials, or the credentials exist but the specified user does not exist in the user's table.
- The user exists, but the stored password is different from that specified in the received credentials.
- The credentials are valid, but that user hasn't got the required privileges (for example, they only have the CanRead access but CanWrite is required).

So, we have now covered a simple authenticated web app.

Summary

In this chapter, we have seen how to use the Tera template engine to create text strings or files (not just in HTML format) containing variable parts, conditional sections, repeated sections, and sections included from another file.

Then, we saw how Actix web—together with HTML code, JavaScript code, CSS styles, and the Tera template engine—can be used to create a complete web app with CRUD capabilities, authentication (to prove who is the current user), and authorization (to forbid some operations to the current user).

This project showed us how to create a single application that performs both client-side code and server-side code.

In the next chapter, we will see how to create a client-side web app using WebAssembly technology and the Yew framework.

Questions

1. What are the possible strategies for creating HTML code containing variable parts?
2. What is the syntax to embed a Tera expression into a text file?
3. What is the syntax to embed a Tera statement into a text file?
4. How are the values of variables in a Tera rendering operation specified?
5. How can the requests to a web server be classified?
6. Why may it be useful to split a web page into parts?
7. Should HTML templates and JavaScript files be deployed separately or are they linked into the executable program?
8. Which JavaScript object can be used to send HTTP requests?
9. Where should the current username be stored when the server does not store user sessions?
10. How are credentials extracted from an HTTP request?

Further reading

- Additional information regarding Tera can be found at `https://tera.netlify.app/`.
- Additional information regarding Actix web can be found at `https://actix.rs/docs/`.
- The status of web development libraries and frameworks can be found at `https://www.arewewebyet.org/`.

5
Creating a Client-Side WebAssembly App Using Yew

In this chapter, you will see how Rust can be used to build the frontend of a web application, as an alternative to using HTML, CSS, and JavaScript (typically using a JavaScript frontend framework, such as React) or another language generating JavaScript code (such as Elm or TypeScript).

To build a Rust app for a web browser, the Rust code must be translated to WebAssembly code, which can be supported by all modern web browsers. The capability to translate Rust code into WebAssembly code is now included in the stable Rust compiler.

To develop large projects, a web frontend framework is needed. In this chapter, the Yew framework will be presented. It is a framework that supports the development of frontend web applications, using the **Model-View-Controller** (**MVC**) architectural pattern, and generating WebAssembly code.

The following topics will be covered in this chapter:

- Understanding the MVC architectural pattern and its usage in web pages
- Building WebAssembly apps using the Yew framework
- How to use the Yew crate to create web pages designed with the MVC pattern (`incr` and `adder`)
- Creating a web app having several pages with a common header and footer (`login` and `yauth`)
- Creating a web app having both a frontend and a backend, in two distinct projects (`yclient` and `persons_db`)

 The frontend is developed using Yew, and the backend, which is an HTTP RESTful service, is developed using Actix web.

Technical requirements

This chapter assumes you have already read the previous chapters, also, prior knowledge of HTML is required.

To run the projects in this chapter, it is enough to install the generator of WebAssembly code (Wasm, for short). Probably the simplest way to do this is by typing the following command:

```
cargo install cargo-web
```

After 13 minutes, your Cargo tool will be enriched by several commands. A few of which are as follows:

- `cargo web build` (or `cargo-web build`): It builds Rust projects designed to run in a web browser. It is similar to the `cargo build` command, but for Wasm.
- `cargo web start` (or `cargo-web start`): It performs a `cargo web build` command, and then starts a web server where every time it is visited by a client, it sends a complete Wasm frontend app to the client. It is similar to the `cargo run` command, but for serving Wasm apps.

The complete source code for this chapter is in the `Chapter05` folder of the repository at: `https://github.com/PacktPublishing/Creative-Projects-for-Rust-Programmers`.

Introducing Wasm

Wasm is a powerful new technology to deliver interactive applications. Before the advent of the web, there were already many developers building client/server applications, where the client apps ran on a PC (typically with Microsoft Windows) and the server apps ran on a company-owned system (typically with NetWare, OS/2, Windows NT, or Unix). In such systems, developers could choose their favorite language for the client app. Some people used Visual Basic, others used FoxPro or Delphi, and many other languages were in wide use.

However, for such systems, the deployment of updates was a kind of hell, because of several possible issues, such as ensuring that every client PC had the proper runtime system and that all clients got the updates at the same time. These problems were solved by JavaScript running in web browsers, as it is a ubiquitous platform on which frontend software could be downloaded and executed. This had some drawbacks though: developers were forced to use HTML + CSS + JavaScript to develop frontend software, and sometimes such software had poor performance.

Here comes Wasm, which is a machine-language-like programming language, like Java bytecode or Microsoft .NET CIL code, but it is a standard accepted by all major web browsers. Version 1.0 of its specification appeared in October 2017, and in 2019 it appears that already more than 80% of web browsers running in the world support it. This means that it can be more efficient and that it can be rather easily generated from several programming languages, including Rust.

So, if Wasm is set as the target architecture of the Rust compiler, a program written in Rust can be run on any major modern web browser.

Understanding the MVC architectural pattern

This chapter is about creating web apps. So, to make things more concrete, let's look straight away at two toy web applications named `incr` and `adder`.

Implementing two toy web apps

To run the first toy application, let's take the following steps:

1. Go into the `incr` folder and type `cargo web start`.
2. After a few minutes, a message will appear on the console, ending with the following line:

   You can access the web server at `http://127.0.0.1:8000`.

3. Now, in the address box of a web browser, type: `127.0.0.1:8000` or `localhost:8000`, and immediately you will see the following contents:

4. Click on the two buttons, or select the following textbox and then press the + or the *0* keys on the keyboard.

- If you click once on the **Increment** button, the contents of the box to the right change from **0** to **1**.
- If you click another time, it changes to **2**, and so on.
- If you click on the **Reset** button, the value changes to **0** (zero).
- If you select the textbox by clicking on it and then press the + key, you increment the number like the **Increment** button does. Instead, if you press the *0* key, the number is set to zero.

5. To stop the server, go to the console and press *Ctrl + C*.
6. To run the `adder` app, go into the `adder` folder and type `cargo web start`.
7. Similarly, for the other app, when the server app has started, you can refresh your web browser page and you will see the following page:

8. Here, you can insert a number in the first box, to the right of the **Addend 1** label, another number in the second box, and then press the **Add** button. After that, you will see the sum of those numbers in the textbox at the bottom, which has turned from yellow to light green, as in the following screenshot:

After the addition, the **Add** button has become disabled. If one of the first two boxes is empty, the sum fails and nothing happens. Also, if you change the value of any of the two first boxes, the **Add** button becomes enabled, and the last textbox becomes empty and yellow.

What is the MVC pattern?

Now that we have seen some very simple web applications, we can explain what the MVC architectural pattern is using these apps as an example. The MVC pattern is an architecture regarding event-driven interactive programs.

Let's see what event-driven interactive programs are. The word **interactive** is the opposite of **batch**. A batch program is a program in which the user prepares all the input at the beginning, and then the program runs without asking for further input. Instead, an interactive program has the following steps:

- Initialization.
- Waiting for some actions from the user.
- When the user acts on an input device, the program processes the related input, and then goes to the preceding step, to wait for further input.

For example, console command interpreters are interactive programs, and all web apps are interactive too.

The phrase *event-driven* means that the application, after initialization, does nothing until the user performs something on the user interface. When the user acts on an input device, the app processes such inputs and updates the screen only as a reaction to the user input. Most web applications are event-driven. The main exceptions are games and virtual reality or augmented reality environments, where animations go on even if the user does nothing.

Our examples in this chapter are all event-driven interactive programs, as after initialization, they do something only when the user clicks with the mouse (or touches the touchscreen) or presses any key on the keyboard. Some such clicks and key presses cause a change on the screen. Therefore, the MVC architecture can be applied to these example projects.

There are several dialects of this pattern. The one used by Yew derives from the one implemented by the Elm language, and so it is named the **Elm Architecture**.

The model

In any MVC program, there is a data structure, named `model`, that contains all the dynamic data required to represent the user interface.

For example, in the `incr` app, the value of the number contained in the box to the right is required to represent the box, and it can change at runtime. Hence, that numeric value must be in the model.

Here, the width and height of the browser window are usually not required to generate the HTML code and so they shouldn't be a part of the model. Also, the sizes and texts of the buttons shouldn't be a part of the model, but for another reason: they cannot change at runtime in this app. Though, if it were an internationalized app, all the texts should be in the model too.

In the `adder` app, the model should contain only the three values contained in the three textboxes. It doesn't matter that two of them are directly inputted by the user and the third one is calculated. The labels and the background color of the textboxes shouldn't be a part of the model.

The view

The next portion of the MVC architecture is the **view**. It is a specification of how to represent (or render) the graphical contents of the screen, depending on the value of the model. It can be a declarative specification, such as pure HTML code, or a procedural specification, such as some JavaScript or Rust code, or a mix of them.

For example, in the `incr` app, the view shows two push-buttons and one read-only textbox, whereas, in the `adder` app, the view shows three labels, three textboxes, and one push-button.

All the shown push-buttons have a constant appearance, but the views must change the display of the numbers when the models change.

The controller

The last portion of the MVC architecture is the *controller*. It is always a routine or a set of routines that are invoked by the view when the user, using an input device, interacts with the app. When a user performs an action with an input device, all the view has to do is to notify the controller that the user has performed that action, specifying which action (for example, which mouse key has been pressed), and where (for example, in which position of the screen).

In the `incr` app, the three possible input actions are as follows:

- A click on the **Increment** button
- A click on the **Reset** button
- A press of a key on the keyboard when the textbox is selected

Usually, it is also possible to press a push-button using the keyboard, but such an action can be considered equivalent to a mouse click, and so a single input action type is notified for each button.

In the `adder` app, the three possible input actions are as follows:

- A change of the value in the **Addend 1** textbox
- A change of the value in the **Addend 2** textbox
- A click on the **Add** button

It is possible to change the value of a textbox in several ways:

- By typing when no text is selected, inserting additional characters
- By typing when some text is selected, and so replacing the selected text with a character
- By pasting some text from the clipboard
- By dragging and dropping some text from another element of the screen
- By using the mouse on the up-down spinner

We are not interested in these, because they are handled by the browser or by the framework. All that matters for application code is that when the user performs an input action, a textbox changes its value.

The job of the controller is just to use such input information to update the model. When the model is completely updated, the framework notifies the view about the need to refresh the look of the screen, taking into account the new values of the model.

In the case of the `incr` app, the controller, when it is notified of the pressing of the **Increment** button, increments the number contained in the model; when it is notified of the pressing of the **Reset** button, it sets to zero that number in the model; when it is notified of the pressing of a key on the textbox, it checks whether the pressed key is +, or *0*, or something else, and the appropriate change is applied to the model. After such changes, the view is notified to update the display of such a number.

In the case of the `adder` app, the controller, when it is notified of the change of the **Addend 1** textbox, updates the model with the new value contained in the edit box. Similar behavior happens for the **Addend 2** textbox; and when the controller is notified of the pressing of the **Add** button, it adds the two addends contained in the model and stores the result in the third field of the model. After such changes, the view is notified to update the display of such a result.

View implementation

Regarding web pages, the representation of pages is usually made up of HTML code, and so, using the Yew framework, the view function must generate HTML code. Such generations contain in themselves the constant portions of HTML code, but they also access the model to get the information that can change at runtime.

In the `incr` app, the view composes the HTML code that defines two buttons and one read-only numeric *input* element and puts in such an *input* element the value taken from the model. The view includes the handling of the HTML *click* events on the two buttons by forwarding them to the controller.

In the `adder` app, the view composes the HTML code that defines three labels, three numeric input elements, and one button, and puts in the last *input* element the value taken from the model. It includes the handling of the HTML *input* events in the first two textboxes and the *click* event on the button, by forwarding them to the controller. Regarding the first two textbox events, the values contained in the boxes are forwarded to the controller.

Controller implementation

Using Yew, the controller is implemented by an *update* routine, which processes the messages regarding user actions coming from the view and uses such input to change the model. After the controller has completed all the required changes to the model, the view must be notified to apply the changes of the model to the user interface.

In some frameworks, such as in Yew, such an invocation of the view is automatic; that mechanism has the following steps:

- For any user action handled by the view, the framework calls the `update` function, that is, the controller. In this call, the framework passes to the controller the details regarding the user action; for example, which value has been typed in a textbox.
- The controller, typically, changes the state of the model.
- If the controller has successfully applied some changes to the model, the framework calls the view function, which is the *view* of the MVC architecture.

Understanding the MVC architecture

The general flow of control of the MVC architecture is shown in the following diagram:

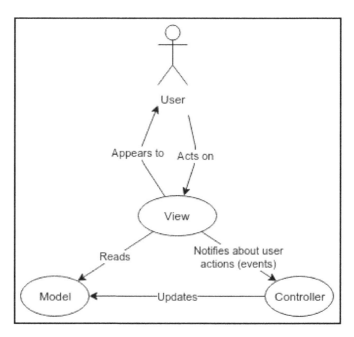

The iteration of every user action is this sequence of operations:

1. The user sees a static representation of graphical elements on the screen.
2. The user acts on the graphical elements using an input device.
3. The view receives a user action and notifies the controller.
4. The controller updates the model.
5. The view reads the new state of the model to update the contents of the screen.
6. The user sees the new state of the screen.

The main concepts of the MVC architecture are as follows:

- All the mutable data that is needed to correctly build the display must be in a single data structure, named **model**. The model may be associated with some code, but such code does not get direct user input, nor does it give output to the user. It may access files, databases, or other processes, though. Because the model does not interact directly with the user interface, the code implementing the model shouldn't change if the application user interface is ported from text mode to GUI/web/mobile.

- The logic that draws on the display and captures user input is named the *view*. The view, of course, must know about screen rendering, input devices and events, and also about the model. Though, the view just *reads* the model, it never changes it directly. When an interesting event happens, the view notifies the controller of that event.
- When the controller is notified of an interesting event by the view, it changes the model accordingly, and when it has finished, the framework notifies the view to refresh itself using the new state of the model.

Project overview

This chapter will present four projects that will get more and more complex. You have already seen the first two projects in action: `incr` and `adder`. The third project, named `login`, shows how to create a login page for authentication on a website.

The fourth project, named `yauth`, extends the `login` project adding the CRUD handling of a list of persons. Its behavior is almost identical to that of the `auth` project in Chapter 4, *Creating a Full Server-Side Web App*. Each project will require from 1 to 3 minutes to download and compile from scratch.

Getting started

To start all the machinery, a very simple statement is enough – the body of the `main` function:

Server
```
yew::start_app::<Model>();
```

It creates a web app based on the specified `Model`, starts it, and waits on the default TCP port. Of course, the TCP port can be changed. It is a server that will serve the app to any browser navigating to it.

The incr app

Here, we'll see the implementation of the `incr` project, which we already saw how to build and use. The only dependency is on the Yew framework, and so, the TOML file contains the following line:

```
yew = "0.6"
```

All the source code is in the `main.rs` file. The model is implemented by the following simple declaration:

```
struct Model {
    value: u64,
}
```

It just has to be a struct that will be instantiated by the framework, read by the view, and read and written by the controller. Its name and the name of its fields are arbitrary.

Then the possible notifications from the view to the controller must be declared as an `enum` type. Here is that of `incr`:

```
enum Msg {
    Increment,
    Reset,
    KeyDown(String),
}
```

Also, here, the names are arbitrary:

- `Msg` is short for *message*, as such notifications are in a sense messages from the view to the controller.
- The `Increment` message notifies a click on the **Increment** button. The `Reset` message notifies a click on the **Reset** button.
- The `KeyDown` message notifies a press of any key on the keyboard; its argument communicates which key has been pressed.

To implement the controller, the `yew::Component` trait must be implemented for our model. The code for our project is as follows:

```
impl Component for Model {
    type Message = Msg;
    type Properties = ();
    fn create(_: Self::Properties, _: ComponentLink<Self>) -> Self {
        Self { value: 0 }
    }
    fn update(&mut self, msg: Self::Message) -> ShouldRender { ... }
}
```

The required implementations are as follows:

- `Message`: It is the `enum` defined before, describing all possible notifications from the view to the controller.
- `Properties`: It is not used in this project. When not used, it must be an empty tuple.
- `create`: It is invoked by the framework to let the controller initialize the model. It can use two arguments, but here we are not interested in them, and it must return an instance of the model with its initial value. As we want to show the number zero at the beginning, we set `value` to `0`.
- `update`: It is invoked by the framework any time the user acts on the page in some way handled by the view. The two arguments are the mutable model itself (`self`) and the notification from the view (`msg`). This method should return a value of type `ShouldRender`, but a `bool` value will be good. Returning `true` means that the model has been changed, and so a refresh of the view is required. Returning `false` means that the model has not been changed, and so a refresh of the view would be a waste of time.

The `update` method contains a `match` on the message type. The first two message types are quite simple:

```
match msg {
    Msg::Increment => {
        self.value += 1;
        true
    }
    Msg::Reset => {
        self.value = 0;
        true
    }
}
```

If the `Increment` message is notified, the value is incremented. If the `Reset` message is notified, the value is zeroed. In both cases, the view must be refreshed.

The handling of the keypress is a bit more complex:

```
Msg::KeyDown(s) => match s.as_ref() {
    "+" => {
        self.value += 1;
        true
    }
    "0" => {
        self.value = 0;
        true
```

```
    }
    _ => false,
}
```

The `KeyDown` match arm assigns the key pressed to the s variable. As we are interested
only in two possible keys, there is a nested `match` statement on the s variable. For the two-
handled keys (+ and 0), the model is updated, and `true` is returned to refresh the view. For
any other key pressed, nothing is done.

To implement the view part of MVC, the `yew::Renderable` trait must be implemented for
our model. The only required method is `view`, which gets an immutable reference to the
model, and returns an object that represents some HTML code, but that is capable of
reading the model and notifying the controller:

```
impl Renderable<Model> for Model {
    fn view(&self) -> Html<Self> {
        html! { ... }
    }
}
```

The body of such a method is constructed with the powerful `yew::html` macro. Here is the
body of such a macro invocation:

```
                                                             literal
<div>
    <button onclick=|_| Msg::Increment,>{"Increment"}</button>
    <button onclick=|_| Msg::Reset,>{"Reset"}</button>
    <input
        readonly="true",
        value={self.value},
        onkeydown=|e| Msg::KeyDown(e.key()),
    />
</div>
```

It looks very similar to the actual HTML code. It is equivalent to the following HTML
pseudo-code:

```
<div>
    <button onclick="notify(Increment)">Increment</button>
    <button onclick="notify(Reset)">Reset</button>
    <input
        readonly="true"
        value="[value]"
        onkeydown="notify(KeyDown, [key])"),
    />
</div>
```

Notice that at any HTML event, in the HTML pseudo-code, a JavaScript function is invoked (here, named `notify`). Instead, in Rust, there is a closure that returns a message for the controller. Such a message must have the arguments of the appropriate type. While the `onclick` event has no arguments, the `onkeydown` event has one argument, captured in the `e` variable, and by calling the `key` method on that argument, the pressed key is passed to the controller.

Also notice in the HTML pseudo-code the `[value]` symbol, which at runtime will be replaced by an actual value.

Finally, notice that the body of the macro has three features that differentiate it from HTML code:

- All the arguments of HTML elements must end with a comma.
- Any Rust expression can be evaluated inside HTML code, as long as it is enclosed in braces.
- Literal strings are not allowed in this HTML code, so they must be inserted as Rust literals (by including them in braces).

The adder app

Here, we'll see the implementation of the `adder` project, which we already saw how to build and use. Only that which differentiates it from the `incr` project will be examined.

First of all, there is a problem with the `html` macro expansion recursion level. It is so deep that it must be increased using the following directives at the beginning of the program:

```
#![recursion_limit = "128"]
#[macro_use]
extern crate yew;
```

Without them, a compilation error is generated. With more complex views, an even larger limit is required. The model contains the following fields:

```
addend1: String,
addend2: String,
sum: Option<f64>,
```

They represent the following, respectively:

- The text inserted in the first box (`addend1`).
- The text inserted in the second box (`addend2`).
- The number calculated and to be displayed in the third box, if the calculation was performed and was successful, or nothing otherwise.

The handled events (that is, the messages) are as follows:

```
ChangedAddend1(String),
ChangedAddend2(String),
ComputeSum,
```

They represent the following, respectively:

- Any change to the contents of the first box, with the new value contained in the box (`ChangedAddend1`).
- Any change to the contents of the second box, with its value (`ChangedAddend2`).
- A click on the **Add** button.

The `create` function initializes the three fields of the model: the two addends are set to empty strings, and the `sum` field is set to `None`. With these initial values, no number is displayed in the **Sum** textbox.

The `update` function processes the three possible messages. For the `ComputeSum` message, it does the following:

```
self.sum = match (self.addend1.parse::<f64>(), self.addend2.parse::<f64>())
{
    (Ok(a1), Ok(a2)) => Some(a1 + a2),
    _ => None,
};
```

The `addend1` and `addend2` fields of the model are parsed to convert them into numbers. If both conversions are successful, the first arm matches, and so the `a1` and `a2` values are added, and their sum is assigned to the `sum` field. If some conversion fails, `None` is assigned to the sum field.

The arm regarding the first addend is as follows:

```
Msg::ChangedAddend1(value) => {
    self.addend1 = value;
    self.sum = None;
}
```

The current value of the textbox is assigned to the addend1 field of the model, and the sum field is set to None. Similar behavior is performed for a change to the other addend.

Let's see the most interesting parts of the view method:

```
let numeric = "text-align: right;";
```

It assigns to a Rust variable a snippet of CSS code. Then, the textbox for the first addend is created by the following code:

```
<input type="number", style=numeric,
    oninput=|e| Msg::ChangedAddend1(e.value),/>
```

Notice that to the style attribute, the value of the numeric variable is assigned. The values of these attributes are just Rust expressions.

The sum textbox is created by the following code:

```
<input type="number",

    style=numeric.to_string()
        + "background-color: "
        + if self.sum.is_some() { "lightgreen;" } else { "yellow;" },
        readonly="true", value={
        match self.sum { Some(n) => n.to_string(), None => "".to_string() }
    },
/>
```

The style attribute is composed by concatenating the numeric string seen before with the background color. Such a color is light green if sum has a numeric value, or yellow if it is None. Also, the value attribute is assigned using an expression, to assign an empty string if sum is None.

The login app

So far, we have seen that an app contains just one model struct, one `enum` of messages, one `create` function, one `update` method, and one `view` method. This is good for very simple apps, but with more complex apps, this simple architecture becomes unwieldy. There is a need to separate different portions of the app in different components, where each component is designed with the MVC pattern and so it has its own model, controller, and view.

Typically, but not necessarily, there is a general component that contains the portions of the app that remain the same for all of the app:

- A header with a logo, a menu, and the name of the current user
- A footer containing copyright information and contact information

And then in the middle of the page, there is the inner part (also named the *body*, although it is not the `body` HTML element). This inner part contains the real information of the app and is one of many possible components or forms (or pages):

1. Let's run the `login` app by typing `cargo web start` in its folder.
2. When navigating to `localhost:8000`, the following page appears:

There are two horizontal lines. The part above the first line is meant to be a header, which must remain for the whole app. The part underneath the second line is meant to be a footer, which must remain for the whole app, too. The median part is the `Login` component, which appears only when the user must be authenticated. This portion will be replaced by other components when the user is authenticated.

First of all, let's see some authentication failures:

- If you click on **Log in** straightaway, a message box appears saying: **User not found**. The same happens if you type some random characters in the **User name** textbox. The only allowed user names are susan and joe.
- If you insert one of the two allowed user names, and then you click on **Log in**, you get the message **Invalid password for the specified user**.
- The same happens if you type some random characters in the **Password** textbox. The only allowed passwords are xsusan for the user susan, and xjoe for the user joe. If you type susan and then xsusan, just before clicking on **Log in**, you will see the following:

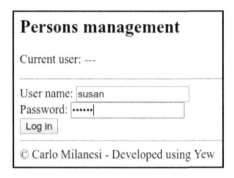

And just after, you will see the following:

Three things have changed:

- At the right of the label—**Current user**—the blue text **---** has been replaced by **susan**.
- At the right of that blue text, the **Change User** button has appeared.
- Between the two horizontal lines, all the HTML elements have been replaced by the large text reading **Page to be implemented**. Of course, this situation would represent a case in which the user has been successfully authenticated and is using the rest of the app.

If you were to click the **Change User** button, you will get the following page:

It is similar to the first page, but the name **susan** appears both as **Current user**, and as **User name**.

Organization of the project

The source code of this project has been split into three files (which you will find in the book's GitHub repository at `Chapter05/login/src/db_access.rs`:

- `db_access.rs`: Contains a stub of a user directory to handle authentication
- `main.rs`: Contains the one-line `main` function, and an MVC component that handles the header and the footer of the page, and delegates the inner section to the authentication component
- `login.rs`: Contains the MVC component to handle the authentication, to be used as an inner section of the main component

The db_access.rs file

The `db_access` module is a subset of that of the previous chapter. It declares a `DbConnection` struct that simulates a connection to a database. Actually, for simplicity, it contains just `Vec<User>`, where `User` is an account of the app:

```
#[derive(PartialEq, Clone)]
pub struct DbConnection {
    users: Vec<User>,
}
```

The definition of the `User` type is this:

```
pub enum DbPrivilege {
    CanRead,
    CanWrite,
}

pub struct User {
    pub username: String,
    pub password: String,
    pub privileges: Vec<DbPrivilege>,
}
```

Any user of the app has a name, a password, and some privileges. In this simple system, there are only two possible privileges:

- `CanRead`, which means that the user can read all of the database
- `CanWrite`, which means that the user can change all of the database (that is, inserting, updating, and deleting records)

Two users are wired in:

- `joe` with the password `xjoe`, capable only of reading from the database
- `susan` with the password `xsusan`, capable of reading and writing the data

The only functions are as follows:

- new, to create a `DbConnection`:

    ```
    pub fn new() -> DbConnection {
        DbConnection {
            users: vec![
                User {
                    username: "joe".to_string(),
                    password: "xjoe".to_string(),
    ```

```
                            privileges: vec![DbPrivilege::CanRead],
                    },
                    User {
                        username: "susan".to_string(),
                        password: "xsusan".to_string(),
                        privileges: vec![DbPrivilege::CanRead,
                         DbPrivilege::CanWrite],
                    },
                ],
            }
        }
```

- `get_user_by_username`, to get a reference to the user having the specified name, or `None` if there is no user with that name:

```
        pub fn get_user_by_username(&self, username: &str) -> Option<&User>
        {
            if let Some(u) = self.users.iter().find(|u|
             u.username == username) {
                Some(u)
            } else {
                None
            }
        }
    }
```

Of course, first, we will create a `DbConnection` object, using the `new` function, and then we will get a `User` from that object, using the `get_user_by_username` method.

The main.rs file

The `main.rs` file begins with the following declarations:

```
mod login;

enum Page {
    Login,
    PersonsList,
}
```

The first declaration imports the `login` module, which will be referenced by the `main` module. Any inner section module must be imported here.

The second statement declares all the components that will be used as inner sections. Here, we have only the authentication component (`Login`) and a component that is not yet implemented (`PersonsList`).

Then, there is the model of the MVC component of the main page:

```
struct MainModel {
    page: Page,
    current_user: Option<String>,
    can_write: bool,
    db_connection: std::rc::Rc<std::cell::RefCell<DbConnection>>,
}
```

As a convention, the name of any model ends with `Model`:

- The first field of the model is the most important one. It represents which inner section (or `page`) is currently active.
- The other fields contain global information, that is, information useful for displaying the header, the footer, or that must be shared with the inner components.
- The `current_user` field contains the name of the logged-in user, or `None` if no user is logged in.
- The `can_write` flag is a simplistic description of user privileges; here, both users can read, but only one can also write, and so this flag is `true` when they are logged in.
- The `db_connection` field is a reference to the database stub. It must be shared with an inner component, and so it is implemented as a reference-counted smart pointer to `RefCell`, containing the actual `DbConnection`. Using this wrapping, any object can be shared with other components, as long as one thread at a time accesses them.

The possible notifications from the view to the controller are these:

```
enum MainMsg {
    LoggedIn(User),
    ChangeUserPressed,
}
```

Remember that the footer has no elements that can get input, and for the header, there is only the **Change User** button that can get input, when it is visible. By pressing such a button, the `ChangeUserPressed` message is sent.

So, it appears there is no way to send the `LoggedIn` message! Actually, the `Login` component can send it to the main component.

The update function of the controller has the following body:

```
match msg {
    MainMsg::LoggedIn(user) => {
        self.page = Page::PersonsList;
        self.current_user = Some(user.username);
        self.can_write = user.privileges.contains(&DbPrivilege::CanWrite);
    }
    MainMsg::ChangeUserPressed => self.page = Page::Login,
```

When the `Login` component notifies the main component of successful authentication, thus specifying the authenticated user, the main controller sets `PersonsList` as the page to go to, saves the name of the newly authenticated user, and extracts the privileges from that user.

When the **Change User** button is clicked, the *page to go to* becomes the `Login` page. The `view` method contains just an invocation of the `html` macro. Such a macro must contain one HTML element, and in this case, it is a `div` element.

That `div` element contains three HTML elements: a `style` element, a `header` element, and a `footer` element. But between the header and the footer, there is some Rust code to create the inner section of the main page.

To insert Rust code inside an `html` macro, there are two possibilities:

- Attributes of HTML elements are just Rust code.
- At any point, a pair of braces encloses Rust code.

In the first case, the evaluation of such Rust code must return a value convertible to a string through the `Display` trait.

In the second case, the evaluation of the Rust code in braces must return an HTML element. And how can you return an HTML element from Rust code? Using an `html` macro!

So, the Rust code that implements the `view` method contains an `html` macro invocation that contains a block of Rust code, which contains an `html` macro invocation, and so on. This recursion is performed at compile time and has a limit that can be overridden using the `recursion_limit` Rust attribute.

 Notice that both the header and the inner section contain a `match` `self.page` expression.

In the header, it is used to show the **Change User** button only if the current page is not the login page, for which it would be pointless.

In the inner section, the body of such a statement is the following:

```
Page::Login => html! {
    <LoginModel:
        current_username=&self.current_user,
        when_logged_in=|u| MainMsg::LoggedIn(u),
        db_connection=Some(self.db_connection.clone()),
    />
},
Page::PersonsList => html! {
    <h2>{ "Page to be implemented" }</h2>
},
```

If the current page is `Login`, an invocation to the `html` macro contains the `LoginModel:` HTML element. Actually, the HTML language doesn't have such an element type. This is the way to embed another Yew component in the current component. The `LoginModel` component is declared in the `login.rs` source file. Its construction requires some arguments:

- `current_username` is the name of the current user.
- `when_logged_in` is a callback that the component should invoke when it has performed a successful authentication.
- `db_connection` is a (reference-counted) copy of the database.

Regarding the callback, notice that it receives a user (`u`) as an argument and returns the message `LoggedIn` decorated by that user. Sending this message to the controller of the main component is the way the `Login` component communicates to the main component who the user is that has just logged in.

The login.rs file

The `login` module begins by defining the model of the `Login` component:

```
pub struct LoginModel {
    dialog: DialogService,
    username: String,
    password: String,
    when_logged_in: Option<Callback<User>>,
    db_connection: std::rc::Rc<std::cell::RefCell<DbConnection>>,
}
```

This model must be used by the main component, and so it must be public.

Its fields are as follows:

- `dialog` is a reference to a Yew service, which is a way to ask the framework to do something more than implementing the MVC architecture. A dialog service is the ability to show message boxes to the user, through the JavaScript engine of the browser.
- `username` and `password` are the values of the text that the user has typed in the two textboxes.
- `when_logged_in` is a possible callback function, to call when a successful authentication is completed.
- `db_connection` is a reference to the database.

The possible notification messages are these:

```
pub enum LoginMsg {
    UsernameChanged(String),
    PasswordChanged(String),
    LoginPressed,
}
```

The first two messages mean that the respective fields have changed values, and the third message says that the push-button has been pressed.

So far, we have seen that this component has a model and some messages, like the components we saw before; but now we'll see that it also has something that we've never seen:

```
pub struct LoginProps {
    pub current_username: Option<String>,
    pub when_logged_in: Option<Callback<User>>,
    pub db_connection:
      Option<std::rc::Rc<std::cell::RefCell<DbConnection>>>,
}
```

This structure represents the arguments that every parent of this component must pass to create the component. In this project, there is only one parent of the `Login` component, that is, the main component, and that component created a `LoginModel:` element having the fields of `LoginProps` as attributes. Notice that all the fields are specializations of `Option`: it is required by the Yew framework, even if you don't pass an `Option` as an attribute.

This `LoginProps` type must be used in four points:

- First, it must implement the `Default` trait, to ensure its fields are properly initialized when the framework needs an object of this type:

```
impl Default for LoginProps {
    fn default() -> Self {
        LoginProps {
            current_username: None,
            when_logged_in: None,
            db_connection: None,
        }
    }
}
```

- Second, we already saw that the implementation of the `Component` trait for the model has to define a `Properties` type. In this case, it must be like so:

```
impl Component for LoginModel {
    type Message = LoginMsg;
    type Properties = LoginProps;
```

That is, this type is passed into the implementation of the `Component` trait for the `LoginModel` type.

- Third, the `create` function must use its first argument, containing the values passed in by the parent component. Here is that function:

```
fn create(props: Self::Properties, _link: ComponentLink<Self>)
-> Self {
    LoginModel {
        dialog: DialogService::new(),
        username: props.current_username.unwrap_or(String::new()),
        password: String::new(),
        when_logged_in: props.when_logged_in,
        db_connection: props.db_connection.unwrap(),
    }
}
```

All the fields of the model are initialized, but while the `dialog` and `password` fields receive default values, the other fields receive a value from the `props` object received from the parent component, that is, `MainModel`. As we are sure that the `db_connection` field of `props` will be `None`, we call `unwrap` for it. Instead, the `current_username` field may be `None`, and so, in that case, an empty string is used.

Then there is the `update` function, which is the controller of the `Login` component.

When the user presses the **Log in** button, the following code is executed:

```
if let Some(user) = self.db_connection.borrow()
    .get_user_by_username(&self.username)
{
    if user.password == self.password {
        if let Some(ref go_to_page) = self.when_logged_in {
            go_to_page.emit(user.clone());
        }
    } else {
        self.dialog.alert("Invalid password for the specified user.");
    }
} else {
    self.dialog.alert("User not found.");
}
```

The connection to the database is extracted from `RefCell` using the `borrow` method, and then the user with the current name is looked for. If the user is found, and if their stored password is the same as that typed by the user, the callback kept in the `when_logged_in` field is extracted, and then its `emit` method is invoked, passing a copy of the user name as argument. So, the routine passed by the parent, that is, the `|u|`
`MainMsg::LoggedIn(u)` closure, is executed.

In the event of a missing user or mismatching password, a message box is displayed using the `alert` method of the dialog service. The controllers that we saw before had just two functions: `create` and `update`. This one has another function, though; it is the `change` method:

```
fn change(&mut self, props: Self::Properties) -> ShouldRender {
    self.username = props.current_username.unwrap_or(String::new());
    self.when_logged_in = props.when_logged_in;
    self.db_connection = props.db_connection.unwrap();
    true
}
```

This method allows the parent to re-send to this component updated arguments using the `Properties` structure. The `create` method is invoked just one time, while the `change` method is invoked any time the parent will need to update the arguments to pass to the child component.

The view is easy to understand by reading its code and does not require explanation.

The yauth app

The `login` app, presented in the previous section, showed how to create a parent component containing one of several possible child components. However, it implemented just one child component, the `Login` component. So, in this section, a more complete example will be presented, having three different possible child components, corresponding to three different pages of a classical web application.

It is named `yauth`, short for **Yew Auth**, as its behavior is almost identical to the `auth` project shown in the previous chapter, although, it is completely based on the Yew framework, instead of being based on Actix web and Tera.

Understanding the behavior of the app

This app is built and launched like the ones in the previous sections, and its first page is identical to the first page of the `login` app. Though, if you type `susan` as the username and `xsusan` as the password, and then click on the **Log in** button, you'll see the following page:

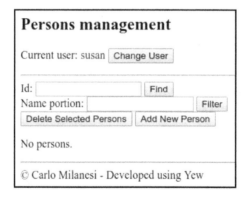

This page and the other page that you will see in this app, and their behavior, are almost identical to those of the `auth` app described in the previous chapter. The only differences are as follows:

- Any error message is not shown as red text embedded in the page but as a pop-up message box.
- The header and the footer are implemented by the main component, and they look and behave as already described in the previous section of this chapter.

So, we just need to examine the implementation of this app.

Organization of the project

The source code of this project has been split into five files:

- `db_access.rs`: It contains a stub of a connection to a database, providing access to a user directory to handle authentication and to a list of persons; it actually contains such data as vectors. It is virtually identical to the file with the same name in the `auth` project of the previous chapter. The only relevant difference is that the `Serialize` trait is not implemented, because it's not required by the Yew framework.
- `main.rs`: It contains the one-line `main` function, and an MVC component that handles the header and the footer of the page, and delegates the inner section to one of the other three components of the app.
- `login.rs`: It contains the MVC component to handle the authentication. It is to be used as an inner section of the main component. It is identical to the module having the same name in the `login` project.
- `persons_list.rs`: It contains the MVC component to handle the list of persons. It is to be used as an inner section of the main component.
- `one_person.rs`: It contains the MVC component to view, edit, or insert a single person; it is to be used as an inner section of the main component.

We will only discuss the files unique to the `yauth` app, as follows.

The persons_list.rs file

This file contains the definition of the component to let the user manage the list of persons, and so it defines the following struct as a model:

```
pub struct PersonsListModel {
    dialog: DialogService,
    id_to_find: Option<u32>,
    name_portion: String,
    filtered_persons: Vec<Person>,
    selected_ids: std::collections::HashSet<u32>,
    can_write: bool,
    go_to_one_person_page: Option<Callback<Option<Person>>>,
    db_connection: std::rc::Rc<std::cell::RefCell<DbConnection>>,
}
```

Let's see what each line in the previous code says:

- The `dialog` field contains a service to open message boxes.
- The `id_to_find` field contains the value typed by the user in the **Id** textbox if the box contains a number, or `None` otherwise.
- The `name_portion` field contains the value contained in the **Name portion:** textbox. In particular, if that box is empty, this field of the model contains an empty string. The `filtered_persons` field contains a list of the persons extracted from the database using the specified filter. Initially, the filter specifies to extract all the persons whose names contain an empty string. Of course, all the persons satisfy that filter, and so all the persons in the database are added to this vector, though the database is empty, and so this vector is too.
- The `selected_ids` field contains the IDs of all the listed people whose checkbox is set, and so they are selected for further operation.
- The `can_write` field specifies whether the current user has the privilege to modify the data.
- The `go_to_one_person_page` field contains the callback to call to pass to the page to view/edit/insert a single person. Such a callback function receives one argument, which is the person to view/edit, or `None` to open the page to insert a new person.
- The `db_connection` field contains a shared reference to the database connection.

The possible notifications from the view to the controllers are defined by this structure:

```
pub enum PersonsListMsg {
    IdChanged(String),
    FindPressed,
    PartialNameChanged(String),
    FilterPressed,
    DeletePressed,
    AddPressed,
    SelectionToggled(u32),
    EditPressed(u32),
}
```

Let's see what we did in the previous code:

- The `IdChanged` message must be sent when the text in the **Id:** textbox is changed. Its argument is the new text value of the field.
- The `FindPressed` message must be sent when the **Find** push-button is clicked.
- The `PartialNameChanged` message must be sent when the text in the **Name portion:** textbox is changed. Its argument is the new text value of the field.
- The `FilterPressed` message must be sent when the **Filter** push-button is clicked.
- The `DeletePressed` message must be sent when the **Delete Selected Persons** push-button is clicked.
- The `AddPressed` message must be sent when the **Add New Person** push-button is clicked.
- The `SelectionToggled` message must be sent when a checkbox in the list of persons is toggled (that is, checked or unchecked). Its argument is the ID of the person specified by that line of the list.
- The `EditPressed` message must be sent when any **Edit** push-button in the list of persons is clicked. Its argument is the ID of the person specified by that line of the list.

Then, the structure of the initialization arguments for the component is defined:

```
pub struct PersonsListProps {
    pub can_write: bool,
    pub go_to_one_person_page: Option<Callback<Option<Person>>>,
    pub db_connection:
      Option<std::rc::Rc<std::cell::RefCell<DbConnection>>>,
}
```

Let's look at how this works:

- Using the `can_write` field, the main component specifies a simple definition of the privileges of the current user. A more complex application could have a more complex definition of privileges.
- Using the `go_to_one_person_page` field, the main component passes a reference to a function, which must be called to go to the page for showing, editing, or inserting a single person.
- Using the `db_connection` field, the main component passes a shared reference to the database connection.

The initialization of the `PersonsListProps` struct by implementing the `Default` trait and of the `PersonsListModel` struct by implementing the `Component` trait is trivial, except for the `filtered_persons` field. Instead of leaving it as an empty vector, it is first set as an empty vector, and then modified by the following statement:

```
model.filtered_persons = model.db_connection.borrow()
    .get_persons_by_partial_name("");
```

Why an empty collection wouldn't be good for filtered_persons

Every time the `PersonsList` page is opened, both from the login page and from the `OnePerson` page, the model is initialized by the `create` function, and all the user interface elements of the page are initialized using that model.

So, if you type something in the `PersonsList` page, and then you go to another page, and then you go back to the `PersonsList` page, everything you typed is cleared unless you set it in the `create` function.

Probably, the fact that the **Id** textbox, the **Name portion** textbox, or the selected persons are cleared is not very annoying, but the fact that the list of persons is cleared means that you will get the following behavior:

- You filter the persons to see some persons listed.
- You click on the **Edit** button in the row of one person, to change the name of that person, and so you go to the `OnePerson` page.
- You change the name and press the **Update** button, and so you go back to the `PersonsList` page.
- You see the text **No persons.** instead of the list of persons.

You don't see the person that you have just modified in the `OnePerson` page anymore. This is inconvenient.

To see that person listed, you need to set `filtered_persons` to a value containing that person. The solution chosen has been to show all the persons existing in the database, and this is performed by calling the `get_persons_by_partial_name("")` function.

Now, let's see how the `update` method handles the messages from the view.

When the `IdChanged` message is received, the following statement is executed:

```
self.id_to_find = id_str.parse::<u32>().ok(),
```

It tries to store in the model the value of the textbox, or None if the value is not convertible to a number.

When the FindPressed message is received, the following statement is executed:

```
match self.id_to_find {
    Some(id) => { self.update(PersonsListMsg::EditPressed(id)); }
    None => { self.dialog.alert("No id specified."); }
},
```

If the **Id** textbox contained a valid number, another message would be sent recursively: it is the EditPressed message. Pressing the **Find** button must have the same behavior as pressing the **Edit** button in the row with the same ID contained in the **Id** textbox, and so the message is forwarded to the same function. If there is no ID in the text field, a message box is displayed.

When the PartialNameChanged message is received, the new partial name is just saved in the name_portion field of the model. When the FilterPressed message is received, the following statement is executed:

```
self.filtered_persons = self
    .db_connection
    .borrow()
    .get_persons_by_partial_name(&self.name_portion);
```

The connection to the database is encapsulated in a RefCell object, which is further encapsulated in an Rc object. The access inside Rc is implicit, but to access inside RefCell, it is required to call the borrow method. Then the database is queried to get the list of all the persons whose names contain the current name portion. This list is finally assigned to the filtered_persons field of the model.

When the DeletePressed message is received, the following statement is executed:

```
if self
    .dialog
    .confirm("Do you confirm to delete the selected persons?") {
    {
        let mut db = self.db_connection.borrow_mut();
        for id in &self.selected_ids {
            db.delete_by_id(*id);
        }
    }
    self.update(PersonsListMsg::FilterPressed);
    self.dialog.alert("Deleted.");
}
```

The following pop-up box is shown for confirmation:

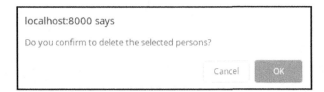

If the user clicks on the **OK** button (or presses *Enter*), then the deletion is performed in the following way: a mutable reference is borrowed from the shared connection to the database, and for any ID selected through the checkboxes, the respective person is deleted from the database.

The closing of the scope releases the borrowing. Then, a recursive call to update triggers the FilterPressed message, whose purpose is to refresh the list of persons shown. Finally, the following message box communicates the completion of the operation:

When the AddPressed message is received, the following code is executed:

```
if let Some(ref go_to_page) = self.go_to_one_person_page {
    go_to_page.emit(None);
}
```

Here, a reference to the go_to_one_person_page callback is taken, and then it is invoked using the emit method. The effect of such an invocation is to go to the OnePerson page. The argument of emit specifies which person will be edited on the page. If it is None, as in this case, the page is opened in insertion mode.

When the SelectionToggled message is received, it specifies an ID of a person, but it does not specify whether that person is to be selected or deselected. So, the following code is executed:

```
if self.selected_ids.contains(&id) {
    self.selected_ids.remove(&id);
} else {
    self.selected_ids.insert(id);
}
```

We want to invert the status of the person on which the user has clicked, that is, to select it if it was not selected, and to unselect it if it was selected. The `selected_ids` field of the model contains the set of all the selected persons. So, if the clicked ID is contained in the set of selected IDs, it is removed from this set by calling the `remove` method; otherwise, it is added to the list, by calling the `insert` method.

At last, when the `EditPressed` message is received (specifying the `id` of the person to view/change), the following code is executed:

```
match self.db_connection.borrow().get_person_by_id(id) {
    Some(person) => {
        if let Some(ref go_to_page) = self.go_to_one_person_page {
            go_to_page.emit(Some(person.clone()));
        }
    }
    None => self.dialog.alert("No person found with the indicated id."),
}
```

The database is searched for a person with the specified ID. If such a person is found, the `go_to_one_person_page` callback is invoked, passing a clone of the person found. Otherwise, a message box explains the error. The `change` method keeps the fields of the model updated when any property coming from the parent component would change.

Then there is the view. The messages sent by the view were described when the messages were presented. The other interesting aspects of the view are the following ones.

The **Delete Selected Persons** button and the **Add New Person** button have the attribute `disabled=!self.can_write`. This enables such commands only if the user has the privilege to change the data.

The `if !self.filtered_persons.is_empty()` clause causes the table of persons to be displayed only if there is at least one person filtered. Otherwise, the text **No persons.** is displayed.

The body of the table begins and ends with the following lines:

```
for self.filtered_persons.iter().map(|p| {
    let id = p.id;
    let name = p.name.clone();
    html! {
        ...
    }
})
```

This is the required syntax for generating sequences of HTML elements based on an iterator.

The `for` keyword is immediately followed by an iterator (in this case, the expression `self.filtered_persons.iter()`), followed by the expression `.map(|p|`, where `p` is the loop variable. In this way, it is possible to insert into the map closure a call to the `html` macro that generates the elements of the sequence. In this case, such elements are the lines of the HTML table.

The last noteworthy point is the way to show which persons are selected. Every checkbox has the attribute `checked=self.selected_ids.contains(&id),`. The checked attribute expects a `bool` value. That expression sets as checked the checkbox relative to the persons whose `id` is contained in the list of the selected IDs.

The one_person.rs file

This file contains the definition of the component to let the user view or edit the details of one person or to fill in the details and insert a new person. Of course, to view the details of an existing record, such details must be passed as arguments to the component; instead, to insert a new person, no data must be passed to the component.

This component does not return its changes directly to the parent that created it. Such changes are saved to the database, if the user requested that, and the parent can retrieve them from the database.

Therefore the model is defined by the following struct:

```
pub struct OnePersonModel {
    id: Option<u32>,
    name: String,
    can_write: bool,
    is_inserting: bool,
    go_to_persons_list_page: Option<Callback<()>>,
    db_connection: std::rc::Rc<std::cell::RefCell<DbConnection>>,
}
```

With the preceding code, we understood the following things:

- The `id` field contains the value contained in the **Id** textbox if the box contains a number, or `None` otherwise.
- The `name` field contains the value contained in the **Name** textbox. In particular, if the box is empty, this field of the model contains an empty string.

- The `can_write` field specifies whether the current privileges allow the user to change the data or only to see it.
- The `is_inserting` field specifies whether this component has received no data, to insert a new person into the database, or whether it has received the data of a person, to view or edit them.
- The `go_to_persons_list_page` field is a callback with no arguments that must be invoked by this component when the user closes this page to go to the page to manage the list of persons.
- The `db_connection` field is a shared connection to the database.

Of course, it is pointless to open a page for insertion without allowing the user to change the values. So, the possible combinations are the following ones:

- **Insertion mode**: The `id` field is `None`, the `can_write` field is `true`, and the `is_inserting` field is `true`.
- **Editing mode**: The `id` field is `Some`, the `can_write` field is `true`, and the `is_inserting` field is `false`.
- **Read-only mode**: The `id` field is `Some`, the `can_write` field is `false`, and the `is_inserting` field is `false`.

The possible notifications from the view to the controller are defined by the following enum:

```
pub enum OnePersonMsg {
    NameChanged(String),
    SavePressed,
    CancelPressed,
}
```

Let's see what happened in the code:

- When the user changes the contents of the **Name** textbox, the `NameChanged` message is sent, which also specifies the current contents of that textbox.
- When the user clicks on the **Insert** button or on the **Update** button, the `SavePressed` message is sent. To distinguish between the two buttons, the `is_inserting` field can be used.
- When the user presses the **Cancel** button, the `CancelPressed` message is sent.

The value of the **Id** textbox can never be changed during the life of this component, and so no message is required for it. The data received from the parent is defined by the following structure:

```
pub struct OnePersonProps {
    pub id: Option<u32>,
    pub name: String,
    pub can_write: bool,
    pub go_to_persons_list_page: Option<Callback<()>>,
    pub db_connection:
     Option<std::rc::Rc<std::cell::RefCell<DbConnection>>>,
}
```

In the preceding code, we have the following things to check:

- The `id` field is `None` in case the parent wants to open the page to let the user insert a new person, and contains the ID of an existing person in case the page is for viewing or editing the data of that person.
- The `name` field is the only changeable data of any person. It is an empty string if the page is created for inserting a new person. Otherwise, the parent passes the current name of the person.
- The `can_write` field specifies whether the user is allowed to change the displayed data. This field should be `true` if the `id` field is `None`.
- `go_to_persons_list_page` is the callback that will activate the `PersonsList` component in the parent.
- The `db_connection` field is the shared database connection.

In the rest of the module, there is nothing new. The only thing to stress is that the use of conditional expressions based on the `can_write` and `is_inserting` flags of the model allows having just one component with a mutant view.

A web app accessing a RESTful service

The previous section described a rather complex software architecture, but still running only in the user's web browser, after having being served by the site where it is installed. This is quite unusual, as most web apps actually communicate with some other process. Typically, the same site that provides the frontend app also provides a backend service, that is, a web service to let the app access shared data residing on the server.

In this section, we'll see a pair of projects that can be downloaded from the repository:

- `yclient`: This is an app quite similar to the `yauth` app. Actually, it is developed using Yew and Wasm, and it has the same look and behavior as `yauth`; though its data, which is the authorized users and the persons stored in the mock database, no longer resides in the app itself, but in another app, which is accessed through an HTTP connection.
- `persons_db`: This is the RESTful service that provides access to the data for the `yclient` app. It is developed using the Actix web framework, as explained in the previous chapter. Even this app does not manage a real database, only a mock, in-memory database.

To run the system, two commands are required: one to run the frontend provider, `yclient`, and one to run the web service, `persons_db`.

To run the frontend provider, go into the `yclient` folder, and type the following:

```
cargo web start
```

After downloading and compiling all the required crates, it will print the following:

```
You can access the web server at `http://127.0.0.1:8000`.
```

To run the backend, in another console window, go into the `db_persons` folder and type the following:

```
cargo run
```

Or, we can use the following command:

```
cargo run --release
```

Both these commands will end by printing the following:

```
Listening at address 127.0.0.1:8080
```

Now you can use your web browser and navigate to `localhost:8000`. The app that will be opened will be quite similar to both the `yauth` app, shown in the previous section, and to the `auth` app, shown in the previous chapter.

Let's first see how `persons_db` is organized.

The persons_db app

This app uses the Actix web framework, described in the previous two chapters. In particular, this project has some features taken from the `json_db` project, described in Chapter 3, *Creating a REST Web Service*, and some from the `auth` project, described in Chapter 4, *Creating a Full Server-Side Web App*.

Here, we'll see only the new features that haven't been described so far. The `Cargo.toml` file contains the following new line:

```
actix-cors = "0.1"
```

This crate allows the handling of the **Cross-Origin Resource Sharing** (**CORS**) checks, usually performed by browsers. When some code running inside a browser tries to access an external resource using a network connection, the browser, for security reasons, checks whether the addressed host is just the one that provided the code that is performing the request. That means that the frontend and the backend are actually the same website.

If the check fails, that is, the frontend app is trying to communicate with a different site, the browser sends an HTTP request using the `OPTION` method to check whether the site agrees to cooperate with that web app on this resource sharing. Only if the response to the `OPTION` request allows the required kind of access can the original request be forwarded.

In our case, both the frontend app and the web service run on localhost; though, they use different TCP ports: `8000` for the frontend and `8080` for the backend. So, they are considered as different origins, and CORS handling is needed. The `actix-cors` crate provides features to allow such cross-origin access for backends developed using Actix web.

One of these features is used in the `main` function, as in the following code snippet:

```
.wrap(
    actix_cors::Cors::new()
        .allowed_methods(vec!["GET", "POST", "PUT", "DELETE"])
)
```

This code is a so-called **middleware**, meaning that it will be run for every request received by the service, and so it is a piece of software that stays in the middle between the client and the server.

The `wrap` method is the one to use to add a piece of middleware. This word means that the following code must be *around* every handler, possibly filtering both requests and responses.

Such code creates an object of type `Cors` and specifies for it which HTTP methods will be accepted.

The rest of this web service should be clear to those who have learned what has already been described about the Actix web framework. It is a RESTful web service that accepts requests as URI paths and queries and returns responses as JSON bodies, and for which authentication is provided in any request by the basic authentication header.

The API has a new route for the `GET` method and the `/authenticate` path, which calls the `authenticate` handler, which is used to get a whole user object with the list of their privileges.

Now let's see how `yclient` is organized.

The yclient app

This app starts from where the `yauth` app left off. The `yauth` apps contain its own in-memory database, while the app described here communicates with the `person_db` web service to access its database.

Here, we'll see only the new features, with respect to the `yauth` project.

The imported crates

The `Cargo.toml` file contains new lines:

```
failure = "0.1"
serde = "1"
serde_derive = "1"
url = "1"
base64 = "0.10"
```

For the preceding code, let's have a look at the following things:

- The `failure` crate is used to encapsulate communication errors.
- The `serde` and `serde_derive` crates are needed to transfer whole objects from server to client, using deserialization. In particular, the whole object of the types `Person`, `User`, and `DbPrivilege` are transferred in server responses.

- The `url` crate is used for encoding information in a URL. In a URL path or a URL query, you can easily put only identifiers or integer numbers, such as, say, `/person/id/478` or `/persons?ids=1,3,39`, but more complex data, such as the name of a person, is not allowed *as is*. You cannot have a URL as `/persons?partial_name=John Doe`, because it contains whitespace. In general, you have to encode it in coding allowed in a URL, and that is provided by the call to `url::form_urlencoded::byte_serialize`, which gets a slice of bytes and returns an iterator generating chars. If you call `collect::<String>()` on this iterator, you get a string that can be safely put into a web URI.
- The `base64` crate is used to perform a similar encoding of binary data into textual data, but for the header or the body of an HTTP request. In particular, it is required to encode usernames and passwords in the basic authentication header.

The source files

The source file names are the same as the `yauth` project, except that the `db_access.rs` file has been renamed as `common.rs`. Actually, in this project, there is no code required to access the database, as access is now performed only by the service. The `common` module contains definitions of a constant, two structs, an enum, and a function needed by several components.

The changes to the models

The models of the components have the following changes.

All the `db_connection` fields have been removed, as the app now does not directly access the database. That has become the responsibility of the server.

The Boolean `fetching` field has been added. It is set to true when a request is sent to the server and reset to false when the response is received, or the request has failed. It is not really necessary in this app, but it may be useful when using a slower communication (with a remote server) or some more lengthy requests. It may be used to show to the user that a request is pending, and also to disable other requests in the meantime.

The `fetch_service` field has been added to provide the communication feature. The `ft` field has been added to contain a reference to the current `FetchTask` object during a request, or `Nothing` when no request has already been sent. This field is not actually used; this is just a trick to keep the current request alive, because otherwise after the request is sent and the `update` function returns, the local variables would be dropped.

The `link` field has been added for forwarding to the current model the callback that will be called when the response is received.

The `console` field has been added to provide a way to print to the console of the browser, for debugging purposes. In Yew, the `print!` and `println!` macros are ineffective, as there is no system console on which to print. But the web browser has a console, which is accessed using the `console.log()` JavaScript function call. This Yew service provides access to such a feature.

The `username` and `password` fields have been added to send authentication data with any requests.

But let's see the changes required to the code because of the need to communicate with the server.

A typical client/server request

For any user command that, in the `yauth` project, required access to the database, such access has been removed, and the following changes have been applied, instead.

Such a user command now sends a request to a web service, and then a response from that service must be handled. In our examples, the time between the user command and the reception of the response from the service is quite short – just a few milliseconds, for the following reasons:

- Both client and server run in the same computer, and so the TCP/IP packets actually don't exit the computer.
- The computer has nothing else to do.
- The database is actually a very short memory vector, and so its operations are very fast.

Though, in a real system, much more time is spent processing a user command that causes communication. If everything is good, a command takes only half a second, but sometimes it may take several seconds. So, synchronous communication is not acceptable. Your app cannot just wait for a response from the server, because it would appear to be stuck.

So, the `FetchService` object of the Yew framework provides an asynchronous communication model.

The controller routine triggered by the user command prepares the request to be sent to the server, and also prepares a callback routine, to handle the response from the server, and then sends the request, and so the app is free to handle other messages.

When the response comes from the server, the response triggers a message that is handled by the controller. The handling of the message invokes the callback prepared in advance.

So, in addition to the messages signaling a user command, other messages have been added. Some of them report the reception of a response, that is, the successful completion of a request; and others report a failure of the request coming from the server, that is, the unsuccessful completion of a request. For example, in the `PersonsListModel` component, implemented in the `persons_list.rs` file, the following user actions required communication:

- Pressing the **Find** button (triggering the `FindPressed` message)
- Pressing the **Filter** button (triggering the `FilterPressed` message)
- Pressing the **Delete Selected Persons** button (triggering the `DeletePressed` message)
- Pressing one of the **Edit** buttons (triggering the `EditPressed` message)

For them, the following messages have been added:

- `ReadyFilteredPersons(Result<Vec<Person>, Error>)`: This is triggered by the `FetchService` instance when a list of filtered persons is received from the service. Such a list is contained in a `Vec` of `Person`. This may happen after processing the `FilterPressed` message.
- `ReadyDeletedPersons(Result<u32, Error>)`: This is triggered by the `FetchService` instance when the report that a command to delete some persons has been completed by the service. The number of deleted persons is contained in `u32`. This may happen after processing the `DeletePressed` message.
- `ReadyPersonToEdit(Result<Person, Error>)`: This is sent by `FetchService` when the requested `Person` object is received from the service, and so it can be edited (or simply displayed). This may happen after processing the `FindPressed` message or the `EditPressed` message.
- `Failure(String)`: This is sent by `FetchService` when any of the preceding requests have failed as the service returns a failure response.

For example, let's see the code that handles the `EditPressed` message. Its first part is as follows:

```
self.fetching = true;
self.console.log(&format!("EditPressed: {:?}.", id));
let callback =
    self.link
        .send_back(move |response: Response<Json<Result<Person, Error>>>| {
            let (meta, Json(data)) = response.into_parts();
            if meta.status.is_success() {
                PersonsListMsg::ReadyPersonToEdit(data)
            } else {
                PersonsListMsg::Failure(
                    "No person found with the indicated id".to_string(),
                )
            }
        });
```

Let's check the working of the code:

- First, the `fetching` state is set to `true`, to take note that communication is underway.
- Then a debug message is printed to the console of the browser.
- Then, a callback is prepared to handle the response. To prepare such a callback, a *move* closure, that is, a closure that gets ownership of all the variables it uses, is passed to the `send_back` function of the `link` object.

 Remember that we come here when the user has pressed a button to edit a person specified by their ID; and so we need the whole of the person data to display it to the user.

The body of the callback is the code that we want to be executed after receiving a response from the server. Such a response, if successful, must contain all the data regarding the person we want to edit. So, this closure gets a `Response` object from the service. This type is actually parameterized by the possible contents of the response. In this project, we always expect a `yew::format::Json` payload and such a payload is a `Result`, which always has `failure::Error` as its error type. Though, the success type varies depending on the request type. In this particular request, we expect a `Person` object as a successful result.

The body of the closure calls the `into_parts` method on the response to destructure the response into the metadata and the data. The metadata is HTTP-specific information, while the data is the JSON payload.

Using the metadata, it is possible to check whether the response was successful (`meta.status.is_success()`). In such a case, the Yew message `ReadyPersonToEdit(data)` is triggered; such a message will handle the response payload. In the event of an error, a Yew message of `Failure` is triggered; such a message will display the specified error message.

You could ask: "Why does the callback forward the payload to the Yew framework, specifying another message, instead of doing anything that should be done upon receipt of the response?"

The reason is that the callback, to be executed out of context by the framework, must be the owner of any variable it accesses after its creation, that is, when the request is sent, up to the time of its destruction (when the response is received). So, it cannot use the model or any other external variable. You cannot even print on the console or open an alert box inside such a callback. So you need to asynchronously forward the response to a message handler, which will be able to access the model.

The remaining part of the handler of the `EditPressed` message is this:

```
let mut request = Request::get(format!("{}person/id/{}", BACKEND_SITE, id))
    .body(Nothing)
    .unwrap();

add_auth(&self.username, &self.password, &mut request);
self.ft = Some(self.fetch_service.fetch(request, callback));
```

First, a web request is prepared, using the `get` method, which uses the GET HTTP method, and optionally specifying a `body`, which in this case is empty (`Nothing`).

Such a request is enriched with authentication information by a call of the `add_auth` common function, and finally, the `fetch` method of the `FetchService` object is invoked. This method uses the request and the callback to begin the communication with the server. It immediately returns a handle, stored in the `ft` field of the model.

Then the control returns to Yew, which can process other messages, until a response comes from the server. Such a response will be forwarded to the callback defined before.

Now, let's see the handler of the `ReadyPersonToEdit(person)` message, forwarded when a person structure is received from the server as a response to the request of editing a person by their `id`. Its code is as follows:

```
self.fetching = false;
let person = person.unwrap_or(Person {
    id: 0,
    name: "".to_string(),
```

```
    });
    if let Some(ref go_to_page) = self.go_to_one_person_page {
        self.console
            .log(&format!("ReadyPersonToEdit: {:?}.", person));
        go_to_page.emit(Some(person.clone()));
    }
```

First, the `fetching` state is set to `false`, to take note that the current communication is ended.

Then, if the received person was `None`, such a value is replaced by a person having zero as `id` and an empty string as a name. Of course, it is an invalid person.

Then, a reference to the `go_to_one_person_page` field of the model is taken. This field can be `None` (in fact, only at the initialization stage), so, if it is not defined, nothing is done. This field is a Yew callback to jump to another page.

At last, a debug message is printed, and the callback is invoked using the `emit` method. This call receives a copy of the person to display on that page.

Now, let's see the handler of the `Failure(msg)` message, forwarded when an error is received from the server. This handler is shared by other requests, as it has the same behavior. Its code is as follows:

```
    self.fetching = false;
    self.console.log(&format!("Failure: {:?}.", msg));
    self.dialog.alert(&msg);
    return false;
```

Again, the fetching state is set to `false` since the communication is ended.

A debug message is printed, and a message box is opened to show the user the error message. As long as such a message box is opened, the component is frozen, as no other message can be processed.

At last, the controller returns `false` to signal that no view needs to be refreshed. Notice that the default return value is `true` as, usually, the controller changes the model, and so the view must be refreshed as a consequence of that.

Summary

We have seen how a complete frontend web app can be built using Rust, by using the `cargo-web` command, the Wasm code generator, and the Yew framework. Such apps are modular and well structured, as they use the Elm Architecture, which is a variant of the MVC architectural pattern.

We created six apps, and we saw how they worked—`incr`, `adder`, `login`, `yauth`, `persons_db`, and `yclient`.

In particular, you learned how to build and run a Wasm project. We looked at the MVC architectural pattern for building interactive apps. We covered how the Yew framework supports the creation of apps implementing an MVC pattern, specifically according to the Elm Architecture. We also saw how to structure an app in several components and how to keep a common header and footer, while the body of the app changes from page to page. And at the end, we learned how to use Yew to communicate with a backend app, possibly running on a different computer, packaging data in JSON format.

In the next chapter, we will see how to build a web game using Wasm and the Quicksilver framework.

Questions

1. What is WebAssembly, and what are its advantages?
2. What is the MVC pattern?
3. What are messages in the Elm Architecture?
4. What are components in the Yew framework?
5. What are properties in the Yew framework?
6. How can you build a web app with a fixed header and footer and change the inner section using the Yew framework?
7. What are callbacks in the Yew framework?
8. How can you pass a shared object, such as a database connection, between Yew components?
9. Why you must keep in the model a field having type FetchTask, when you communicate with a server, even if you don't need to use it?
10. How can you open JavaScript-style alert boxes and confirm boxes using the Yew framework?

Further reading

- The Yew project can be downloaded from here: `https://github.com/DenisKolodin/yew`. The repository contains a very short tutorial and many examples.
- You can find other info about generating Wasm code from a Rust project at: `https://github.com/koute/cargo-web`.
- The status of web development libraries and frameworks: `https://www.arewewebyet.org/`
- The status of game development libraries and frameworks: `https://arewegameyet.com/`
- The status of programmers' editors and IDEs: `https://areweideyet.com/`
- The status of asynchronous programming libraries: `https://areweasyncyet.rs/`
- The status of GUI development libraries and frameworks: `https://areweguiyet.com/`

6
Creating a WebAssembly Game Using Quicksilver

In this chapter, you will see how Rust can be used to build a simple 2D game that can be compiled to run as a desktop app or as a web app. To run it as a web app, we will use the tools seen in the previous chapter to generate a **WebAssembly (Wasm)** application. As seen in that chapter, Wasm is a powerful new technology to run applications inside a browser. The appropriate tools translate Rust source code into a pseudo-machine language, named Wasm, that is loaded and run at top speed by browsers.

The Quicksilver open source framework will be described and used in this chapter. It has the powerful feature of being able to generate the following applications from a single source code:

- A standalone **graphical user interface (GUI)** application, to be run in a desktop system such as Windows, macOS, or Linux
- A Wasm app that runs in a JavaScript-enabled web browser

Quicksilver is oriented toward game programming, and so, as an example, we will develop an interactive graphical game using it: a slalom ski race, in which the player must drive a ski along a slope, entering the gates found along the ski run.

The following topics will be covered in this chapter:

- Understanding the animation loop architecture
- Building an animated application (`ski`) using the Quicksilver framework
- Building a simple game using the Quicksilver framework (`silent_slalom`)
- Adding text and sound to a game (`assets_slalom`)

Technical requirements

You need to read the section on Wasm of the previous chapter, but no other knowledge is required. To run the projects in this chapter, it is enough to install a Wasm code generator.

The complete source code for this chapter is in the `Chapter06` folder of the repository, found at `https://github.com/PacktPublishing/Creative-Projects-for-Rust-Programmers`.

For macOS users, you may struggle to install `coreaudio-sys`. Upgrading the patch version of `coreaudio-sys` to 0.2.3 resolves this issue.

Project overview

In this chapter, we will see how to develop games to be run in modern web browsers, or in GUI windows.

For that purpose, we will first describe the typical architecture of any interactive game that is based on the animation loop concept.

Then, the Quicksilver crate will be introduced. This is a framework that allows us to create a graphical application based on an animation loop. It allows us to generate a Wasm executable to be run in a web browser, or a native executable to be run in a desktop environment.

The first project (`ski`) will be very simple: just a page containing one ski that can be rotated by pressing arrow keys. This project will show the general architecture of a game, how to draw on a page, and how to handle input.

The second project (`silent_slalom`) will add features to the first project, creating a complete—albeit very simple—game. However, it will not use loadable resources such as images, fonts, or sounds.

The third project (`assets_slalom`) will add features to the second project, loading a font and some recorded sounds, and showing how to display some text on the page, and how to play the loaded sound files.

Understanding the animation loop architecture

As described in the previous chapter, the typical architecture of interactive software is **event-driven architecture**. In such an architecture, the software just waits for input commands, and it responds to such commands when they arrive. Until any command arrives, the software does nothing.

This architecture is efficient and responsive for many kinds of applications, but it is not optimal for some other kinds of applications, such as the following:

- Games with animations
- Continuous-simulation software
- Multimedia software
- Some kind of educational software
- Machine monitoring software (known as **Human-Machine Interface** (HMI) software)
- Systems monitoring software (known as **Supervisory Control and Data Acquisition** (SCADA) software)

In such systems, the software has always something to do, as in the following examples:

- In games with animations, such as sports games or combat games or racing games, both those against other human players and those against machine-simulated players, even if the user does nothing, the opponents move, and time flows; so, the screen must be constantly updated to show what the opponents have done, and what the current time is.
- In continuous-simulation software, such as the graphical simulation of a car crash, the objects continue to move, even if you don't press any key; so, the screen must show the new positions of the objects at any time.
- In multimedia software, such as software that reproduces an audio or video clip, the data continues to flow, until you pause or stop the reproduction.
- There are many kinds of educational software, but some of them are just games with animations, continuous-simulation software, or multimedia software.

- Most mechanical machines, to let a user monitor them, display on a screen a constantly updated representation of their internal status, even when the user does not request an update.
- Many complex systems, such as industrial plants, office buildings, and—recently—also residential buildings, display on a screen a constantly updated representation of the status of the devices operating in the system.

Actually, such kinds of software can even be developed using an event-driven architecture. It is enough to use a specific widget known as a *timer*. A timer is a software component that triggers an event at a fixed time interval.

For example, in an electronic thermometer, there is a timer that executes a routine every minute. Such a routine reads the temperature from a sensor and displays the read value on the small screen.

For some kinds of applications, the use of an event-driven environment, possibly including one or more timers, is appropriate. For example, event-driven programming is optimal for business applications such as an accounting application. In such applications, the user screen is split into several input widgets, such as labels, buttons, and textboxes. In such software, no application code is run until the user clicks the mouse or presses a key. Such input events trigger the action.

However, event-driven programming is not quite appropriate for the kind of software that displays a scene that fills the window, with no widgets, and that always has some code running even if the user does not act on input devices.

For such software, the so-called **animation loop architecture** is more appropriate. Its simplest structure is the following one:

1. First, a draw routine is defined as the one responsible for checking the status of the input devices and for redrawing the screen according to the status.
2. Then, a screen area is defined as a scene, and an update rate is defined for it.
3. When the program starts, it first opens a window (or a subwindow) for the scene, and then invokes the draw routine at regular intervals, using an internal timer.
4. Such periodic invocations of the draw routine are usually named *frames*, and the invocation rate is measured in **Frames Per Second (FPS)**.

The animation loop is sometimes named *game-loop*, as it is very often used for games. This is quite a misnomer, however, for the following two reasons:

- There are several other kinds of apps that should use an animation loop, such as continuous-simulation software, industrial machine monitoring software, or multimedia software. So, an animation loop is not only for games.
- There are some games that do not need an animation loop. For example, a chess game, a card game, or an adventure game, provided they are not based on animations, can be implemented perfectly well using an event-driven architecture. So, games are not necessarily based on animation loop.

 Notice that, while in an event-driven architecture user input triggers the action, in an animation loop architecture some action happens anyway, but if there is some user input such actions change accordingly.

Consider a user who presses a keyboard key or a mouse button. In event-driven programming, that input operation sends exactly one command. Instead, in animation loop programming, the program, at any frame, checks whether any key is pressed. If the key is pressed for a very short time, it is possible that such an operation goes unnoticed as, when the keyboard is checked in one cycle, that key has not been pressed yet, and when the keyboard is checked in the next cycle, that key has been already released.

This is quite unusual, though. Typical frame rates are from 20 to 60 FPS, and so the corresponding intervals are from 50 to 16.7 milliseconds. It is very difficult to press a key for a shorter time than that. Instead, it is quite typical that a key-press is much longer than a frame, and so the key is seen pressed in several successive frames.

If you use such a key-press to insert text, you would want to allow the user to press a key to insert just one letter. If you use a mouse click to press a button on the screen, you want that screen button to be pressed just once. To avoid such multiple hits, you must disable input for a short time the first time you get it. This is quite a nuisance, and so, for typical widget-based GUI apps, event-driven programming is more appropriate.

Instead, animation loop programming is appropriate whenever a key-press must have an effect proportional to the duration of the press. For example, if the arrow keys are used to move a character on the screen, and if you keep the right arrow pressed for 1 second, that character moves by a short distance; while if you keep pressed that key for 2 seconds, that character moves double that distance. In general, a short press should change little, and a long press should change much.

Regarding the output, when using event-driven programming, the effect of the operation is usually shown by changing some property of a widget (such as changing the text contents in a textbox, or loading a bitmap in a picture box). After that change, the widget is capable of refreshing itself whenever it needs, using its internal state. The event that triggers refreshing is the invalidation of the screen portion containing the widget. For example, if another window overlaps our window, and then it moves away, the discovered portion of our window is invalidated, and so it must be refreshed.

This kind of graphic is named **retained-mode**, as there is an inner data structure that retains the information needed to refresh the screen when there is a need. Instead, when using animation loop programming, all the images must be regenerated at every frame, and so there is no need to wait for a specific event. This kind of graphic is named **immediate-mode**, as the drawing is performed immediately by application code when it must be seen.

In the previous chapter, we saw that for event-driven applications, the **Model-View-Controller** (**MVC**) architectural pattern allows you to give a better structure to your code. Also, for animation loop applications, there is a kind of MVC architectural pattern.

The **Model** is the data structure that contains all the variables that must persist between frames.

The **Controller** is a function that has input but no output. It checks the status of input devices (which keyboard keys are pressed; which mouse keys are pressed; where the mouse is; which are the values of possible other input channels), reads the fields of the model, and updates them.

The **View** is a function that has output but no input. It reads the fields of the model and draws on the screen according to the read values.

Here is how the Quicksilver framework implements this pattern.

The model is any data type, typically a struct, that must implement the `State` trait. Such a trait contains the following three functions:

- `fn new() -> Result<Screen>`: This is the only way to create the model. It will return a valid model (if it can) or an error.
- `fn update(&mut self, window: &mut Window) -> Result<()>`: This is the controller. It is invoked periodically by the framework. The `window` argument allows you to get some context information. In this framework, it is mutable, but in the proper implementation of the MVC pattern, it shouldn't be changed. Instead, `self`—that is, the model—is rightly mutable.

- `fn draw(&mut self, window: &mut Window) -> Result<()>`: This is the view. It is invoked periodically by the framework. The `self` argument allows information to be obtained from the model. In this framework, it is mutable, but in the proper implementation of the MVC pattern, it shouldn't be changed. Instead, the `window` argument—that is, the output device—is rightly mutable.

Now, let's examine the first project in the repository using the Quicksilver framework.

Implementing the ski project

The first project we are going to see is quite simple. It just shows a geometric shape on the screen and it allows the user to rotate it using the arrow keys:

1. To run it as a desktop app, go into the `ski` folder, and type the following command:

   ```
   cargo run --release
   ```

   The `--release` argument is recommended to optimize the generated code. For this simple example, it is pointless, but in more complex examples, the code generated without specifying it is so inefficient that the resulting app is noticeably slowed down.

2. After a few minutes of download and compilation, the following desktop window will appear:

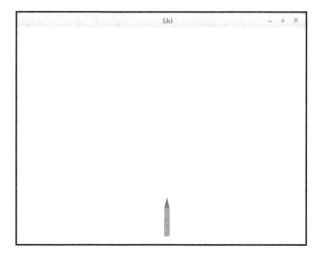

It is just an 800 x 600-pixels white rectangle, with a small purple rectangle and a small indigo triangle on top of it. They represent a monoski with its pointed end, in a snowy ski slope.

3. If you press the left or right arrow keys (←/→) on your keyboard, you will see the ski rotate around its tip.
4. Now, close this window using the appropriate command in your windowing environment. Typically, you click on a cross icon in the caption bar or press the *Alt + F4* key combination.
5. Now, let's see another way to launch this application. Type the following command:

```
cargo web start --release
```

We saw in the previous chapter that this command helps us to create a Wasm app and to launch a command-line program that serves it through the HTTP protocol.

At the end of the compilation, a server program starts and suggests the address where you can access the app. On your preferred browser, you can type this address: `localhost:8000`. Only modern 64-bit browsers support WebGL2. If this is not true in your case, then nothing happens; instead, if your browser supports this standard, you will see in the browser just the same graphics that before were shown in the desktop window.

This is possible as the Quicksilver framework, used by our app, has multi-target capability. When compiled for the Wasm target, it generates a web browser application; and when compiled for a **central processing unit** (**CPU**) target, it generates a desktop application.

This compile-time portability is very useful for debugging purposes. Actually, it is not easy to debug a Wasm application; but if you first debug the desktop application, a few bugs will remain in the Wasm version.

Understanding the code behind this

Now, let's see the code used to create such a project.

Before starting the project, a note about this is required. All the projects in this chapter show a monoski on a ski slope. There is a convention about the coordinates of the ski and other objects: the horizontal coordinate, usually named *X*, is actually named *across*; and the vertical coordinate, usually named *Y*, is actually named *along*.

So, the *across speed* is the speed of a movement from left to right (or vice versa, if negative), and the *along speed* is the speed of a movement from bottom to top (or vice versa, if negative).

First of all, the `Cargo.toml` file must contain the `quicksilver = "0.3"` dependency. Then, there is just a `main.rs` source file. It contains some constants, as shown in the following code snippet:

```
const SCREEN_WIDTH: f32 = 800.;
const SCREEN_HEIGHT: f32 = 600.;
const SKI_WIDTH: f32 = 10.;
const SKI_LENGTH: f32 = 50.;
const SKI_TIP_LEN: f32 = 20.;
const STEERING_SPEED: f32 = 3.5;
const MAX_ANGLE: f32 = 75.;
```

Let's look at what the terms suggest in this code, as follows:

- `SCREEN_WIDTH` and `SCREEN_HEIGHT` are the size in pixels of the client area in the desktop window or the size of the canvas in the web page.
- `SKI_WIDTH`, `SKI_LENGTH`, and `SKI_TIP_LEN` are the sizes of the ski.
- `STEERING_SPEED` is the number of degrees by which the ski is rotated at every step. Steps have a frequency (that is, 25 per second), and so this constant represents an angular speed (3.5 degrees per step * 25 steps per second = 87.5 degrees per second).
- `MAX_ANGLE` is a limit to rotational capability, both to the right and to the left, to ensure the ski is always downhill.

Then, there is the model of our MVC architecture, as shown in the following code snippet:

```
struct Screen {
    ski_across_offset: f32,
    direction: f32,
}
```

The meaning of these fields is as follows:

- `ski_across_offset` represents the across displacement of the tip of the ski with respect to the center of the screen. Actually, in this project, it is always zero, as the tip of the ski never moves. It is a variable just because in future projects, it will change.
- `direction` is the angle in degrees of the ski with respect to the downhill direction. It is initially zero but can vary from -75 to +75. It is the only portion of our model that can change.

The constructor of the model is quite simple, as illustrated in the following code snippet:

```
Ok(Screen {
    ski_across_offset: 0.,
    direction: 0.,
})
```

It simply initializes to zero both fields of the model. The body of the controller (the `update` function) is created with this code:

```
if window.keyboard()[Key::Right].is_down() {
    self.steer(1.);
}
if window.keyboard()[Key::Left].is_down() {
    self.steer(-1.);
}
Ok(())
```

The purpose of this routine is to steer the ski a bit to the right, if the right-arrow key is pressed, and a bit to the left if the left-arrow key is pressed.

The `window.keyboard()` expression gets a reference to the keyboard associated with the current window, and then the `[Key::Right]` expression gets a reference to the right-arrow key of such a keyboard. The `is_down` function returns `true` if the specified key is in a pressed state in this instant.

The steering is performed by the `steer` method, whose body consists of the following code:

```
self.direction += STEERING_SPEED * side;
if self.direction > MAX_ANGLE {
    self.direction = MAX_ANGLE;
}
else if self.direction < -MAX_ANGLE {
    self.direction = -MAX_ANGLE;
}
```

First, the value of the `direction` field of the model is incremented or decremented by the `STEERING_SPEED` constant. Then, it is ensured that the new value does not exceed the designed limits.

The view is more complex. It must redraw all the scene even if it has not changed at all. The first drawing operation is always to draw the white background, as follows:

```
window.clear(Color::WHITE)?;
```

Then, the rectangle is drawn, like this:

```
window.draw_ex(&Rectangle::new((
    SCREEN_WIDTH / 2. + self.ski_across_offset - SKI_WIDTH / 2.,
    SCREEN_HEIGHT * 15. / 16. - SKI_LENGTH / 2.),
    (SKI_WIDTH, SKI_LENGTH)),
    Background::Col(Color::PURPLE),
    Transform::translate(Vector::new(0, - SKI_LENGTH / 2. - SKI_TIP_LEN)) *
        Transform::rotate(self.direction) *
        Transform::translate(Vector::new(0, SKI_LENGTH / 2.
        + SKI_TIP_LEN)),
    0);
```

The `draw_ex` method is used to draw shapes. Its first argument is a reference to the shape to draw; in this case, it is `Rectangle`. Its second argument, in the fifth line, is the background color of the shape; in this case, it is `PURPLE`. Its third argument is a plane affine transformation matrix; in this case, it is a translation, followed by a rotation, followed by a translation. And its fourth argument, in the last line, is a Z elevation; its purpose is to give an overlapping order to shapes. Let's examine these arguments in more detail.

The `Rectangle::new` method receives two arguments. The first argument is a tuple made up of the x and y coordinates on the top-left vertex of the rectangle. The second argument is a tuple made up of the width and height of the rectangle. The origin of the coordinate system is the top left of the window, with the x coordinate that grows toward the right, and the y coordinate that grows downward.

In those formulas, the only variable is `self.ski_across_offset`, which represents the displacement of the ski to the right of the center of the window when positive, and to the left when negative. In this project, it is always zero, and so the ski's x coordinate is always at the center of the window. The vertical position is such that the center of the rectangle is near the bottom of the window, at 15/16 of the height of the window.

Rectangles are always created with their sides parallel to the sides of the window. To have a rotated angle, a geometric transformation must be applied. There are several elementary transformations that can be combined by multiplying them. To draw a shape in a translated position, a transformation is created using the `Transform::translate` method, which receives a `Vector` (not a `Vec`!) specifying the displacements along *x* and *y*. To draw a shape in a rotated position, a transformation is created using the `Transform::rotate` method, which receives an angle in degrees specifying the angle by which to rotate the shape.

The rotation is performed around the centroid of the shape, but we want to rotate around the tip of the ski. So, we need first to translate the rectangle so that its centroid is where the tip of the ski was, then rotate it around its centroid, and then translate it back to the original centroid. By multiplying the three transformations, a rotation around the tip of the ski is obtained. In the case of a rectangle, the centroid is just the center of the rectangle.

The last argument of `draw_ex` is a *z* coordinate. This is a 2D framework, and so no *z* coordinate would be required, but this coordinate allows us to specify the order of the appearance of the shapes. Actually, if two shapes overlap, and they have the same *z* coordinate, WebGL (used by Quicksilver) does not necessarily draw them in the order in which you have drawn them. The actual order is undefined. To specify that a shape must appear above another, it must have a larger *z* coordinate. It doesn't matter how much larger.

To draw the triangular-pointed end on top of the rectangle, a similar statement is executed. The `Triangle::new` method creates a `Triangle` shape, using three `Vector` variables as its vertices. To rotate it around its tip, we need to know the centroid of the triangle. With a bit of geometry, you can calculate that the centroid of that triangle is the point above the center of the base of the triangle by a distance equal to one-third of the height of the triangle.

By the end of the program, there is a `main` function that must initialize the app. The body of the function contains this:

```
run::<Screen>("Ski",
    Vector::new(SCREEN_WIDTH, SCREEN_HEIGHT), Settings {
        draw_rate: 40.,
        update_rate: 40.,
        ..Settings::default()
    }
);
```

This statement just runs the model, with some arguments. The first argument is the caption of the title bar, the second one is the size of the window, and the third one is a structure containing some optional settings.

The following two settings are specified here:

- `draw_rate`: This is the interval in milliseconds between each successive invocation of the `draw` function
- `update_rate`: This is the interval in milliseconds between each successive invocation of the `update` function

This project was quite trivial, but it showed many concepts that will be used in the other projects of this chapter.

Implementing the silent_slalom project

The previous project just showed a ski on a ski slope. In this section, we will show a possibly amusing game using a ski—a slalom. For simplicity, no text is displayed and no sound effects are played in this project. Its source code is contained in the `silent_slalom` folder.

After compiling and running its desktop version, a window similar to this will appear to you:

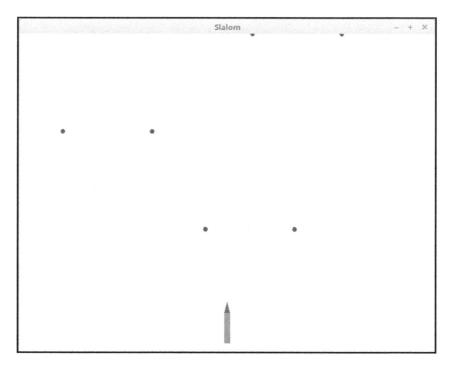

In addition to the ski, some blue dots are drawn. There are four dots in the middle of the window, and two half dots that come out at the top border. Each pair of blue dots is the poles of a slalom gate. The purpose of the game is to make the ski pass through each of the gates. Now, you can see just three gates, but the course contains seven intermediate gates, plus the finish gate. The remaining five gates will appear when the ski proceeds along the slope.

The actual position of the poles will be different in your case because their horizontal (across) position is generated at random. If you stop and relaunch the program, you will see other poles' positions. The size of the gates—that is, the distance between the two poles of any gate—is kept constant, though; and also, the distance, along the y coordinate, between any gate and the gate following it is constant.

To start the game, press the spacebar. The blue dots will begin to move slowly downward, giving the impression of the ski going forward. By rotating the ski, you change its direction, and you should try to ensure that its tip passes between the poles of every gate.

The finish gate is distinguished by having green poles instead of blue. If you pass through it, the game finishes, showing a window similar to this:

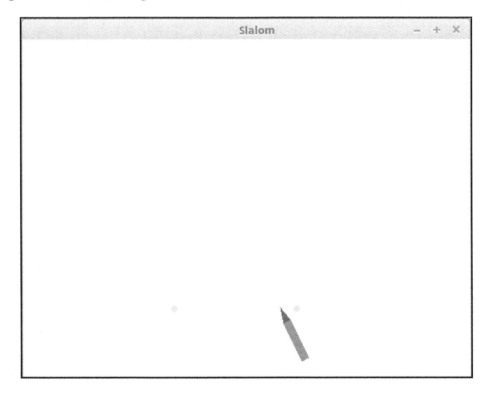

You can restart the game by pressing the *R* key. If you fail to pass a gate correctly, the game stops and ends. You can restart it by pressing the *R* key.

Of course, this project has something in common with the previous project. Let's see the differences within it.

The first difference is the insertion into the `Cargo.toml` file of the `rand = "0.6"` dependency. The gates are positioned at a random *x* position, and so the random number generator contained in this crate is required.

Then, the following constants are defined:

```
const N_GATES_IN_SCREEN: usize = 3;
const GATE_POLE_RADIUS: f32 = 4.;
const GATE_WIDTH: f32 = 150.;
const SKI_MARGIN: f32 = 12.;
const ALONG_ACCELERATION: f32 = 0.06;
const DRAG_FACTOR: f32 = 0.02;
const TOTAL_N_GATES: usize = 8;
```

Let's have a look at these constants in detail, as follows:

- `N_GATES_IN_SCREEN` is the number of gates that will appear in the window at once. The along separation between successive gates is the window height divided by this number. Therefore, this number must be positive.

- `GATE_POLE_RADIUS` is the radius in pixels of each circle drawn to represent a pole.

- `GATE_WIDTH` is the distance in pixels between the centers of the poles in each gate. This number must be positive.

- `SKI_MARGIN` is the distance in pixels between the leftmost position that can be reached by the tip of the ski to the left border of the window, and between the rightmost position that can be reached by the tip of the ski to the right border of the window.

- `ALONG_ACCELERATION` is the acceleration, in pixels per frame for each frame, for the movement of the ski, due to the slope, when the ski is in downhill position—that is, vertical. For example, for an acceleration value of 0.06 and an update rate of 40 milliseconds, or 25 frames per second, in a second the speed would go from zero to $0.06 * 25 = 1.5$ pixels per frame—that is, a speed of $1.5 * 25 = 37.5$ pixels per second. The actual acceleration will be lower if the ski has an inclination with respect to the slope.

- DRAG_FACTOR represents the deceleration caused by air friction. The actual deceleration is this factor multiplied by the module of the speed.

- TOTAL_N_GATES is the number of gates, including the finish gate.

While in the previous project you could do just one thing all the time—that is, rotate the ski—in this project, you can do different things according to the current situation. So, there is a need to distinguish among four possible states, as follows:

```
enum Mode {
    Ready,
    Running,
    Finished,
    Failed,
}
```

The initial mode is Ready, when you are eager to start the run, at the top of the slope. After the start command, you are in Running mode, until you complete the run correctly, ending in Finished mode, or get out of a gate, ending in Failed mode.

Some fields have been added to the model of the application, to track some other state information, as illustrated in the following code block:

```
gates: Vec<(f32, f32)>,
forward_speed: f32,
gates_along_offset: f32,
mode: Mode,
entered_gate: bool,
disappeared_gates: usize,
```

The meaning of these fields is described as follows:

- gates is a list of the along positions of the poles. For them, the origin is the center of the window.
- forward_speed is the module of the velocity in pixels per frame.
- gates_along_offset is the *Y* translation of all the shown gates toward the bottom, which represents the advancement of the ski. It is a number between zero and the along spacing between successive gates.
- mode is the state described previously.

- `entered_gate` indicates whether the tip of the ski has already entered the lowest gate shown in the window. This flag is initialized as `false`; it becomes `true` when the ski passes a gate correctly and becomes `false` again when that gate exits the window from the bottom because now it refers to the next gate.
- `disappeared_gates` counts the gates exited from the window. Of course, it is initialized at zero and is incremented every time a gate exits the window.

A function added to the `Screen` type generates a random gate, as illustrated in the following code block:

```
fn get_random_gate(gate_is_at_right: bool) -> (f32, f32) {
    let mut rng = thread_rng();
    let pole_pos = rng.gen_range(-GATE_WIDTH / 2., SCREEN_WIDTH / 2. -
        GATE_WIDTH * 1.5);
    if gate_is_at_right {
        (pole_pos, pole_pos + GATE_WIDTH)
    } else {
        (-pole_pos - GATE_WIDTH, -pole_pos)
    }
}
```

This function receives the `gate_is_at_right` flag, which indicates in which part of the slope the generated gate will be. If such an argument is `true`, the new gate will be at the right of the center of the window; otherwise, it will be at the left of the center of the window. This function creates a random number generator and uses it to generate a reasonable position for a pole. The other pole position is computed using the argument of the function and the fixed gate size (`GATE_WIDTH`).

Another utility function is `deg_to_rad`, which converts angles from degrees to radians. It is needed because Quicksilver uses degrees, but trigonometric functions use radians. The `new` method creates all the gates, alternating them at right and at left, and initializes the model. The `update` function does a lot more than the function with that name seen in the previous project. Let's look at the following code snippet:

```
match self.mode {
    Mode::Ready => {
        if window.keyboard()[Key::Space].is_down() {
            self.mode = Mode::Running;
        }
    }
```

According to the current mode, different operations are performed. If the mode is `Ready`, it checks whether the spacebar key is pressed, and, in such a case, it sets the current mode to `Running`. This means that it starts the race. If the mode is `Running`, the following code is executed:

```
Mode::Running => {
    let angle = deg_to_rad(self.direction);
    self.forward_speed +=
        ALONG_ACCELERATION * angle.cos() - DRAG_FACTOR
          * self.forward_speed;
    let along_speed = self.forward_speed * angle.cos();
    self.ski_across_offset += self.forward_speed * angle.sin();
```

In this mode, a lot of things are computed. First, the ski direction is converted from degrees to radians.

Then, the forward speed is incremented because of the slope, and it is decremented because of the friction of the air, which is proportional to the speed itself. The net effect is that the speed will tend to a maximum value. In addition, the more the ski direction is rotated with respect to the slope, the slower it is. This effect is implemented using the `cos` cosine trigonometric function.

Then, the forward speed is split into its components: the along speed, which causes the downward movement of the poles, and the across speed, which increments the across ski offset. They are computed by applying, respectively, the `cos` and `sin` trigonometric functions to the forward speed, as shown in the following code snippet:

```
if self.ski_across_offset < -SCREEN_WIDTH / 2. + SKI_MARGIN {
    self.ski_across_offset = -SCREEN_WIDTH / 2. + SKI_MARGIN;
}
if self.ski_across_offset > SCREEN_WIDTH / 2. - SKI_MARGIN {
    self.ski_across_offset = SCREEN_WIDTH / 2. - SKI_MARGIN;
}
```

Then, it checks that the ski position is not too far to the left or to the right, and, if it is so, it is kept within the defined margins, as illustrated in the following code snippet:

```
self.gates_along_offset += along_speed;
let max_gates_along_offset = SCREEN_HEIGHT / N_GATES_IN_SCREEN as f32;
if self.gates_along_offset > max_gates_along_offset {
    self.gates_along_offset -= max_gates_along_offset;
    self.disappeared_gates += 1;
}
```

The new along speed is used to move down the gates, by incrementing
the `gates_along_offset` field. If its new value is larger than the distance between
successive gates, one gate is dropped out of the bottom of the window, and all the gates are
moved backward by one step and the number of disappeared gates is incremented, as
illustrated in the following code snippet:

```
let ski_tip_along = SCREEN_HEIGHT * 15. / 16. - SKI_LENGTH / 2. -
SKI_TIP_LEN;
let ski_tip_across = SCREEN_WIDTH / 2. + self.ski_across_offset;
let n_next_gate = self.disappeared_gates;
let next_gate = &self.gates[n_next_gate];
let left_pole_offset = SCREEN_WIDTH / 2. + next_gate.0 + GATE_POLE_RADIUS;
let right_pole_offset = SCREEN_WIDTH / 2. + next_gate.1 - GATE_POLE_RADIUS;
let next_gate_along = self.gates_along_offset + SCREEN_HEIGHT
    - SCREEN_HEIGHT / N_GATES_IN_SCREEN as f32;
```

Then, the two coordinates of the tip of the ski are computed: `ski_tip_along` is the
constant y coordinate, from the top of the window, and `ski_tip_across` is the variable x
coordinate, from the center of the window.

Then, the positions inside the next gate are computed: `left_pole_offset` is the x position
of the right side of the left pole, and `right_pole_offset` is the x position of the left side of
the right pole. These coordinates are computed from the left border of the window. And
then, `next_gate_along` is the y position of such points, as illustrated in the following code
snippet:

```
if ski_tip_along <= next_gate_along {
    if !self.entered_gate {
        if ski_tip_across < left_pole_offset ||
          ski_tip_across > right_pole_offset {
            self.mode = Mode::Failed;
        } else if self.disappeared_gates == TOTAL_N_GATES - 1 {
            self.mode = Mode::Finished;
        }
        self.entered_gate = true;
    }
} else {
    self.entered_gate = false;
}
```

If the *y* coordinate of the tip of the ski (`ski_tip_along`) is less than that of the gate (`next_gate_along`), then we can say that the tip of the ski has passed to the next gate. Though, if the `entered_gate` field, which records such passing, is still `false`, we can say that in the previous frame the ski hadn't yet passed the gate. Therefore, in such a case, we are in the situation in which the ski has just passed a gate. So, we must check whether the gate has been passed correctly or wrongly.

If the *x* coordinate of the tip is *not* between the two coordinates of the poles, we are outside the gate, and so we go into the `Failed` mode. Otherwise, we must check whether this gate is the last gate of the course—that is, the finish gate. If it is the case, we go into the `Finish` mode; otherwise, we make a note that we have entered the gate, to avoid checking it again at the next frame, and the race goes on.

If the *y* coordinate is such that we haven't reached the next gate yet, we take note that `entered_gate` is still false. With this, we have completed the computations for the `Running` case.

Two modes remain to be considered, as illustrated in the following code snippet:

```
Mode::Failed | Mode::Finished => {
    if window.keyboard()[Key::R].is_down() {
        *self = Screen::new().unwrap();
    }
}
```

Both in the `Failed` mode and in the `Finished` mode, the *R* key is checked. If it is pressed, the model is reinitialized, going to the same state as when the game was just launched.

Lastly, the steering key is checked for any mode, just as in the previous project. Regarding the `draw` function, what has been added in this project, with respect to the previous project, is the drawing of the poles. The code can be seen in the following snippet:

```
for i_gate in self.disappeared_gates..self.disappeared_gates +
N_GATES_IN_SCREEN {
    if i_gate >= TOTAL_N_GATES {
        break;
    }
}
```

A loop scans the gates that appear in the window. The indices of the gates go from zero to `TOTAL_N_GATES`, but we must ski the ones that have already exited from the bottom, whose number is `self.disappeared_gates`. We must show at least the `N_GATES_IN_SCREEN` gates and must stop at the last gate.

To show the player which is the finish gate, it has a different color, as can be seen in the following code snippet:

```
let pole_color = Background::Col(if i_gate == TOTAL_N_GATES - 1 {
    Color::GREEN
} else {
    Color::BLUE
});
```

The last gate is green. To compute the *y* coordinate of the poles of a gate, the following formula is used:

```
let gates_along_pos = self.gates_along_offset
    + SCREEN_HEIGHT / N_GATES_IN_SCREEN as f32
        * (self.disappeared_gates + N_GATES_IN_SCREEN - 1 - i_gate) as f32;
```

It adds the position of the ski between two successive gates (`gates_along_offset`) to the initial position of the first three gates.

And then, two small circles are drawn for each gate. The left circle is drawn by executing the following statement:

```
window.draw(
    &Circle::new(
        (SCREEN_WIDTH / 2. + gate.0, gates_along_pos),
        GATE_POLE_RADIUS,
    ),
    pole_color,
);
```

The argument of the `Circle` constructor is a tuple composed of the *x* and *y* coordinates of the center and the radius. Here, the `draw` method of the window object is used, instead of the `draw_ex` method. It is simpler, as it does not require a transformation nor a *z* coordinate.

And so, we have examined all the code of this project. In the next project, we'll show how we can add text and sound to our game.

Implementing the assets_slalom project

The previous project built was a valid slalom race, but that game had no sound or text to explain what was happening. This project, contained in the `assets_slalom` folder, just adds sound and text to the game of the previous project.

Here is a screenshot that was taken during a race:

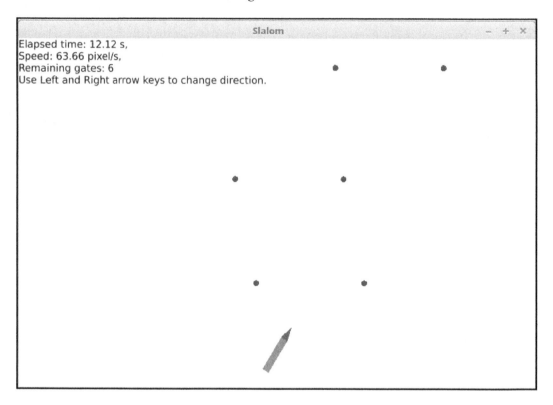

In the top left of the window, there is the following information:

- **Elapsed time**: This tells us how many seconds or hundreds of seconds have elapsed since the start of the current race.
- **Speed**: This tells us how much is the current forward speed in pixels per second.
- **Remaining gates**: This tells us how many gates remain to pass.

Then, a help message explains which commands are available.

In addition, four sounds have been added, as follows:

- A tick at any start of a race
- A whoosh at any turn
- A bump at any fail
- A chime at any finish

You have to run the game to hear them. Notice that not all web browsers are equally capable of reproducing sounds.

Now, let's see how Quicksilver can show text and play sounds. Sounds and text are not so simple to use because of the fact that they need files; for text, one or more font files are needed; and for sounds, a sound file for any sound effect is needed. Such files must be stored in a folder named `static` in the root of the project. If you look in the said folder, you'll find the following files:

- `font.ttf`: This is a font in TrueType format.
- `click.ogg`: This is a short click sound, to be played at the start of a race.
- `whoosh.ogg`: This is a short friction sound, to be played when the ski is turning during a race.
- `bump.ogg`: This is a bump sound to express disapproval, to be played when the ski misses a gate.
- `two_notes.ogg`: This is a pair of notes to express satisfaction, to be played when the ski passes the finish gate.

Such a `static` folder and its contained files must be deployed together with the executable program, as they are loaded at runtime by the program. They are usually also named *assets* as they are just data, not executable code.

Quicksilver has chosen to load such assets in an asynchronous way, using the *future concept*. To load a sound from a file, the `Sound::load(«filename»)` expression is used. It receives a value implementing a reference to a path, such as a string, and it returns an object implementing the `Future` trait.

An asset—that is, an object that encapsulates a future that is loading a file—is created by the `Asset::new(«future value»)` expression. It receives a value implementing a future, and it returns an `Asset` instance of the specific type. For instance, the `Asset::new(Sound::load("bump.ogg"))` expression returns a value of the `Asset<Sound>` type. Such a value is an asset that encapsulates a future—that is, reading a sound from the `bump.ogg` file. The sounds in this project are in the `.ogg` format, but Quicksilver is capable of reading several audio formats.

Once you have an asset encapsulating a future loading a file, you can access such a file in an expression such as `sound_future.execute(|sound_resource| sound_resource.play())`. Here, the `sound_future` variable is our asset. As it is a future, you have to wait for it to be ready. This is done using the `execute` method of the `Asset` type. It invokes the closure received as an argument, passing to it the encapsulated resource, which in this case is of the `Sound` type.

The `Sound` type has the `play` method, which starts to reproduce the sound. As usual in multimedia systems, such reproduction is asynchronous: you don't have to wait for the end of the sound to proceed with the game. If you call `play` on a sound when the previous sound is still reproducing, the two sounds overlap, and if you play many of them, the resulting volume typically becomes very high. Therefore, you should keep your sounds very short, or play them seldom.

Similarly, the `Asset::new(Font::load("font.ttf"))` expression returns a value of the `Asset<Font>`. type. Such a value is an asset that encapsulates a future—that is, reading a font from the `font.ttf` file. You can use that font with the `font_future.execute(|font_resource| image = font_resource.render(&"Hello", &style))` expression. Here, the `font_future` variable is our asset. As it is a future, you have to wait for it using the `execute` method of the `Asset` type, which invokes the closure received as an argument, passing to it the encapsulated resource, which in this case is of the `Font` type.

The `Font` type has the `render` method, which receives a string and a reference to a `FontStyle` value and creates an image containing that text, printed using that font and that font style.

Analyzing the code

And now, let's see all the code of the project that differs from the previous project. There is a new constant, as can be seen in the following code snippet:

```
const MIN_TIME_DURATION: f64 = 0.1;
```

This is to solve the following problem. If the game has a frame rate of 50 FPS, the window is redrawn 50 times per second, and each time using the latest values of the variables. Regarding time, it is a number that would change so rapidly that it would be impossible to read. Therefore, this constant sets the maximum rate of change of the displayed time.

The model has several new fields, as can be seen in the following code snippet:

```
elapsed_sec: f64,
elapsed_shown_sec: f64,
font_style: FontStyle,
font: Asset<Font>,
whoosh_sound: Asset<Sound>,
bump_sound: Asset<Sound>,
click_sound: Asset<Sound>,
two_notes_sound: Asset<Sound>,
```

The meaning of these fields is described as follows:

- `elapsed_sec` is the fractional number of seconds elapsed since the start of the current race, using the maximum resolution available.
- `elapsed_shown_sec` is the fractional number to show to the user as the number of elapsed seconds since the start of the current race.
- `font_style` contains the size and color of the text to print.
- `font` is the future value of the font to use to print the text of the screen.
- `whoosh_sound` is the future value of the sound to play during the turns of the running ski.
- `bump_sound` is the future value of the sound to play when a gate is missed.
- `click_sound` is the future value of the sound to play when a race is started.
- `two_notes_sound` is the future value of the sound to play when the finish gate is crossed.

A routine to play sounds has been defined, as follows:

```
fn play_sound(sound: &mut Asset<Sound>, volume: f32) {
    let _ = sound.execute(|sound| {
        sound.set_volume(volume);
        let _ = sound.play();
        Ok(())
    });
}
```

It receives a future value of a sound and a volume. It calls `execute` to ensure the sound is loaded, and then sets the specified volume and plays that sound. Notice that the `execute` method returns a `Result`, to allow for possible errors. As in games sounds are not essential, we want to ignore possible errors regarding sounds, and so, we always return `Ok(())`.

In the `steer` function, when a turn operation is performed and the ski is not already at an extreme angle, the following statement is performed:

```
play_sound(&mut self.whoosh_sound, self.forward_speed * 0.1);
```

It plays the whoosh sound and a volume that is proportional to the speed of the ski. In this way, if you rotate the ski when you are not running, you are silent.

The new fields of the model are initialized like this:

```
elapsed_sec: 0.,
elapsed_shown_sec: 0.,
font_style: FontStyle::new(16.0, Color::BLACK),
font: Asset::new(Font::load("font.ttf")),
whoosh_sound: Asset::new(Sound::load("whoosh.ogg")),
bump_sound: Asset::new(Sound::load("bump.ogg")),
click_sound: Asset::new(Sound::load("click.ogg")),
two_notes_sound: Asset::new(Sound::load("two_notes.ogg")),
```

Notice that, as `font_style`, a size of 16 points and a black color are set. We already described the other kind of expressions.

In the `update` function, when the race is started by pressing the spacebar, the following statement is executed:

```
play_sound(&mut self.click_sound, 1.)
```

It plays a click sound with a normal volume. When running, the elapsed time is computed like this:

```
self.elapsed_sec += window.update_rate() / 1000.;
if self.elapsed_sec - self.elapsed_shown_sec >= MIN_TIME_DURATION {
    self.elapsed_shown_sec = self.elapsed_sec;
}
```

The `update_rate` function actually returns the time between frames, in milliseconds. So, if you divide it by 1,000, you get the seconds between each frame.

If there is a high frame rate, such as 25 frames per second or more, showing the user different text at any frame can be confusing, as people cannot read a text that changes so rapidly. So, the second statement in the previous code snippet shows a technique to update the text at a lower rate. The `elapsed_shown_sec` field keeps the time of the last update, and the `elapsed_sec` field keeps the current time.

The `MIN_TIME_DURATION` constant keeps the minimum duration by which a text must remain unchanged on screen before it can be updated. So, if the time elapsed from the time of the previous update to the current time is larger than such minimum duration, the text can be updated. In this particular case, the text to update is just the elapsed time in seconds, and so, if enough time has passed, the `elapsed_shown_sec` field is set to the current time. The `draw` routine will use that value to print the elapsed time on the screen.

Two other sounds are emitted. When the `mode` becomes `Failed`, the `play_sound` is called to play a bump sound. And when the `mode` becomes `Finished`, the `play_sound` is called to play a chime.

Then, it's up to the draw routine to print all the text. First, the text is formatted in a new multi-line string, as follows:

```
let elapsed_shown_text = format!(
    "Elapsed time: {:.2} s,\n\
     Speed: {:.2} pixel/s,\n\
     Remaining gates: {}\n\
     Use Left and Right arrow keys to change direction.\n\
     {}",
    self.elapsed_shown_sec,
    self.forward_speed * 1000f32 / window.update_rate() as f32,
    TOTAL_N_GATES - self.disappeared_gates - if self.entered_gate { 1 }
else { 0 },
    match self.mode {
        Mode::Ready => "Press Space to start.",
        Mode::Running => "",
        Mode::Finished => "Finished: Press R to reset.",
        Mode::Failed => "Failed: Press R to reset.",
    }
);
```

The elapsed time and the speed are printed using two decimals; the remaining gates are computed by subtracting the disappeared gates to the total number of gates. In addition, if the current gate has been entered, the count of remaining gates is decremented by one. Then, some different words are printed according to the current mode.

After having prepared the multiline string, the string is printed on a new image and stored in the `image` local variable, and the image is drawn on the window using the `draw` method, as a textured background. The method receives as a first argument the rectangular area to print, large as the whole bitmap, and, as a second argument, the `Img` variant of the `Background` type, constructed using the image, as illustrated in the following code snippet:

```
let style = self.font_style;
self.font.execute(|font| {
    let image = font.render(&elapsed_shown_text, &style).unwrap();
    window.draw(&image.area(), Img(&image));
    Ok(())
})?;
```

So, we have completed our examination of this simple but interesting framework.

Summary

We have seen how a complete game, running both on desktop and on the web, can be built using Rust and the Quicksilver framework, with the web version using the `cargo-web` command and the Wasm code generator. This game was structured according to the animation loop architecture and the MVC architectural pattern. We created three apps—`ski`, `silent_slalom`, and `assets_slalom`—and understood the implementation behind them.

In the next chapter, we will be seeing another 2D game framework, the `ggez` framework, oriented toward desktop applications.

Questions

1. What is the animation loop, and what are its advantages with respect to an event-driven architecture?
2. When is an event-driven architecture better than an animation loop architecture?
3. Which kinds of software can use the animation loop?
4. How can you draw triangles, rectangles, and circles using Quicksilver?
5. How can you receive input from the keyboard using Quicksilver?
6. How are the controller and the view of MVC implemented using Quicksilver?
7. How can you vary the frame rate of animation using Quicksilver?
8. How can you load assets from files using Quicksilver, and where should you keep such assets?
9. How can you play sounds using Quicksilver?
10. How can you draw text on the screen using Quicksilver?

Further reading

The Quicksilver project can be downloaded from here: `https://github.com/ryanisaacg/quicksilver`. This repository contains a link to a very short tutorial and some examples.

You can find more information about generating Wasm code from a Rust project at `https://github.com/koute/cargo-web`.

7
Creating a Desktop Two-Dimensional Game Using ggez

In the preceding chapter, we saw how to build interactive software based on the animation-loop architecture (typically, animated games) for desktops or for web browsers from a single set of source codes using the `quicksilver` framework. A drawback of this approach is that many input/output functions available on the desktop are not available on web browsers, and so a framework for web browsers does not necessarily provide as many features to desktop applications that are offered on desktop platforms, such as file storage.

In addition, when using the animation-loop architecture, it is quite awkward to get discrete input, such as mouse clicks, typed letters, or digits. For this, an event-driven architecture is more appropriate.

In this chapter, another application framework will be introduced—the `ggez` framework. This handles both animation-loop and discrete events, but at the time of writing, it only supports two-dimensional desktop applications.

In the previous chapter, we saw that to compute the position and orientation of various graphical objects, some analytical geometry and trigonometry is required. For more complex applications, these mathematical computations can become overwhelming. To simplify the code, it is useful to encapsulate positions in point objects and translations in vector objects, and so in this chapter, we will look at how to perform these encapsulations. The `nalgebra` mathematical library helps us to do this and will be introduced in this chapter, too.

The following topics will be covered in this chapter:

- Understanding linear algebra
- Implementing the `gg_ski` project
- Implementing the `gg_silent_slalom` project
- Implementing the `gg_assets_slalom` project
- Implementing the `gg_whac` project

In particular, you will see the implementation of the same three projects we looked at in the previous chapter (`gg_ski`, `gg_silent_slalom`, and `gg_assets_slalom`) to demonstrate the animation loop, as well as a Whac-A-Mole game (`gg_whac`) to demonstrate the handling of discrete events.

Technical requirements

This chapter uses references to the animation-loop architecture and the slalom game implemented in the preceding chapter. The `ggez` framework requires (for correctly rendering graphical objects) the OpenGL 3.2 API to be well supported by the operating system. Therefore, old operating systems such as Windows XP cannot be used.

The complete source code for this chapter is found in the `Chapter07` folder of the repository at `https://github.com/PacktPublishing/Creative-Projects-for-Rust-Programmers`.

 macOS users may struggle to install `coreaudio-sys`. Upgrading the patch version of `coreaudio-sys` to `0.2.3` resolves this issue.

Project overview

In this chapter, we will first look at what linear algebra is and why it is useful to describe and manipulate the objects drawn in any graphical game. Then, we will look at how to use the `nalgebra` library to perform linear algebra operations in our programs.

After that, we will recreate the same projects used in the previous chapter, but using the `nalgebra` library and the `ggez` framework instead of the `quicksilver` framework. `gg_ski` is a rewrite of `ski`, `gg_silent_slalom` is a rewrite of `silent_slalom`, and `gg_assets_slalom` is a rewrite of `assets_slalom`.

At the end of the chapter, we will look at the implementation of a completely different game with the `gg_whac` project to see how to handle discrete events in an architecture that mixes the animation loop with an event-driven architecture. This will also show how widgets (such as buttons) can be created and added to a window.

Understanding linear algebra

Linear algebra is the sector of mathematics regarding systems of first-degree equations, such as the following:

$$\begin{cases} 3x + 2y = 8 \\ -x + 5y = -6 \end{cases}$$

This system of equations has a solution to certain values (that is, $x = \frac{52}{17}, y = -\frac{10}{17}$). In addition to being useful for solving systems of equations, the concepts and methods of linear algebra are also useful for representing and manipulating geometrical entities.

In particular, any position on a plane can be represented by two coordinates, x and y, and any position in space can be represented by three coordinates, x, y, and z. In addition, any translation of a position on a plane can be represented by two coordinates, Δx and Δy, and any translation of a position in space can be represented by three coordinates, Δx, Δy, and Δz.

For example, consider two positions on a plane:

- p_1: Its coordinates are $x = 4$, $y = 7$.
- p_2: Its coordinates are $x = 10$, $y = 16$.

Consider two translations on that plane:

- t_1: Its coordinates are $\Delta x = 6, \Delta y = 9$.
- t_2: Its coordinates are $\Delta x = -3, \Delta y = 8$.

You can say that if you translate the p_1 position by the t_1 translation, you get to the p_2 position. The computation is done by adding the corresponding coordinates: $p_{1x} + t_{1x} = p_{2x}$ (or, in numbers, $4 + 6 = 10$) and $p_{1y} + t_{1y} = p_{2y}$ (or, in numbers, $7 + 9 = 16$).

If you apply two translations sequentially to the p_1 position—the t_1 translation and the t_2 translation—then you will obtain another position (say, p_3). You will also obtain the same result if you first sum the two translations (by summing their components memberwise) and then applying the resulting translation to p_1.

So, for the x coordinate, we have $(p_{1x} + t_{1x}) + t_{2x} = p_{1x} + (t_{1x} + t_{2x})$ and a similar equation also holds for the y coordinate. So, translations can be added. You can add a translation to another one by summing their respective coordinates, instead, it does not make sense to add one position to another position.

You can simplify your geometric computations by applying the computations to the position and translation entities themselves using the following formula:

$$(p_1 + t_1) + t_2 = p_1 + (t_1 + t_2)$$

In linear algebra, there are two concepts that can be applied to these sorts of operations:

- **Vectors**: An algebraic *vector* is a tuple of numbers that can be added to another vector, obtaining another vector, which is what is needed to *represent translations*.
- **Points**: An algebraic *point* is a tuple of numbers that cannot be added to another point, but that can be incremented by a vector, thereby obtaining another point, which is what is needed to *represent a position*.

Therefore, linear algebraic *N-dimensional vectors* are fit to represent *translations* in an N-dimensional geometric space, whereas linear algebraic *N-dimensional points* are fit to represent *positions* in an N-dimensional geometric space.

The `nalgebra` library (pronounced *en-algebra*) is a collection of to many algebraic algorithms that provide implementations for these kinds of two-dimensional point and vector types, and so it will be used in all of the following projects.

Using this library, you can write the following program, which shows which operations are allowed and which are forbidden, using vectors and points:

```
use nalgebra::{Point2, Vector2};
fn main() {
    let p1: Point2<f32> = Point2::new(4., 7.);
    let p2: Point2<f32> = Point2::new(10., 16.);
    let v: Vector2<f32> = Vector2::new(6., 9.);
```

```
        assert!(p1.x == 4.);
        assert!(p1.y == 7.);
        assert!(v.x == 6.);
        assert!(v.y == 9.);
        assert!(p1 + v == p2);
        assert!(p2 - p1 == v);
        assert!(v + v - v == v);
        assert!(v == (2. * v) / 2.);
        //let _ = p1 + p2;
        let _ = 2. * p1;
}
```

The first three statements of the `main` function create two two-dimensional points and one two-dimensional vector whose coordinates are `f32` numbers. This sort of inner numeric type can often be *inferred*, but here it is specified for clarity.

The next four statements show that both the `Point2` and `Vector2` types contain the x and y fields, initialized by the arguments of the `new` function. So, the `Point2` and `Vector2` types look quite similar, and actually many libraries and many developers use just one type to store both positions and translations.

However, these types differ for the allowed operations. The following four statements show which operations can be carried out:

- Sum a vector to a point (`p1 + v`), obtaining another point.
- Subtract two points (`p2 - p1`), obtaining a vector.
- Sum two vectors or subtract two vectors (`v + v - v`), obtaining a vector in both cases.
- Multiply a vector by a number or divide a vector by a number (`(2. * v) / 2.`), obtaining a vector in both cases.

There are some operations allowed on vectors that shouldn't be allowed on points (because they make no sense for them), which the last two statements show. You cannot add two points (`p1 + p2`) and actually, this operation is commented out to prevent a compilation error. You shouldn't multiply a point by a number (`2. * p1`), although, for some reason, the `nalgebra` library allows this.

If you want to learn more about the `nalgebra` library, you can find its documentation at `https://www.nalgebra.org/`.

Now that we have looked at a good way to handle geometric coordinates using the `nalgebra` library, let's see how to use them in game applications.

Implementing the gg_ski project

The first three projects in this chapter are just a rewrite of the three projects covered in the preceding chapter but are converted so that they use the `ggez` framework and the `nalgebra` library instead. They are as follows:

- The `ski` project has become `gg_ski`.
- The `silent_slalom` project has become `gg_silent_slalom`.
- The `assets_slalom` project has become `gg_assets_slalom`.

Each project's behavior is very similar to its respective project in Chapter 6, *Creating a WebAssembly Game Using Quicksilver*, and so you can go back to that chapter to see the screenshots accompanying each one. For all three projects, `gg_ski`, `gg_silent_slalom`, and `gg_assets_slalom`, the `Cargo.toml` file has the following change. Instead of the `quicksilver` dependency, there are the following dependencies:

```
ggez = "0.5"
nalgebra = "0.18"
```

The term `ggez` (pronounced *G. G. easy*) is a slang term used by multiplayer online gamers.

The `ggez` framework was admittedly inspired by the **LÖVE game framework**. The main difference between them lies in the programming languages. LÖVE is implemented in C++ and is programmable in Lua, while `ggez` is both implemented and programmable in Rust.

Now, let's compare the `main.rs` source code of the `ski` project to that of the `gg_ski` project.

The main function

At the end of the file, there is the `main` function, which prepares the context for the game and then runs the game:

```
fn main() -> GameResult {
    let (context, animation_loop) = &mut ContextBuilder::new
      ("slalom", "ggez")
        .window_setup(conf::WindowSetup::default().title("Slalom"))
        .window_mode(conf::WindowMode::default().dimensions(SCREEN_WIDTH,
```

```
        SCREEN_HEIGHT))
      .add_resource_path("static")
      .build()?;
    let game = &mut Screen::new(context)?;
    event::run(context, animation_loop, game)
}
```

model

In this function, you can see that, when you use the `ggez` framework, you don't just run the model. First, you should create three objects:

- A context, which, in our case, is a window. It is assigned to the `context` variable.
- An animation loop, which animates that context. It is assigned to the `animation_loop` variable.
- The model, in our case, is of `Screen` type. It is assigned to the `game` variable.

After creating these objects, you can call the `run` function with these three objects as arguments.

To create the context and the animation loop, a `ContextBuilder` object is first created by calling the `ContextBuilder::new` function; then, this builder is modified by calling its methods—`window_setup`, `window_mode`, and `add_resource_path`. Finally, the call to the `build` method returns both a context and an animation loop.

However, notice the following things:

- The call to `new` specifies a name for the app (`"slalom"`) and a name for its creator (`"ggez"`).
- The call to `window_setup` specifies the text in the title bar of the window (`"Slalom"`).
- The call to `window_mode` specifies the desired size of the window.
- The call to `add_resource_path` specifies the name of the folder that will contain the assets loaded at runtime (`"static"`), even if we are not going to use assets in this project.

Regarding the `Screen` model, notice that it is created using the `new` method, and so we will have to provide this method; however, we could use any other name for this sort of creation method.

Patterns of input handling

Both `quicksilver` and `ggez` adopt an animation loop-based **Model-View-Controller** (**MVC**) pattern. This is done by requiring the model to implement a trait that has two required methods:

- `update` is the controller.
- `draw` is the view.

Both frameworks run an implicit loop that periodically (many times per second) calls the following:

- The controller to update the model, using possible input data and the preceding values of the model
- The view to update the screen, using the updated values of the model

However, there is a substantial difference in the technique used by these frameworks to get input. `quicksilver` is a complete animation loop-oriented framework. The controller (or the `update` function) gets input accessing the state of input devices—it can check where the mouse is and which mouse buttons and keyboard keys are being pressed.

Instead, `ggez` input handling is event-driven because it captures input device *transitions*, not input device *states*. There are several kinds of possible input device transitions:

- A movement of the mouse (*mouse moves*)
- A press of a mouse button (*mouse button down*)
- A release of a pressed mouse button (*mouse button up*)
- A press of keyboard key (*key down*)
- A release of a pressed keyboard key (*key up*)

In `ggez`, for each of these possible input device transitions, the trait declares an optional handler routine that can be implemented for the model by the application code. These routines are called `mouse_motion_event`, `mouse_button_down_event`, `mouse_button_up_event`, `key_down_event`, and `key_up_event`.

If an event happens in an animation-loop time frame, the corresponding handlers are invoked just before the `update` function is invoked. In these event handlers, the application code should store (in the model) the information gathered from the event, such as which key has been pressed or in which position the mouse has been moved. Then, the `update` function can process this input data to prepare the information needed by the view.

To better understand these techniques, consider, as an example, the following sequence of events or timeline:

- The `update` function is invoked 10 times per second—that is, once every tenth of a second—so, frames per second = 10.
- The user presses the *A* key at `0.020` seconds and releases it 50 milliseconds later at `0.070` seconds, and then they press the *B* key at `0.140` seconds and release it 240 milliseconds later at `0.380` seconds.

For `quicksilver`, we have the following timeline:

At time	Input device state	Input processing in the update function
0.0	No key is pressed.	Nothing.
0.1	No key is pressed.	Nothing.
0.2	The *B* key is pressed.	The *B* key is processed.
0.3	The *B* key is pressed.	The *B* key is processed.
0.4	No key is pressed.	Nothing.
0.5	No key is pressed.	Nothing.

For `ggez`, we have the following timeline:

At time	Input events	Input processing in the update function
0.0	No input events.	No key info is stored in the model.
0.1	The `key_down_event` function is invoked with the *A* key as an argument. It stores the *A* key in the model. The `key_up_event` function is invoked with the *A* key as an argument. It does nothing.	The *A* key is read from the model. It is processed and reset.
0.2	The `key_down_event` function is invoked with the *B* key as an argument. It stores the *B* key in the model.	The *B* key is read from the model. It is processed and reset.
0.3	No input events.	No key info is stored in the model.
0.4	The `key_up_event` function is invoked with the *B* key as an argument. It does nothing.	No key info is stored in the model.
0.5	No input events.	No key info is stored in the model.

Notice that for `quicksilver`, the *A* key has never been pressed, while the *B* key has been pressed twice. This can be good for continuous events, such as using a joystick, but not for discrete events, such as clicking a command button or typing text into a textbox.

However, `quicksilver` has the advantage of capturing all simultaneous events. For example, `quicksilver` can easily handle a chord, which is when several keys are continually pressed at the same time.

Instead, for `ggez`, as long as only one key is pressed in a time frame, all key presses are handled the appropriate number of times. This is expected for buttons and textboxes; however, chords are not handled correctly. The only key combinations handled by `ggez` are those involving the *Shift*, *Ctrl*, and *Alt* special keys.

Input handling in the gg_ski project

Among the many events that can be captured by a `ggez` application, the `gg_ski` game captures only two events—the press of the right or left arrow keys and their release. The handling of these events stores the relevant input information in the model so that the `update` function can use it. Therefore, the model must contain some additional fields, with respect to those contained for the `quicksilver ski` project.

So, we now have a model that contains some fields updated by the event functions, to be used by the `update` function, and some other fields updated by the `update` function, to be used by the `draw` function. To distinguish these input fields, it's better to encapsulate them in a structure defined as follows:

```
struct InputState {
    to_turn: f32,
    started: bool,
}
```

The `to_turn` field indicates that the user has pressed an arrow key to change the direction of the ski. If only the left key is pressed, the direction angle should be decremented, and so the value of this field should be -1.0. If only the right key is pressed, the direction angle should be incremented, and so the value of this field should be 1.0. If the user has not pressed any arrow key, the direction should remain unchanged, and so the value of this field should be 0.0.

The `started` field indicates that the race has started. It is not used in this project. An instance of this structure is added to the model using the following line:

```
input: InputState,
```

The capture of key presses is done through the following code:

```
fn key_down_event(
    &mut self,
    _ctx: &mut Context,
    keycode: KeyCode,
    _keymod: KeyMods,
    _repeat: bool,
) {
    match keycode {
        KeyCode::Left  => { self.input.to_turn = -1.0; }
        KeyCode::Right => { self.input.to_turn = 1.0; }
        _ => (),
    }
}
```

The `keycode` argument specifies which key has been pressed. If the left or the right arrow keys have been pressed, the `to_turn` field is set to −1.0 or to +1.0, respectively. Any other keys that are pressed are ignored.

Capturing the release of the keys is done through the following code:

```
fn key_up_event(&mut self, _ctx: &mut Context, keycode: KeyCode, _keymod:
KeyMods) {
    match keycode {
        KeyCode::Left | KeyCode::Right => {
            self.input.to_turn = 0.0;
        }
        _ => (),
    }
}
```

If the left or the right arrow keys are released, the `to_turn` field is set to 0.0 to stop the change of direction. The release of any other key is ignored.

Other differences with quicksilver

Between `quicksilver` and `ggez`, in addition to the described conceptual differences, there are some minor differences, which I have covered in the following subsections.

Name of the trait

The name of the trait to be implemented by the model is `State` for `quicksilver` and `EventHandler` for `ggez`. So, for `quicksilver` we had the following line:

```
impl State for Screen {
```

But in `ggez`, we have the following:

```
impl EventHandler for Screen {
```

The type of context

Using both `quicksilver` and `ggez`, you need to implement the `update` method and the `draw` method. Both of these methods receive an argument for both frameworks that describes the input/output context. This context is the object used to receive interactive input (by the `update` method) and to emit graphical output (by the `draw` method).

However, for `quicksilver` the type of this context argument is `Window`, as in the following function signatures:

```
fn update(&mut self, window: &mut Window) -> Result<()> {
...
fn draw(&mut self, window: &mut Window) -> Result<()> {
```

For `ggez`, it is `Context`. So, now we have the following signatures:

```
fn update(&mut self, ctx: &mut Context) -> GameResult {
...
fn draw(&mut self, ctx: &mut Context) -> GameResult {
```

The new method

The `State` trait of `quicksilver` requires the implementation of the `new` method, used by the framework to create the model instance. The `EventHandler` trait of `ggez` has no such method because the model instance is created explicitly by application code in the `main` function, as we have seen.

The angle's unit of measurement

While `quicksilver` rotation angles must be specified in degrees, `ggez` rotation angles must be specified in radians, and so angular constants and variables are specified in these units of measurement. So, now we have the following lines:

```
const STEERING_SPEED: f32 = 110. / 180. * PI; // in radians/second
const MAX_ANGLE: f32 = 75. / 180. * PI; // in radians
```

How to specify the FPS rate

To specify the desired **Frames Per Second** (**FPS**) rate, two parameters are specified in the `main` function when using `quicksilver`, whereas `ggez` uses another technique. For `ggez`, the `update` function is always invoked 60 times per second (if possible), but the application code can simulate a different rate by writing the following body of the `update` function:

```
const DESIRED_FPS: u32 = 25;
while timer::check_update_time(ctx, DESIRED_FPS) {
    ...
}
```

The purpose of this code is to ensure that the body of the `while` loop is executed with the specified rate, which in this case is 25 frames per second. Let's see how this is accomplished.

The required rate specified in our code means that the body should be executed once every *1000 / 25 = 40* milliseconds. When the `update` function is executed, if less than 40 milliseconds have elapsed since the preceding execution, the `check_update_time` function returns `false`, and so the body of the `while` loop is not executed this time. It is likely that even at the next `update` call, not enough time will have elapsed, and so the `check_update_time` function will return `false` again. In a later execution, when at least 40 milliseconds have elapsed since the last time the body was executed, `true` will be returned, and so the body will be executed.

This allows a rate that is lower than 60 FPS. However, there is another feature. If a frame, for some reason, takes longer than the allotted time—say, 130 milliseconds—causing the animation to stutter, then the `check_update_time` function returns `true` several times in a row to make up for the lost time.

Of course, you cannot obtain the desired rate if every frame is so slow to take too much time. Tough, as long as your frames are processed within the required time, this technique ensures that the average frame rate will be the specified one.

To say that the actual average rate approximates the desired rate, it is enough that the average time taken by a frame is less than the one allotted for a frame. Instead, if your frames take, on average, 100 milliseconds, the actual frame rate will be 10 FPS.

Handling the ski steering

The ski steering is handled differently in the body of the `update` loop. In the `ski` project, the `steer` function is only called if an arrow key is kept pressed down at that time. Instead, in the `gg_sky` project, the following statement is always executed:

```
self.steer(self.input.to_turn);
```

The `steer` function is called at any time frame, passing the value set before by the input handling methods. If this value is `0`, the ski doesn't steer.

Computation of new position and speed

In addition, the body of the `update` function now contains the following statements:

```
let now = timer::time_since_start(ctx);
self.period_in_sec = (now - self.previous_frame_time)
    .as_millis() as f32 / 1000.;
self.previous_frame_time = now;
```

Their purpose is to compute the correct kinematics of the ski. In mechanics, to compute a position variation ($\triangle p$), you have to multiply the current speed (also called **velocity**, v) by the time elapsed since the previous frame ($\triangle t$). This results in the following equation:

$$\triangle p = v \cdot \triangle t$$

To compute a speed variation ($\triangle v$), you have to multiply the current acceleration (a) by the time elapsed since the preceding frame ($\triangle t$), which results in the following equation:

$$\triangle v = a. \triangle t$$

So, to compute the position variation and the speed variation, we need the time elapsed since the preceding frame. The ggez framework provides the `timer::time_since_start` function, which returns the duration since the start of the application. We subtract the time of the preceding frame from the duration to obtain the time elapsed between the two frames. The duration is then converted into seconds. Finally, the current time is saved, to be used in the next frame computation.

Drawing the background

The MVC view implemented by the `draw` method draws the white background by using the following statement:

```
graphics::clear(ctx, graphics::WHITE);
```

Now, let's check how to draw the composite shapes.

Drawing composite shapes

To draw a composite shape, instead of individually drawing all of its components, first create a `Mesh` object, which is a composite shape containing all the component shapes, and then draw the `Mesh` object. To create a `Mesh` object, the `MeshBuilder` class is used with this code:

```
let ski = graphics::MeshBuilder::new()
    .rectangle(
        DrawMode::fill(),
        Rect {
            x: -SKI_WIDTH / 2.,
            y: SKI_TIP_LEN,
            w: SKI_WIDTH,
            h: SKI_LENGTH,
        },
        [1., 0., 1., 1.].into(),
    )
    .polygon(
        DrawMode::fill(),
        &[
            Point2::new(-SKI_WIDTH / 2., SKI_TIP_LEN),
            Point2::new(SKI_WIDTH / 2., SKI_TIP_LEN),
            Point2::new(0., 0.),
        ],
        [0.5, 0., 1., 1.].into(),
    )?
    .build(ctx)?;
```

Let's now check what this code does:

1. First, the `new` function creates a `MeshBuilder` object.

2. Then, the methods instruct these mesh builders how to create the mesh components. The `rectangle` method explains how to create a rectangle, which will be the ski body, and the `polygon` method explains how to create a polygon, which will be the ski tip. The features of the rectangle are its draw mode (`DrawMode::fill()`), its position and size (`x`, `y`, `w`, and `h`), and its color (`1.`, `0.`, `1.`, `1.`). The features of the polygon are its draw mode, the list of its vertices, and its color. It has just three vertices, so it is a triangle.

3. Then, the `build` method creates and returns the specified mesh. Notice that the method calls ending with a question mark are fallible and that the colors are specified by the quadruple red-green-blue-alpha model, where each number is in the range `0` to `1`.

To draw a mesh, the following statement is used:

```
graphics::draw(
    ctx,
    &ski,
    graphics::DrawParam::new()
        .dest(Point2::new(
            SCREEN_WIDTH / 2. + self.ski_across_offset,
            SCREEN_HEIGHT * 15. / 16. - SKI_LENGTH / 2.
                - SKI_TIP_LEN,
        ))
        .rotation(self.direction),
)?;
```

This `draw` method is not the same as the `draw` method that defines the view of the MVC architecture. This is found in the `ggez::graphics` module, while the containing method (the view) is part of the `ggez::event::EventHandler` trait.

The first argument of the `graphics::draw` method—`ctx`—is the context on which we are drawing. The second argument—`&ski`—is the mesh we are drawing. The third argument is a collection of parameters, encapsulated in a `DrawParam` object. This type allows us to specify numerous parameters, two of which are specified as follows:

• The point to draw the mesh, specified using the `dest` method
• The angle (in radians) by which the mesh must be rotated, specified using the `rotation` method

So, we have now seen how to draw on the screen. However, after calling these statements, nothing actually appears on the screen because the statements just prepare the output off-screen. To get the output, a finalization statement is needed, which is described in the next section.

Ending the draw method

The view (that is, the `draw` method) should end with the following statements:

```
graphics::present(ctx)?;
timer::yield_now();
```

In the typical double-buffering technique used by OpenGL, all the `ggez` drawing operations do not output graphics directly on the screen but in a hidden buffer. The `present` function quickly swaps the shown screen buffer with the hidden drawn buffer, with the effect of immediately displaying the scene and avoiding the flicker that could appear otherwise. The last statement tells the operating system to stop using the CPU for this process until the next frame must be drawn. By doing this, if the processing of a frame is quicker than a time frame, the application avoids using 100% of the CPU cycles.

So, we have finished examining the `gg_ski` project. In the next section, we will examine how the `gg_silent_slalom` project builds on this project to create a slalom game with no sound or text.

Implementing the gg_silent_slalom project

In this section, we will examine the `gg_silent_slalom` project, which is an implementation of the `ggez` framework of the `gg_silent_slalom` game presented in the preceding chapter. Here, we will only examine the differences between the `gg_ski` project and the `silent_slalom` project.

As we saw in the preceding section, `ggez` handles input as events. In this project, two other key events are handled—`Space` and `R`:

```
KeyCode::Space => {
    self.input.started = true;
}
KeyCode::R => {
    self.input.started = false;
}
```

The spacebar is used to command the start of the race, and so it sets the `started` flag to `true`. The *R* key is used to reposition the ski at the beginning of the slope, and so it sets the `started` flag to `false`.

This flag is then used in the `update` method, as in the following code:

```
match self.mode {
    Mode::Ready => {
        if self.input.started {
            self.mode = Mode::Running;
        }
    }
}
```

When in `Ready` mode, instead of directly checking the keyboard state, the `started` flag is checked. The computation of speed and acceleration takes into account the time that has actually elapsed since the preceding frame computation:

```
self.forward_speed = (self.forward_speed
    + ALONG_ACCELERATION * self.period_in_sec * self.direction.cos())
    * DRAG_FACTOR.powf(self.period_in_sec);
```

To compute the new forward speed, the acceleration along the slope (`ALONG_ACCELERATION`) is projected on the ski direction using the cosine function (`self.direction.cos()`), and then the result is multiplied by the elapsed time (`self.period_in_sec`) to get the speed increment.

The incremented speed is then multiplied by a factor that is less than 1 to take friction into account. This factor is the `DRAG_FACTOR` constant for a time of 1 second. To get the decrease factor for the actual time elapsed, the exponential function must be used (`powf`).

To compute the new horizontal position of the ski tip, the following statement is executed:

```
self.ski_across_offset +=
    self.forward_speed * self.period_in_sec * self.direction.sin();
```

This multiplies the speed (`self.forward_speed`) by the time elapsed (`self.period_in_sec`) to obtain the space increment. This increment is projected on the horizontal direction using the sine function (`self.direction.sin()`) to get the horizontal position variation.

A similar computation is performed to compute the movement along the slope, which is actually the offset of the position of the gates as the ski is always drawn at the same *Y* coordinate.

To draw the poles of the gates in the `draw` method, first, two meshes are created by using the following statements:

```
let normal_pole = graphics::Mesh::new_circle(
    ctx,
    DrawMode::fill(),
    Point2::new(0., 0.),
    GATE_POLE_RADIUS,
    0.05,
    [0., 0., 1., 1.].into(),
)?;
let finish_pole = graphics::Mesh::new_circle(
    ctx,
    DrawMode::fill(),
    Point2::new(0., 0.),
    GATE_POLE_RADIUS,
    0.05,
    [0., 1., 0., 1.].into(),
)?;
```

Here, the meshes are created directly without using a `MeshBuilder` object. The `new_circle` method requires the context, the fill mode, the center, the radius, a tolerance, and the color as parameters. Tolerance is a trade-off between performance and graphic quality. The former mesh is used to draw all the poles, except those of the finish gate, and the latter mesh is used to draw the poles of the finish gate.

Then, these meshes are drawn to show all the poles using statements such as the following:

```
graphics::draw(
    ctx,
    pole,
    (Point2::new(SCREEN_WIDTH / 2. + gate.0, gates_along_pos),),
)?;
```

Here, the third argument (with the `DrawParam` type) is specified in a simple but somewhat obscure way; it is a tuple containing just one element. This element is interpreted as the position where the mesh will be drawn, corresponding to the `dest` method call seen in the preceding section.

So, we have now also seen the peculiarities of the `gg_silent_slalom` project. In the next section, we will look at the `gg_assets_slalom` project, which adds sound and text to our project.

Implementing the gg_assets_slalom project

In this chapter, we will examine the `gg_assets_slalom` project, which is an implementation of the `ggez` framework of the `assets_slalom` game presented in the preceding chapter. Here, we will only examine the differences between the `gg_silent_slalom` project and the `assets_slalom` project.

The main difference is found in how the assets are loaded. The assets of these projects are of two kinds—fonts and sounds. To encapsulate these assets, instead of using objects with the `Asset<Font>` and `Asset<Sound>` types, `ggez` uses objects with the `graphics::Font` and `audio::Source` types, respectively. These assets are loaded into the constructor of the model. For example, the constructor of the `Screen` object contains the following statements:

```
font: Font::new(ctx, "/font.ttf")?,
whoosh_sound: audio::Source::new(ctx, "/whoosh.ogg")?,
```

The first one loads a file containing a `TrueType` font for the `ctx` context and returns an object encapsulating this font. The second one loads (for the `ctx` context) a file containing an OGG sound and returns an object encapsulating this sound. Both files must be present in the `asset` folder that was specified in the `main` function using the `add_resource_path` method, and they must be in one of the supported formats.

There is an important difference in how `quicksilver` and `ggez` load their assets. `quicksilver` loads them asynchronously, creating future objects whose access function must ensure that the asset is loaded. On the other hand, `ggez` is synchronous; when it loads the assets, it blocks the application until the assets are completely loaded. The objects created are not future objects, and so they can be used immediately.

Because it uses future objects, `quicksilver` is more sophisticated, but this sophistication is probably useless on a desktop application because, provided your application has no more than a few megabytes of assets, loading them from local storage is quite fast, and so some blocking statements at application startup are not going to be inconvenient. Of course, to prevent slowing down animations, the assets must be loaded only at application startup, when changing the level of a game, or when the game is ending. Once an asset is loaded, it is immediately available.

The easiest asset to use is sound. To play a sound, the following function is defined:

```
fn play_sound(sound: &mut audio::Source, volume: f32) {
    sound.set_volume(volume);
    let _ = sound.play_detached();
}
```

Its first argument is the `sound` asset and the second argument is the desired `volume` level. This function simply sets the volume and then plays the sound using the `play_detached` method. This method overlaps the new sound with any other sounds that are already playing. There is also a `play` method, which automatically stops playing the old sounds before starting the new one.

To play a fixed-volume sound, such as one that signals the failure to enter a gate, the following statement is used:

```
play_sound(&mut self.bump_sound, 1.);
```

In addition, to make a sound proportional to the speed, the following statement is used:

```
play_sound(&mut self.whoosh_sound, self.forward_speed * 0.005);
```

The font is quite easy to use, too:

```
let text = graphics::Text::new((elapsed_shown_text, self.font, 16.0));
graphics::draw(ctx, &text, (Point2::new(4.0, 4.0), graphics::BLACK))?;
```

The first statement creates a text shape by calling the new function. It has a tuple with three fields as an argument:

- The string to print (`elapsed_shown_text`)
- The scalable font object to use for this text (`self.font`)
- The desired size of the generated text (`16.0`)

The second statement draws the created text shape on the `ctx` context. This statement specifies a tuple that will be converted to a `DrawParam` value as a third parameter. The specified sub-arguments are the destination point (`Point2::new(4.0, 4.0)`) and the color to use (`graphics::BLACK`).

So, we have now covered the whole game. In the next section, we will look at another game, which uses mouse clicks and other kinds of assets—images.

Implementing the gg_whac project

In this section, we will examine the `gg_whac` project, which is an implementation in the `ggez` framework of the famous **Whack-A-Mole** arcade game. First of all, let's try to play it.

After running `cargo run --release` in the `gg_whac` folder, the following window will appear, which shows a lawn:

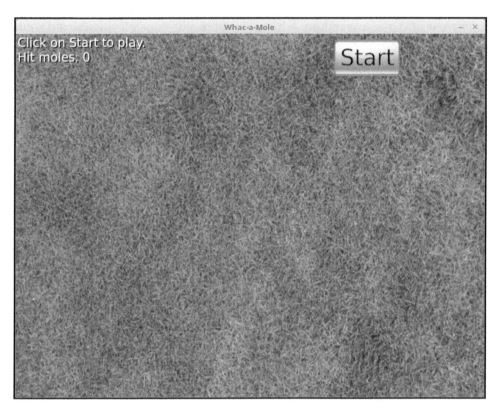

For those of you who aren't familiar with this game, here are the rules. When you click on the **Start** button, the following things happen:

1. The **Start** button disappears.
2. The countdown begins at the top left from **40** seconds to **0**.
3. A nice mole pops up in a random position of the lawn.
4. The mouse cursor becomes a barred circle.
5. If you move your mouse cursor over the mole, it becomes a cross and a big mallet appears; this mallet can be dragged by the mouse as long as you remain over the mole.

Your window should look similar to the following:

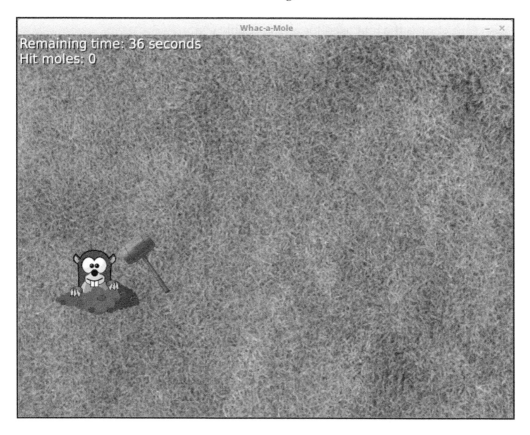

If you click the main mouse button when the mouse cursor hovers over the mole, the mole disappears and another one appears in another position. In the meantime, a counter tells you how many moles you have managed to whack. When the countdown reaches 0, you are presented with your score.

The assets

To understand the behavior of this application, first, let's look at the content of the `assets` folder:

- `cry.ogg` is the sound produced by the mole when it pops up out of the lawn.
- `click.ogg` is the sound of the mallet when it hits the mole.
- `bump.ogg` is the sound of the mallet when it hits the lawn but misses the mole.

- `two_notes.ogg` is the jingle produced when the game ends because the countdown has elapsed.
- `font.ttf` is the font used for all the visible text.
- `mole.png` is the image of the moles.
- `mallet.png` is the image of the mallet.
- `lawn.jpg` is the image used to fill the background.
- `button.png` is the image used for the **Start** button.

We already saw, in the preceding section, how to load and use sounds and fonts. Here, there is a new kind of asset—images. Images are declared by statements such as the following:

```
lawn_image: graphics::Image,
```

They are loaded, at application initialization time, by statements such as the following:

```
lawn_image: graphics::Image::new(ctx, "/lawn.jpg")?
```

They are displayed by statements such as the following:

```
graphics::draw(ctx, &self.lawn_image, lawn_params)?;
```

Here, the `lawn_params` argument, with a type of `DrawParam`, can specify a position, a scale, a rotation, and even a crop.

The general structure of the application and events

Now, let's examine the structure of the source code. Like the preceding projects we have seen in this chapter, this project does the following:

- Defines some constants
- Defines a model with the `struct Screen` type
- Implements the `EventHandler` trait with its required `update` and `draw` methods and its optional `mouse_button_down_event` and `mouse_button_up_event` methods
- Defines the `main` function

The most important field of the model is `mode`, whose type is defined by the following code:

```
enum Mode {
    Ready,
    Raising,
    Lowering,
}
```

The initial mode is `Ready`, where the countdown is stopped and the game is ready to start. When the game is running, there are the following states:

- No mole appears.
- One mole rises from the ground.
- One mole rises and waits to be hit.
- A blow of the mallet is about to hit the mole.
- The mole that has been hit lowers into the ground.

Well, actually, the first state does not exists, because as soon as the game starts, a mole pops up, and also, as soon as you hit a mole, another mole pops up. The second and third states are represented by `Mode::Raising`. Simply put, when the mole reaches its full height, it is not raised.

The fourth and fifth states are represented by `Mode::Lowering`. Simply put, the mole lowers simultaneously with the mallet.

Regarding the input operations, it should be noted that for the `EventHandler` trait, no key handling methods are implemented as this game does not use the keyboard. Instead, it uses the mouse, and so there is the following code:

```
fn mouse_button_down_event(&mut self, _ctx: &mut Context,
    button: MouseButton, x: f32, y: f32) {
    if button == MouseButton::Left {
        self.mouse_down_at = Some(Point2::new(x, y));
    }
}

fn mouse_button_up_event(&mut self, _ctx: &mut Context,
    button: MouseButton, x: f32, y: f32) {
    if button == MouseButton::Left {
        self.mouse_up_at = Some(Point2::new(x, y));
    }
}
```

The first method is invoked when a mouse button is pressed and the second one is invoked when a mouse button is released.

The third argument of these methods (button) is an enum indicating which button has been pressed; MouseButton::Left actually represents the main mouse button.

The fourth and fifth arguments of these methods (x and y) are the coordinates of the position of the mouse when its button has been pressed. Their unit of measurement is pixels and the origin of their coordinate system is the top-left vertex of the context, which in our case is the client area of the window.

Only the main mouse button is handled. When it is pressed, the point representing the current mouse position is stored in the mouse_down_at field of the model, and when it is released, it is stored in the mouse_up_at field of the model.

These fields are defined in the model in the following way:

```
mouse_down_at: Option<Point2>,
mouse_up_at: Option<Point2>,
```

Their value is initialized to None and is only set to a Point2 value by the preceding code; it is reset to None as soon as these events are processed by the update method. So, each mouse event is only processed once.

Other fields of the model

In addition to the fields that we have already described, the model has the following other fields:

```
start_time: Option<Duration>,
active_mole_column: usize,
active_mole_row: usize,
active_mole_position: f32,
n_hit_moles: u32,
random_generator: ThreadRng,
start_button: Button,
```

The start_time field is used to show the current remaining time during the game and to show the **Game finished** text when the game ends. It is initialized to None, and then any time the **Start** button is pressed, the current time is stored in it.

The moles do not appear in totally random positions. The lawn is covertly organized into three rows and five columns. A mole appears in 1 of these 15 positions, chosen at random. The `active_mole_column` and `active_mole_row` fields contain the zero-based column and the row of the currently displayed mole.

The `active_mole_position` field contains the fraction of the appearance of the current mole. A `0` value means that the mole is totally hidden. A value of `1` means that the image of the mole (representing a part of its body) has completely appeared. The `n_hit_moles` field counts how many moles have been hit.

The `random_generator` field is a pseudo-random number generator used to generate the position of the next mole to show. Finally, `start_button` is a field representing the **Start** button. However, its type is not defined in a library. It is defined in this application, as we are going to explain.

Defining a widget

Business applications have windows full of small, interactive graphical elements, such as buttons and textboxes. These elements are usually named **controls** by Microsoft Windows documentation and **widgets** (from window objects) in Unix-like environments. Defining widgets using graphics primitives is a rather complex feat, so if you want to develop a business application, you should probably use a library that defines a set of widgets.

Neither the Rust standard library nor the `ggez` framework defines widgets. However, if you need just a few very simple widgets, you can develop them yourself, such as the button we will develop for this project. Let's see how this is implemented.

First of all, there is a definition of the `Button` type that can be instantiated for any button you want to add to your window:

```
struct Button {
    base_image: Rc<graphics::Image>,
    bounding_box: Rect,
    drawable_text: graphics::Text,
}
```

Our button is just an image resized as we want with text centered on it. This image is the same for all the buttons, and so it should be shared throughout the program to save memory. This is why the `base_image` field is a reference-counted pointer to an image.

The `bounding_box` field indicates the desired position and size of the button. The image will be stretched or shrunk to fit this size. The `drawable_text` field is a text shape that will be drawn over the image of the button as its caption. The `Button` type implements several methods:

- `new` to create a new button
- `contains` to check whether a given point is inside the button
- `draw` to display itself in the specified context

The `new` method has many arguments:

```
fn new(
    ctx: &mut Context,
    caption: &str,
    center: Point2,
    font: Font,
    base_image: Rc<graphics::Image>,
) -> Self {
```

The `caption` argument is the text to display inside the button. The `center` argument is the desired position of the center of the button. The `font` and `base_image` arguments are the font and image to use.

To create our button, the following expression is used:

```
start_button: Button::new(
    ctx,
    "Start",
    Point2::new(600., 40.),
    font,
    button_image.clone(),
),
```

It specifies `"Start"` as the caption, a width of 600 pixels, and a height of 40 pixels.

To draw the button, first, we check whether the main mouse button is currently pressed using this expression:

```
mouse::button_pressed(ctx, MouseButton::Left)
```

By doing this, it is possible to make the button appear like it is being pressed to give visual feedback of the button's operation. Then, we check whether the mouse cursor is inside the button using this expression:

```
rect.contains(mouse::position(ctx))
```

This turns the color of the button caption red when the mouse hovers over the button to show the user that the button can be clicked on. So, we have now looked at the most interesting parts of this project, which ends our look into the `ggez` framework.

Summary

We have seen how to build two-dimensional games for the desktop using the `ggez` framework. This framework not only allows us to structure the application according to the animation-loop architecture and the MVC architectural pattern but also to get discrete input events. In addition, we have seen why a linear algebra library can be useful for graphical applications.

We created and looked at four apps—`gg_ski`, `gg_silent_slalom`, `gg_assets_slalom`, and `gg_whac`.

In particular, we learned how to build a graphical desktop app using the `ggez` framework, which is structured according to the MVC architecture, and how to implement both an animation-loop architecture and an event-driven architecture, possibly in the same window. Additionally, we also learned to draw graphical elements on a web page using `ggez`, as well as loading and using static resources using `ggez`. At the end of the chapter, we encapsulated two-dimensional points and vectors in a structure and saw how to manipulate them using the `nalgebra` library.

In the next chapter, we will look at a completely different technology: parsing. Parsing text files is useful for many purposes, in particular for interpreting or compiling a source code program. We will take a look at the `nom` library, which makes parsing tasks easier.

Questions

1. What is the difference between a vector and a point in linear algebra?
2. What are the geometrical concepts corresponding to algebraic vectors and points?
3. Why can capturing events be useful, even in an animation loop-oriented application?
4. Why can loading synchronous assets be a good idea in a desktop game?
5. How does `ggez` get input from the keyboard and mouse?
6. What are the meshes used in the `ggez` framework?

7. How can you build a ggez mesh?
8. How do you obtain a desired animation frame rate using ggez?
9. How do you draw a mesh in the desired position using ggez, with the desired scale and rotation values?
10. How do you play sound using ggez?

Further reading

The ggez project can be downloaded from https://github.com/ggez/ggez. This repository contains many example projects, including a complete asteroid arcade game.

8
Using a Parser Combinator for Interpreting and Compiling

Rust is a system programming language. A typical task of system programming is processing *formal languages*. Formal languages are languages specified by well-defined logical rules and used everywhere in computer technology. They can be broadly classified into command, programming, and markup languages.

To process formal languages, the first step is to parse. **Parsing** means analyzing the grammatical structure of a piece of code to check whether it respects the rules of the grammar it is supposed to use, and then, if the grammar is respected, to generate a data structure that describes the structure of the parsed piece of code, in a way that such code can be further processed.

In this chapter, we will see how to process text written in a formal language, starting from the parsing step and proceeding with several possible outcomes—simply checking the grammar, interpreting a program, and translating a program into the Rust language.

To show such features, an extremely simple programming language will be defined, and four tools (syntax checker, semantic checker, interpreter, and translator) will be built around it.

In this chapter, you will learn about the following topics:

- Defining a programming language using a formal grammar
- Classifying programming languages into three categories
- Learning two popular techniques for building parsers—compiler-compilers and parser combinators
- Using a parser combinator library for Rust named **Nom**
- Processing a source code to check its syntax following a **context-free grammar**, using the Nom library (`calc_parser`)

- Verifying the consistency of variable declarations and their usage in some source code, and at the same time preparing the required structure for optimal execution of the code (`calc_analyzer`)
- Executing the preprocessed code, in a process named **interpretation** (`calc_interpreter`)
- Translating the preprocessed code into another programming language, in a process named **compilation** (`calc_compiler`); as an example, translation to Rust code will be shown

After reading this chapter, you will be able to write the grammar for a simple formal language or understand the grammar for an existing formal language. You will also be able to write an interpreter for any programming language by following its grammar. Also, you will be able to write a translator for a formal language into another formal language, following their grammar.

Technical requirements

To read this chapter, knowledge of the preceding chapters is not required. Some knowledge of formal language theory and techniques is useful but not required, because the required knowledge will be explained in this chapter. The Nom library will be used to build such tools, and so it will be described in this chapter.

The complete source code for this chapter is in the `Chapter08` folder of the GitHub repository, located at `https://github.com/PacktPublishing/Creative-Projects-for-Rust-Programmers`.

Project overview

In this chapter, we will build four projects of increasing complexity, listed as follows:

- The first project (`calc_parser`) will just be a syntax checker for the `Calc` language. Actually, it is just a parser, followed by a formatted debugging print of the parsing result.
- The second project (`calc_analyzer`) uses the parsing result of the first project to add the verification of the consistency of the variable declarations and of their usage, followed by a formatted debugging print of the analysis result.

- The third project (`calc_interpreter`) uses the analysis result to execute the preprocessed code, in an interactive interpreter.
- The fourth project (`calc_compiler`) uses the analysis result again to translate the preprocessed code into equivalent Rust code.

Introducing Calc

To make the following explanations, we will first define a *toy* programming language that we will name `Calc` (from the calculator). A toy programming language is a programming language used to demonstrate or prove something, not designed to develop real-world software. A simple program written in `Calc` is shown as follows:

```
@first
@second
> first
> second
@sum
sum := first + second
< sum
< first * second
```

The preceding program asks the user to type two numbers and then prints the sum and the product of those numbers on the console. Let's examine one statement at a time, as follows:

- The first two statements (`@first` and `@second`) declare two variables. Any variable in `Calc` represents a 64-bit floating-point number.
- The third and fourth statements (`> first` and `> second`) are input statements. Each of these prints a question mark and waits for the user to type a number and press *Enter*. Such a number, if valid, is stored in the specified variable. If no number or an invalid number is typed before pressing *Enter*, the value 0 is assigned to the variable.
- The fifth statement declares the `sum` variable.
- The sixth statement (`sum := first + second`) is a Pascal-style assignment. It computes the sum of the `first` and `second` variables and assigns the result to the `sum` variable.
- The seventh and eight statements perform output. The seventh statement (`< sum`) prints on the console the current value of the `sum` variable. The eighth statement (`< first * second`) computes the multiplication between the current values of the `first` and `second` variables, and then prints on the console the result of such multiplication.

The `Calc` language has two other operators—- (minus) and / (divide)— to specify subtraction and division, respectively. In addition, the following code shows that the operations can be combined in expressions, and so these are valid assignment statements:

```
y := m * x + q
a := a + b - c / d
```

Operations are performed left to right, but multiplication and division have higher precedence than addition and subtraction.

In addition to variables, numeric literals are also allowed. So, you can write the following code:

```
a := 2.1 + 4 * 5
```

This statement assigns 22.1 to a, as multiplication is performed before addition. To force different precedence, parentheses are allowed, as illustrated in the following code snippet:

```
a := (2.1 + 4) * 5
```

The preceding code snippet assigns 30.5 to a.

In the preceding code snippet, there are no characters that separate a statement from the next one, in addition to the newline characters. Actually, the `Calc` language has no symbols used to separate statements, and also, it does not need them. So, the first program should be equivalent to this:

```
@first@second>first>second@sum sum:=first+second<sum<first*second
```

In the preceding code snippet, there is no ambiguity because the @ character marks the start of a declaration, the > character marks the start of an input operation, the < character marks the start of an output operation, and a variable in a location where the current statement does not allow a variable marks the start of an assignment.

To understand this syntax, some grammatical terms must be explained, as follows:

- The whole text is a **program**.
- Any program is a sequence of **statements**. In the first example program, there is exactly one statement for each line.
- In some statements, there can be an arithmetic formula that can be evaluated, such as a * 3 + 2. This formula is an **expression**.

- Any expression can contain sums or subtractions of simpler expressions. The simpler expressions that contain neither sums nor subtractions are named **terms**. Therefore, any expression can be a term (if it contains neither sums nor subtractions), or it can be the sum of an expression and a term, or it can be the subtraction of an expression and a term.
- Any term can contain multiplications or divisions of simpler expressions. The simpler expressions that contain neither multiplications nor divisions are named **factors**. Therefore, any term can be a factor (if it contains neither multiplications nor divisions), or it can be the multiplication of a term and a factor, or it can be the division of a term and a factor. There are three possible kinds of factors, listed here:
    - Names of variables, named **identifiers**
    - Numerical constants, represented by sequences of digits, named **literals**
    - Full expressions enclosed in parentheses, to force their precedence

In the `Calc` language, for the sake of simplicity and unlike in most programming languages, digits and underscores are not allowed in identifiers. So, any identifier is a non-empty sequence of letters. Or, put another way, any identifier can be a letter or an identifier followed by a letter.

The syntax of formal languages can be specified by a notation that is known as **Backus–Naur** form. Using this notation, our `Calc` language can be specified by the following rules:

```
<program> ::= "" | <program> <statement>
<statement> ::= "@" <identifier> | ">" <identifier> | "<" <expr> |
<identifier> ":=" <expr>
<expr> ::= <term> | <expr> "+" <term> | <expr> "-" <term>
<term> ::= <factor> | <term> "*" <factor> | <term> "/" <factor>
<factor> ::= <identifier> | <literal> | "(" <expr> ")"    ← <sub_expr>
<identifier> := <letter> | <identifier> <letter>
```

The explanation for all the rules used in the preceding code snippet is described as follows:

- The first rule specifies that a program is an empty string or a program followed by a statement. This amounts to saying that a program is a list of zero or more statements.
- The second rule specifies that a statement is either a @ character followed by an identifier, a > character followed by an identifier, a < character followed by an expression, or an identifier followed by the := pair of characters and then by an expression.

- The third rule specifies that an expression is either a term or an expression followed by the + character and a term, or an expression followed by the – character and a term. This amounts to saying that an expression is a term followed by zero or more term items, where a term-item is a + or a – operator followed by a term.
- Similarly, the fourth rule specifies that a term is either a factor or a term followed by the * character and a factor, or a term followed by the / character and a factor. This amounts to saying that a term is a factor followed by zero or more factor items, where a factor-item is a multiply or a divide operator followed by a factor.
- The fifth rule specifies that a factor is either an identifier or a literal, or an expression enclosed in parentheses. This rule is satisfied only if the parentheses are correctly paired in code.
- The sixth rule specifies that an identifier is a letter or an identifier followed by a letter. This amounts to saying that an identifier is a sequence of one or more letters. This syntax does not specify how case-sensitiveness is handled, but we will assume identifiers are case-sensitive.

This syntax leaves undefined what is meant by the `<letter>` symbol and by the `<literal>` symbol, therefore these are explained here:

- The `<letter>` symbol means any character for which the `is_alphabetic` Rust standard library function returns `true`.
- The `<literal>` symbol means any floating-point number. In fact, as we are going to use Rust code to parse it, store it, and handle it, the `Calc` definition of `literal` is the same as the Rust definition of `f64` literals. For example `-4.56e300` will be allowed, but `1_000` and `3f64` will not be allowed.

Another simplification has been done regarding white spaces. Spaces, tabs, and newline characters are allowed in all positions of code, except inside an identifier, inside a literal, and inside the `:=` symbol. They are optional, but the only position where white space is required is between the ending identifier of a statement and the beginning identifier of an assignment because, otherwise, the two identifiers would merge into one.

In this section, we have defined the syntax of the `Calc` language. Such a formal definition is called a **grammar**. It is a very simple grammar, but it is similar to the grammar of real-world programming languages. Having a formal grammar for a language is useful for building software that processes code written in such a language.

Now that we have seen our toy language, we are ready to process code written in it. The first task is to build a syntax checker that verifies the structural validity of any program in this language.

Understanding formal languages and their parsers

As we've seen, a typical task of system programming is processing *formal languages*. Several kinds of operations are customarily performed in such formal languages. The most typical ones are listed here:

- To check the syntax validity of a line or of a file
- To format a file according to formatting rules
- To execute a command written in a command language
- To interpret a file written in a programming language—that is, execute it immediately
- To compile a file written in a programming language—that is, translate it into another programming language, such as an assembly language or a machine language
- To translate a markup file into another markup language
- To render a markup file in a browser

All these operations have in common the first step of the procedure—parsing. The process of examining a string to extract its structure according to the grammar is called **parsing**. There are at least three kinds of possible parsing techniques, according to the category of the formal language we want to parse. These categories, which we are going to see in this section, are: **regular languages**, **context-free languages**, and **context-dependent languages**.

Regular languages

The category of the simplest languages is that of regular languages, which can be defined using regular expressions.

In the simplest way, a regular expression is a pattern using the following operators between substrings:

- **Concatenation (or sequence)**: This means that a substring must follow another substring; for example, ab means that b must follow a.
- **Alternation (or choice)**: This means that a substring can be used instead of another substring; for example, a|b means that a or b can be used alternatively.
- **Kleene star (or repetition)**: This means that a substring can be used zero or more times; for example, a* means that a can be used zero, one, two, or more times.

To apply such operators, parentheses can be used. So, the following is a regular expression:

$$a(bcd \mid (ef)^*)g$$

This means that a valid string must begin with an *a*, followed by two possible substrings— one is the string *bcd* and the other is an empty string or the string *ef*, or any multiple repetitions of the string *ef*, and then, there must be *g*. The following are some strings belonging to such regular languages:

- *abcdg*
- *ag*
- *aefg*
- *aefefg*
- *aefefefg*
- *aefefefefg*

An advantage of regular languages is that their parsing requires an amount of memory that depends only on the grammar and does not depend on the text being parsed; so, typically, they require little memory even to parse huge texts.

The regex crate is the most popular way to parse regular languages using regular expressions. If you have regular languages to parse, then it is recommended to use such a library. For example, detecting a valid identifier or a valid floating-point number is a regular language parser's job.

Context-free languages

Since programming languages are not simply regular languages, regular expressions cannot be used to parse them. A typical language feature that does not belong to regular languages is the use of parentheses. Most programming languages allow the
`((5))` string but not the `((5)` string because any open parenthesis must be matched by a closing parenthesis. Such a rule cannot be expressed by a regular expression.

A more general (and so more powerful) category of languages is that of context-free languages. These languages are defined by grammar, as with the one seen in the preceding section on the `Calc` language, including the fact that some elements must be matched (such as parentheses, brackets, braces, and quotes).

Differing from regular languages, context-free languages require a variable amount of memory depending on the parsed text. Every time an open parenthesis is encountered, it must be stored somewhere to match it with the corresponding closed parentheses. Although such memory usage is usually quite small and it is accessed in a **Last-In-First-Out (LIFO)** fashion (as it would be in a stack data structure), it is quite efficient because no heap allocation is required.

Even context-free languages are enough for real-world usage, though, because real-world languages need to be context-dependent, as explained in the following section.

Context-dependent languages

Unfortunately, even CFGs are not powerful enough to represent real-world programming languages. The problem lies in the usage of identifiers.

In many programming languages, before using a variable, you must declare it. In any location of the code, only the variables defined up to that point can be used. Such a set of available identifiers is taken as the context in which the next statement is parsed. In many programming languages, such a context contains not only the name of the variable but also its type, and the fact that it surely has already received a value or it may be still uninitialized.

To capture such constraints, context-dependent languages can be defined, though such formalism is quite unwieldy and the resulting grammar is inefficient to parse.

Therefore, the usual way to parse a programming language text is to split parsing into several conceptual passes, as follows:

- **Pass 1**: Use regular expressions where you can—that is, to parse identifiers, literals, operators, and separators. This pass generates a stream of *tokens*, where each token represents one of the parsed items. So, for example, any identifier is a different token, while white space and comments are skipped. This pass is usually named **lexical analysis** or **lexing**.
- **Pass 2**: Use a context-free parser where you can—that is, to apply the grammar rules to the stream of tokens. This pass creates a tree-shaped structure representing the program. This structure is named a **syntax tree**. The tokens are stored as the leaves (that is, terminal nodes) of this tree. This tree can still contain context-dependent errors, such as the usage of an undeclared identifier. This pass is usually named **syntax analysis**.

- **Pass 3**: Process the syntax tree to associate any variable use with the declaration of such a variable, and possibly check its type. This pass creates a new data structure, named **symbol table**, that describes all the identifiers found in the syntax tree, and it decorates the syntax tree with references to such a symbol table. This pass is usually named **semantic analysis** because it usually also regards type checking.

When we have a decorated syntax tree and its relative symbol table, the parsing operation is completed. Now, the developer can perform the following operations with such data structures:

- Get the syntax errors, in case the code is invalid
- Get suggestions about how to improve the code
- Get some metrics about the code
- Interpret the code (in case the language is a programming language)
- Translate the code into another language

In this chapter, the following operations will be performed:

- The lexical analysis pass and the syntax analysis pass will be grouped in a single pass that will process source code and will generate a syntax tree (in the `calc_parser` project).
- The semantic analysis pass will use the syntax tree generated by the parser to create a symbol table and a decorated syntax tree (in the `calc_analyser` project).
- The symbol table and the decorated syntax tree will be used to execute the program written in the `Calc` language (in the `calc_interpreter` project).
- The symbol table and the decorated syntax tree will also be used to translate the program into the Rust language (in the `calc_complier` project).

In this section, we have seen a useful classification of programming languages. Even if every programming language belongs to the context-dependent category, the other categories are still useful because interpreters and compilers use regular grammars and CFGs as a part of their operation.

But before seeing a complete project, let's have a look at the techniques used to build a parser, and in particular, the technique used by the Nom library.

Using Nom to build parsers

Before starting to write a parser for the `Calc` language, let's have a look at the most popular parsing techniques used for building both interpreters and compilers. This is needed to understand the Nom library, which uses one of these techniques.

Learning about compiler-compilers and parser combinators

To obtain an extremely fast and flexible parser, you need to build it from scratch. But for decades, an easier approach was used to build parsers by using tools named **compiler-compilers** or **compiler generators**: programs that generate compilers. These programs get input as a decorated specification of the syntax and generate the source code of a parser for such a syntax. These generated source code must then be compiled, together with other source files, to get an executable compiler.

This traditional approach is now somewhat out of fashion and another one has emerged, named **parser combinator**. A parser combinator is a set of functions that allow several parsers to be combined to obtain another parser.

We have seen that any `Calc` program is just a sequence of `Calc` statements. If we had a parser of single `Calc` statements and the ability to apply such a parser in sequence, then we could parse any `Calc` program.

We should know that any `Calc` statement is either a `Calc` declaration, a `Calc` assignment, a `Calc` input operation, or a `Calc` output operation. If we had a parser for each of such statements and the ability to apply any such parsers alternatively, we could parse any `Calc` statement. We can go on until we get to single characters (or to tokens if we use the output of a lexical analyzer). So, a parser of a program can be obtained by combining the parsers of its component items.

But what is a parser written in Rust? It is a function that gets a string of source code as input and returns a result. The result can be `Err` (if that string couldn't be parsed) or `Ok` (containing a data structure representing the parsed item).

So, while normal functions receive data as input and return data as output, our parser combinators receive one or more parsers that have functions as input and return a parser as output. Functions that receive functions as input and return a function as output are named **second-order functions** because they process functions instead of data. In computer science, the concept of second-order functions originates from functional languages, and the concept of parser combinators also comes from such languages.

In Rust, second-order functions were not feasible before the 2018 edition, because Rust functions could not return functions without allocating a closure. Therefore, the Nom library (up to version 4) used macros instead of functions as combinators to maintain top performance. When Rust introduced the `impl Trait` feature (included in the 2018 edition), an efficient implementation of parser combinators using functions instead of macros became possible. So, version 5 of Nom is entirely based on functions, keeping macros only for backward compatibility.

In the next section, we will see the basic features of the Nom library, which we are going to use to build both an interpreter and a compiler.

Learning the basics of Nom

The Nom crate is essentially a collection of functions. Most of them are parser combinators—that is, they get one or more parsers as arguments and return a parser as a return value. You can think of them as machines that get one or more parsers as input and emit a combined parser as output.

Some of the Nom function are parsers—that is, they get a sequence of `char` values as an argument and return an error if the parse fails, or a data structure representing the parsed text, in the case of success.

Now, we'll see the most basic features of Nom, using very simple programs. In particular, we'll see the following:

- The `char` parser: To parse single fixed characters
- The `alt` parser combinator: To accept alternative parsers
- The `tuple` parser combinator: To accept a fixed sequence of parsers
- The `tag` parser: To parse fixed strings of a character
- The `map` parser combinator: To transform the output value of parsers
- The `Result::map` function: To apply more complex transformations on the output of a parser

- The `preceded`, `terminated`, and `delimited` parser combinators: To accept a fixed sequence of parsers and discard some of them from the output
- The `take` parser: To accept a defined number of characters
- The `many1` parser combinator: To accept a sequence of one or more repetitions of a parser

Parsing an alternative of characters

As an example of a parser, let's see how to parse an alternative of fixed characters. We want to parse an extremely simple language, a language that has only three words—*a*, *b*, and *c*. Such a parser would succeed only if its input is the string *a* or the string *b* or the string *c*.

If the parsing is successful, we want a couple of things as a result—the remaining input (that is, after the valid part has been processed) and a representation of the processed text. As our words are made up of single characters, we want (as a representation of that) a value of the `char` type, containing just the parsed character.

The following snippet is our first code using Nom:

```
extern crate nom;
use nom::{branch::alt, character::complete::char, IResult};

fn parse_abc(input: &str) -> IResult<&str, char> {
    alt((char('a'), char('b'), char('c')))(input)
}

fn main() {
    println!("a: {:?}", parse_abc("a"));
    println!("x: {:?}", parse_abc("x"));
    println!("bjk: {:?}", parse_abc("bjk"));
}
```

(handwritten annotations: "remain" and "payload" pointing to the IResult type parameters; circle around `alt`)

If you compile this program, including the dependency of the Nom crate, and you run it, it should print the following output:

```
a: Ok(("", 'a'))
x: Err(Error(("x", Char)))
bjk: Ok(("jk", 'b'))
```

We named our parser `parse_abc`. It gets a string slice as input and returns a value of the `IResult<&str, char>` type. Such a return value type is a kind of `Result`. The `Ok` case of such a `Result` type is a tuple of two values—a string slice containing the remaining input, and a character—that is, the information we got by parsing the text. The `Err` case of such a `Result` type is defined internally by the Nom crate.

As you can see in the output, the `parse_abc("a")` expression returns `Ok(("", 'a'))`. This means that when the a string is parsed, the parsing is successful; no input is left to process, and the character extracted is `'a'`.

Instead, the `parse_abc("x")` expression returns `Err(Error(("x", Char)))`. This means that when the x string is parsed, the parsing fails; the x string remains to process, and the kind of error is `Char`, meaning that a `Char` item was expected. Notice that `Char` is a type defined by Nom.

Lastly, the `parse_abc("bjk")` expression returns `Ok(("jk", 'b'))`. This means that when the string `bjk` is parsed, the parsing is successful; the `jk` input remains to be processed, and the character extracted is `'b'`.

And now, let's see how our parser is implemented. The signature of all parsers built for Nom must have a similar signature, and their body must be a function call that has the function argument as its argument (in this case, `(input)`).

The interesting part is `alt((char('a'), char('b'), char('c')))`. This expression means that we want to build a parser by combining the three parsers, `char('a')`, `char('b')`, and `char('c')`. The char function (not to be confused with the Rust type having the same name) is a built-in Nom parser that recognizes the specified character and returns a value of the `char` type containing that character. The `alt` function (short for alternative) is a parser combinator. It has just one argument, which is a tuple composed of several parsers. The `alt` parser chooses one of the specified parsers that match the input.

It's your responsibility to guarantee that there is at most one parser accepting the input, for any given input. Otherwise, the grammar is ambiguous. Here is an example of an ambiguous parser—`alt((char('a'), char('b'), char('a')))`. The `char('a')` sub-parser is repeated, but this will not be spotted by the Rust compiler.

In the next section, we will see how to parse a sequence of characters.

Parsing a sequence of characters

Now, let's see another parser, given as follows:

```
extern crate nom;
use nom::{character::complete::char, sequence::tuple, IResult};

fn parse_abc_sequence(input: &str)
    -> IResult<&str, (char, char, char)> {
    tuple((char('a'), char('b'), char('c')))(input)
}

fn main() {
    println!("abc: {:?}", parse_abc_sequence("abc"));
    println!("bca: {:?}", parse_abc_sequence("bca"));
    println!("abcjk: {:?}", parse_abc_sequence("abcjk"));
}
```

After running it, it should print the following:

```
abc: Ok(("", ('a', 'b', 'c')))
bca: Err(Error(("bca", Char)))
abcjk: Ok(("jk", ('a', 'b', 'c')))
```

This time, the letters a, b, and c must be in this exact sequence, and a tuple containing these characters is returned by the parse_abc_sequence function. For the abc input, there is no remaining input, and the ('a', 'b', 'c') tuple is returned. The bca input is not accepted, as it starts with a b character instead of a. The abcjk input is accepted, as in the first case, but this time, there is a remaining input.

The combination of parsers is tuple((char('a'), char('b'), char('c'))). This is similar to the preceding program, but by using the tuple parser combinator, a parser is obtained that requires that all the specified parsers are satisfied, in their order.

In the next section, we'll see how to parse a fixed string of text.

Parsing a fixed string

In the parse_abc_sequence function discussed previously, to recognize the abc sequence, the char parser had to be specified three times, and the result was a tuple of char values.

For longer strings (such as the keywords of a language), this is inconvenient, as they are more easily seen as strings than as sequences of characters. The Nom library also contains a parser for fixed strings, named `tag`. The preceding program can be rewritten using this built-in parser, shown in the following code block:

```
extern crate nom;
use nom::{bytes::complete::tag, IResult};

fn parse_abc_string(input: &str) -> IResult<&str, &str> {
    tag("abc")(input)
}

fn main() {
    println!("abc: {:?}", parse_abc_string("abc"));
    println!("bca: {:?}", parse_abc_string("bca"));
    println!("abcjk: {:?}", parse_abc_string("abcjk"));
}
```

It will print the following output:

```
abc: Ok(("", "abc"))
bca: Err(Error(("bca", Tag)))
abcjk: Ok(("jk", "abc"))
```

Instead of the `tuple((char('a'), char('b'), char('c')))` expression, there is now a simple call to `tag("abc")`, and the parser returns a string slice, instead of a tuple of `char` values.

In the next section, we'll see how to transform the value resulting from a parser to another value, possibly of another type.

Mapping parsed items to other objects

So far, we get as a result just what we found in the input. But often, we want to transform the parsed input before returning its result.

Say that we want to parse alternatively three letters (a, b, or c) but we want, as a result of the parsing, the number 5 for the letter a, the number 16 for the letter b, and the number 8 for the letter c.

So, we want a parser that parses a letter, but, instead of returning that letter, it returns a number, if the parsing is successful. We also want to map the character a to the number 5, the character b to the number 16, and the character c to the number 8. The original result type was char, while the mapped result type is u8. The following code block shows the program that performs such a transformation:

```
extern crate nom;
use nom::{branch::alt, character::complete::char, combinator::map,
IResult};

fn parse_abc_as_numbers(input: &str)
    -> IResult<&str, u8> {
    alt((
        map(char('a'), |_| 5),
        map(char('b'), |_| 16),
        map(char('c'), |_| 8),
    ))(input)
}

fn main() {
    println!("a: {:?}", parse_abc_as_numbers("a"));
    println!("x: {:?}", parse_abc_as_numbers("x"));
    println!("bjk: {:?}", parse_abc_as_numbers("bjk"));
}
```

When it runs, it should print the following output:

```
a: Ok(("", 5))
x: Err(Error(("x", Char)))
bjk: Ok(("jk", 16))
```

For the a input, 5 is extracted. For the x input, a parse error is obtained. For the bjk input, 16 is extracted, and the jk string remains as input to be parsed.

The implementation, for each one of the three characters, contains something such as map(char('a'), |_| 5). The map function is another parser combinator that takes a parser and a closure. If the parser matches, then it generates a value. The closure is invoked on such a value, and it returns a transformed value. In this case, the argument of the closure was not needed.

An alternative equivalent implementation of the same parser is given as follows:

```
fn parse_abc_as_numbers(input: &str) -> IResult<&str, u8> {
    fn transform_letter(ch: char) -> u8 {
        match ch {
            'a' => 5,
```

```
                    'b' => 16,
                    'c' => 8,
                    _ => 0,
                }
        }
        alt((
            map(char('a'), transform_letter),
            map(char('b'), transform_letter),
            map(char('c'), transform_letter),
        ))(input)
    }
```

It defines the `transform_letter` inner function that applies the transformation and passes just that function as the second argument of the `map` combinator.

In the next section, we'll see how to manipulate the output of a parser in a more complex way, as we will be omitting or swapping some fields of the resulting tuple.

Creating custom parsing results

So far, the results of parsing have been determined by the parsers and combinators used in it—if a parser uses the `tuple` combinator with three items, the result is a tuple of three items. This is seldom what is desired. For example, we want to either omit some items of the resulting tuple or add a fixed item, or to swap the items.

Assume that we want to parse the `abc` string, but in the result we want to omit `b`, keeping only `ac`. For that purpose, we must postprocess the result of the parsing in the following way:

```
extern crate nom;
use nom::{character::complete::char, sequence::tuple, IResult};

fn parse_abc_to_ac(input: &str) -> IResult<&str, (char, char)> {
    tuple((char('a'), char('b'), char('c')))(input)
        .map(|(rest, result)| (rest, (result.0, result.2)))
}

fn main() {
    println!("abc: {:?}", parse_abc_to_ac("abc"));
}
```

It will print the following output:

```
abc: Ok(("", ('a', 'c')))
```

Of course, the result of our parser now contains just a pair—(char, char). The postprocessing is seen in the second line of the body. It uses a map function that is not the one seen in the preceding example; it belongs to the Result type. Such a method receives a closure that gets the Ok variant of the result and returns a new Ok variant with the appropriate types. If the type had been made explicit, then that code would have been as follows:

```
.map(|(rest, result): (&str, (char, char, char))|
    -> (&str, (char, char)) {
    (rest, (result.0, result.2))
}
```

From the preceding code, the call to tuple returns a result whose Ok variant has the (&str, (char, char, char)) type. The first element is the remaining input, assigned to the rest variable, and the second element is the sequence of parsed char values, assigned to the result variable.

Then, we must construct a pair with two items—that is, what we want as the *remaining input*, and the pair of characters that we want as a *result*. As a remaining input, we specify the same pair provided by tuple, while as a result, we specify (result.0, result.2)—that is, the first and third parsed characters, which will be 'a' and 'c'.

Some of the following cases are quite typical:

- A sequence of two parsers, needing to keep the result of the first parser and discard the result of the second parser.
- A sequence of two parsers, needing to discard the result of the first parser and keep the result of the second parser.
- A sequence of three parsers, needing to keep the result of the second parser and discard the results of the first and third parsers. This is typical of parenthesized expressions or quoted text.

For these previous cases, the mapping technique can be applied too, but Nom contains some specific combinators, detailed as follows:

- preceded(a, b): This keeps only the result of b.
- terminated(a, b): This keeps only the result of a.
- delimited(a, b, c): This keeps only the result of b.

In the next section, we'll see how to parse a specified number of characters and return the parsed characters.

Parsing a variable text

The parsing we have done so far is of very limited usefulness, as we just checked that the input respected a language, without the possibility of accepting arbitrary text or numbers.

Say we want to parse a text that begins with an n character followed by two other arbitrary characters, and we want to process only the latter two characters. This can be done with the take built-in parser, shown in the following code snippet:

```
extern crate nom;
use nom::{bytes::complete::take, character::complete::char,
sequence::tuple, IResult};

fn parse_variable_text(input: &str)
    -> IResult<&str, (char, &str)> {
    tuple((char('n'), take(2usize)))(input)
}

fn main() {
    println!("nghj: {:?}", parse_variable_text("nghj"));
    println!("xghj: {:?}", parse_variable_text("xghj"));
    println!("ng: {:?}", parse_variable_text("ng"));
}
```

It will print the following output:

```
nghj: Ok(("j", ('n', "gh")))
xghj: Err(Error(("xghj", Char)))
ng: Err(Error(("g", Eof)))
```

The first invocation is a successful one. The n character is skipped by char('n'), and two other characters are read by take(2usize). This parser reads as many characters as specified by its argument (that must be an unsigned number), and it returns this sequence of bytes as a string slice. To read a single character, just call take(1usize), which will return a string slice anyway.

The second invocation fails because the starting n is missing. The third invocation fails because after the starting n, there are fewer than two characters, and so the Eof (short for **End-Of-File**) error is generated.

In the next section, we will see how to parse a sequence of one or more patterns by applying a given parser repeatedly.

Repeating a parser

It is quite common to need to parse a sequence of repeated expressions, each recognized by a parser. So, that parser must be applied several times, until it fails. Such repetition is done by a couple of combinators—namely, many0 and many1.

The former will succeed even if no occurrence of the expression is parsed—that is, it is a zero-or-more combinator. The latter will succeed only if at least one occurrence of the expression is parsed—that is, it is a one-or-more combinator. Let's see how to recognize a sequence of one or more abc strings, as follows:

```
extern crate nom;
use nom::{bytes::complete::take, multi::many1, IResult};

fn repeated_text(input: &str) -> IResult<&str, Vec<&str>> {
    many1(take(3usize))(input)
}

fn main() {
    println!(": {:?}", repeated_text(""));
    println!("ab: {:?}", repeated_text("abc"));
    println!("abcabcabc: {:?}", repeated_text("abcabcabc"));
}
```

It will print the following output:

```
: Err(Error(("", Eof)))
abc: Ok(("", ["abc"]))
abcabcabcx: Ok(("x", ["abc", "abc", "abc"]))
```

The first invocation fails because the empty string does not contain any occurrences of abc. If the many0 combinator had been used, this invocation would have succeeded.

The two other invocations succeed anyway and return a Vec of the occurrences found.

In this section, we have presented the most popular parsing techniques: compiler-compilers and parser combinators. They are useful both to build interpreters and compilers. Then, we introduced the Nom parser combinator library that will be used in the rest of this chapter, and also in part of the next chapter.

Now, we have seen enough of Nom to begin to see the first project of this chapter.

The calc_parser project

This project is a parser of the `Calc` language. It is a program that can examine a string and detect if it respects the syntax of the `Calc` language, using a context-free parser, and, in such cases, extracts the logical structure of such a string, according to the grammar of the language. Such a structure is often named a **syntax tree** as it has the shape of a tree, and it represents the syntax of the parsed text.

A syntax tree is an internal data structure, and so usually it is not to be seen by a user, nor to be exported. For debugging purposes, though, this program will pretty-print this data structure to the console.

The program built by this project expects a `Calc` language file as a command-line argument. In the `data` folder of the project, there are two example programs—namely, `sum.calc` and `bad_sum.calc`.

The first one is `sum.calc`, given as follows:

```
@a
@b
>a
>b
<a+b
```

It declares the two variables `a` and `b`, then it asks the user to enter values for them, and it prints the sum of their value.

The other program, `bad_sum.calc`, is identical to the former, except for the second line—that is, `@d`—representing a typo because later on, the undeclared `b` variable is used.

To run the project on the first example `Calc` program, go into the `calc_parser` folder, and type the following:

```
cargo run data/sum.calc
```

Such a command should print the following text on the console:

```
Parsed program: [
    Declaration(
        "a",
    ),
    Declaration(
        "b",
    ),
    InputOperation(
```

```
        "a",
    ),
    InputOperation(
        "b",
    ),
    OutputOperation(
        (
            (
                Identifier(
                    "a",
                ),
                [],
            ),
            [
                (
                    Add,
                    (
                        Identifier(
                            "b",
                        ),
                        [],
                    ),
                ),
            ],
        ),
    ),
]
```

From the preceding code, first, there is a declaration of the "a" identifier, then of the "b" identifier, then an input operation on a variable named "a", then one on a variable named "b", and then there is an output operation with a lot of parentheses.

The first open parenthesis under OutputOperation represents the beginning of the expression item that, according to the grammar presented previously, must appear in any output operation statement. Such an expression contains two items—a term and a list of operator-term pairs.

The first term contains two items—a factor and a list of operator-factor pairs. The factor is the "a" identifier, and the list of operator-factor pairs is empty. Then, let's pass this to the list of operator-term pairs. It contains just one item, in which the operator is Add, and the term is again a factor followed by a list of operator-factor pairs. The factor is the "b" identifier, and the list is empty.

If the `cargo run data/bad_sum.calc` command runs, no error is detected, as this program only performs a syntax analysis without checking the semantic context. The output is the same, except for the sixth line—that is, "d" instead of "b".

Now, let's examine the source code of the Rust program. The only external crate is **Nom**, a library used just for the lexical and syntax analysis passes (and therefore used by all the projects of this chapter, because all of them need parsing).

There are two source files—`main.rs` and `parser.rs`. Let's look at the `main.rs` source file first.

Understanding the main.rs source file

The `main.rs` source file contains just the `main` function and the `process_file` function. The `main` function just checks if the command line contains an argument and passes it to the `process_file` function, together with the path of the executable Rust program.

The `process_file` function checks that the command-line argument ends with `.calc`—that is, the only expected file type, then it reads the contents of that file into the `source_code` string and parses that string by calling `parser::parse_program(&source_code)`, contained in the `parser.rs` source file.

Such a file is, of course, a parser for the whole program, and so it returns a `Result` value. The `Ok` variant of such a return value is a pair composed of the remaining code and the syntax tree. The syntax tree is then pretty-printed by the statement given as follows:

```
println!("Parsed program: {:#?}", parsed_program);
```

When the small `sum.calc` file, having only five lines and 17 characters, is processed, this single `println!` statement emits the long output shown before, having 35 lines and 604 bytes. Of course, the output is longer for longer programs.

Next, let's look at the `parser.rs` source file.

Learning about the parser.rs source file

The `parser.rs` source file contains a parser function for each syntax element of the grammar of the language. These functions are detailed as follows:

Function	Description
parse_program	This parses a whole `Calc` program.
parse_declaration	This parses a `Calc` declaration statement, such as @total.
parse_input_statement	This parses a `Calc` input statement, such as >addend.
parse_output_statement	This parses a `Calc` output statement, such as <total.
parse_assignment	This parses a `Calc` assignment statement, such as total := addend * 2.
parse_expr	This parses a `Calc` expression, such as addend * 2 + val / (incr + 1).
parse_term	This parses a `Calc` term, such as val / (incr + 1).
parse_factor	This parses a `Calc` factor, such as incr, or 4.56e12, or (incr + 1).
parse_subexpr	This parses a `Calc` parenthesized expression, such as (incr + 1).
parse_identifier	This parses a `Calc` identifier, such as addend.
skip_spaces	This parses a sequence of zero or more white spaces.

P231

With respect to the grammar previously declared, some explanation is due—the `parse_subexpr` parser has the task to parse the (<expr>) sequence, discarding the parentheses and parsing the <expr> initial expression using `parse_expr`.
The `skip_spaces` function is a parser whose task is to parse zero or more white spaces (spaces, tabs, newline characters), with the purpose of ignoring them.

All the other preceding functions, in the case of success, return a data structure representing the parsed code.

There is no parser for literal numbers, as the built-in `double` parser will be used to parse floating-point numbers.

Understanding the types needed by the parser

In this file, in addition to the parsers, several types are defined to represent the structure of the parsed program. The most important type is defined as follows:

```
type ParsedProgram<'a> = Vec<ParsedStatement<'a>>;
```

The preceding code snippet just says that a parsed program is a vector of parsed statements.

Notice the lifetime specification. To keep the best performance, memory allocation is minimized. Of course, vectors are allocated, but the parsed string is not allocated; they are string slices referencing the input string. Therefore, the syntax tree is dependent on the input string, and its lifetime must be shorter than that of the input string.

The preceding declaration uses the `ParsedStatement` type, which is declared in the following way:

```
enum ParsedStatement<'a> {
    Declaration(&'a str),
    InputOperation(&'a str),
    OutputOperation(ParsedExpr<'a>),
    Assignment(&'a str, ParsedExpr<'a>),
}
```

The preceding code snippet says that a parsed statement can be one of the following:

- A declaration encapsulating the name of the variable that is being declared
- An input statement encapsulating the name of the variable that is going to receive an input value
- An output operation encapsulating a parsed expression whose value is going to be printed
- An assignment encapsulating the name of the variable that is going to receive a calculated value and a parsed expression, whose value is going to be assigned to the variable

This declaration uses the `ParsedExpr` type, which is declared as follows:

```
type ParsedExpr<'a> = (ParsedTerm<'a>, Vec<(ExprOperator,
ParsedTerm<'a>)>);
```

From the preceding code snippet, a parsed expression is a pair composed of a parsed term and zero or more pairs, with each pair composed of an expression operator and a parsed term.

An expression operator is defined as `enum ExprOperator { Add, Subtract }`, while a parsed term is defined as follows:

```
type ParsedTerm<'a> = (ParsedFactor<'a>, Vec<(TermOperator,
ParsedFactor<'a>)>);
```

We can see that a parsed term is a pair composed of a parsed factor and zero or more pairs, with each pair composed of a term operator and a parsed factor. A term operator is defined as `enum TermOperator { Multiply, Divide }`, while a parsed factor is defined as follows:

```
enum ParsedFactor<'a> {
    Literal(f64),
    Identifier(&'a str),
    SubExpression(Box<ParsedExpr<'a>>),
}
```

This declaration says that a parsed factor can be a literal encapsulating a number, or an identifier encapsulating the name of that variable, or a subexpression encapsulating a parsed expression.

Notice the use of `Box`. This is required because any parsed expression contains a parsed term that contains a parsed factor of an `enum` capable of containing a parsed expression. And so, we have an endless recursion of containment. If we use a `Box`, we allocate memory out of the main structure.

So, we have seen all the definitions of the types that will be used by the parser code. Now, let's see the code, in a top-down fashion.

Looking at the parser code

We can now see the code used to parse a whole program. The following code snippet shows the entry point of the parser:

```
pub fn parse_program(input: &str) -> IResult<&str, ParsedProgram> {
    many0(preceded(
        skip_spaces,
        alt((
            parse_declaration,
            parse_input_statement,
            parse_output_statement,
            parse_assignment,
        )),
    ))(input)
}
```

Notice that its result type is `ParsedProgram`, which is a vector of parsed statements.

The body uses the `many0` parser combinator to accept zero or more statements (an empty program is considered valid). Actually, to parse a statement, the `preceded` combinator is used, to combine two parsers and discard the output of the first one. Its first argument is the `skip_spaces` parser, and so it simply skips possible spaces between statements. The second argument is the `alt` combinator, to accept alternatively one of the four possible statements.

The `many0` combinator generates a vector of objects, with such objects generated by the argument of the combinator. Such arguments generate parsed statements, and so we have the needed vector of parsed statements.

So, to summarize, this function accepts zero or more statements, possibly separated by white spaces. The accepted statements can be declarations, input statements, output statements, or assignments. The value returned by the function in the case of success is a vector whose elements are representations of the parsed statements.

The parser of `Calc` declarations is given as follows:

```
fn parse_declaration(input: &str) -> IResult<&str, ParsedStatement> {
    tuple((char('@'), skip_spaces, parse_identifier))(input)
        .map(|(input, output)| (input,
    ParsedStatement::Declaration(output.2)))
}
```

From the preceding code snippet, a declaration must be a sequence of the @ character, optional spaces, and an identifier; so, the `tuple` combinator is used to chain such parsers. However, we are not interested in that initial character nor in those white spaces. We want just the text of the identifier, encapsulated in `ParsedStatement`.

Therefore, after applying the `tuple`, the result is mapped to a `Declaration` object whose argument is the third item generated by the `tuple`.

The following code snippet shows the parser of a `Calc` input statement:

```
fn parse_input_statement(input: &str) -> IResult<&str, ParsedStatement> {
    tuple((char('>'), skip_spaces, parse_identifier))(input)
        .map(|(input, output)| (input,
    ParsedStatement::InputOperation(output.2)))
}
```

The parser of a `Calc` input statement is quite similar to the preceding parser. It just looks for the > character and returns an `InputOperation` variant that encapsulates the string returned by `parse_identifier`.

The following code snippet shows the parser of a `Calc` output statement:

```
fn parse_output_statement(input: &str) -> IResult<&str, ParsedStatement> {
    tuple((char('<'), skip_spaces, parse_expr))(input)
        .map(|(input, output)| (input,
ParsedStatement::OutputOperation(output.2)))
}
```

Also, the parser from the preceding code is similar to the two preceding parsers. It just looks for the < character, parses an expression instead of an identifier, and returns an `OutputOperation` that encapsulates the parsed expression returned by `parse_expr`.

The last kind of `Calc` statement is an assignment. Its parser is shown in the following code snippet:

```
fn parse_assignment(input: &str) -> IResult<&str, ParsedStatement> {
    tuple((
        parse_identifier,
        skip_spaces,
        tag(":="),
        skip_spaces,
        parse_expr,
    ))(input)
        .map(|(input, output)| (input, ParsedStatement::Assignment(output.0,
output.4)))
}
```

This is somewhat different from the preceding statement's parsers. It chains five parsers—for an identifier, some possible spaces, the := string, some possible spaces, and an expression. The result is an `Assignment` variant that encapsulates the first and the last parsed items of the tuple—that is, the identifier string and the parsed expression.

We have encountered the use of the expression parser, which is defined as follows:

```
fn parse_expr(input: &str) -> IResult<&str, ParsedExpr> {
    tuple((
        parse_term,
        many0(tuple((
            preceded(
                skip_spaces,
                alt((
                    map(char('+'), |_| ExprOperator::Add),
                    map(char('-'), |_| ExprOperator::Subtract),
                )),
            ),
            parse_term,
        ))),
```

```
    )) (input)
}
```

From the preceding code, to parse an expression, a term must first be parsed
(`parse_term`), and then zero or more (`many0`) pairs (`tuple`) of an operator and a term
(`parse_term`). The operator can be preceded by white spaces (`skip_spaces`) that must be
discarded (`preceded`), and it can be alternatively (`alt`) a plus character (`char('+')`) or a
minus character (`char('-')`). But we want to replace (`map`) such characters with
the `ExprOperator` values. The resulting object already has the expected type, and so no
other `map` transformation is needed.

The parser of a term is similar to the parser of an expression. Here it is:

```
fn parse_term(input: &str) -> IResult<&str, ParsedTerm> {
    tuple((
        parse_factor,
        many0(tuple((
            preceded(
                skip_spaces,
                alt((
                    map(char('*'), |_| TermOperator::Multiply),
                    map(char('/'), |_| TermOperator::Divide),
                )),
            ),
            parse_factor,
        ))),
    )) (input)
}
```

The only differences between `parse_expr` and `parse_term` are the following ones:

- Where `parse_expr` calls `parse_term`, `parse_term` calls `parse_factor`.
- Where `parse_expr` maps the `'+'` character to the `ExprOperator::Add` value,
  and the `'-'` character to the `ExprOperator::Subtract` value, `parse_term`
  maps the `'*'` character to the `TermOperator::Multiply` value,
  and the `'/'` character to the `TermOperator::Divide` value.
- Where `parse_expr` has a `ParsedExpr` type in the return value type,
  `parse_term` has a `ParsedTerm` type.

The parser of a factor again follows the relative grammar rule, and the definition of its
return type, `ParsedFactor`, as illustrated in the following code snippet:

```
fn parse_factor(input: &str) -> IResult<&str, ParsedFactor> {
    preceded(
        skip_spaces,
```

```
        alt((
            map(parse_identifier, ParsedFactor::Identifier),
            map(double, ParsedFactor::Literal),
            map(parse_subexpr, |expr|
                ParsedFactor::SubExpression(Box::new(expr))
            ),
        )),
    )(input)
}
```

This parser discards possible initial spaces and then parses alternatively an identifier, a number, or a subexpression. The parser of the number is `double`, a Nom built-in function that parses numbers according to the syntax of Rust `f64` literals.

All the returned types of these parses are wrong, so, the `map` combinator is used to generate their return value. For identifiers, it is enough to cite the `Identifier` variant that will be constructed automatically using as an argument the value returned by the `parse_identifier` function. An equivalent and more verbose code would be `map(parse_identifier, |id| ParsedFactor::Identifier(id))`.

Similarly, literals are converted from the `f64` type to the `ParsedFactor::Literal(f64)` type, and subexpressions are boxed and encapsulated in a `SubExpression` variant.

The parse of the subexpression must just match and discard spaces and parentheses, shown in the following code snippet:

```
fn parse_subexpr(input: &str) -> IResult<&str, ParsedExpr> {
    delimited(
        preceded(skip_spaces, char('(')),
        parse_expr,
        preceded(skip_spaces, char(')')),
    )(input)
```

The inner `parse_expr` parser is the only one that passes its output to the result. To parse an identifier, a built-in parser is used, shown as follows:

```
fn parse_identifier(input: &str) -> IResult<&str, &str> {
    alpha1(input)
}
```

The `alpha1` parser returns a string of one or more letters. Digits and other characters are not allowed. Usually, this would not be named *parser*, but lexical analyzer, or lexer, or scanner, or tokenizer, but Nom makes no distinction.

And lastly, the small parser (or lexer) to process spaces is shown as follows:

```
fn skip_spaces(input: &str) -> IResult<&str, &str> {
    let chars = " \t\r\n";
    take_while(move |ch| chars.contains(ch))(input)
}
```

It uses a combinator we have not yet seen—`take_while`. It receives as argument a closure returning a Boolean (that is, predicate). Such a closure is invoked on any input character. If the closure returns `true`, the parser goes on or otherwise stops. So, it returns the maximum sequence of input characters for which the predicate value is *true*.

In our case, the predicate checks whether the character is contained in a slice of four characters.

So, we have seen all our parsers for the `Calc` language. Of course, real-world parsers are much more complex, but the concepts are the same.

In this section, we have seen how the Nom library can be used to parse a program written in the `Calc` language, using a CFG. This is preliminary to applying a **context-sensitive grammar (CSG)**, and then an interpreter or a compiler.

Notice that this program parser considers any sequence of characters to be a valid identifier, without checking whether a variable is defined before being used, or whether a variable is not defined several times. For such checks, further processing must be performed. This will be seen in the next project.

The calc_analyzer project

The preceding project followed a CFG to construct a parser. This is very nice, but there is a big problem: the `Calc` language is not context-free. In fact, there are two problems, as follows:

- Any use of a variable in input statements, output statements, and assignments must be preceded by a declaration of that variable.
- Any variable must not be declared more than once.

Such requirements cannot be expressed in a context-free language.

In addition, `Calc` has just one data type—that is, floating-point numbers—but consider if it also had a string type. You can add subtract two numbers, but you cannot subtract two strings. If a variable named `a` is declared of type `number` and a variable named `b` is declared of type `string`, you cannot assign `a` to `b`, or vice versa.

In general, the operations allowed on a variable depend on the type used to declare that variable. And also, this constraint cannot be expressed in a CFG.

Instead of defining a formal **context-dependent grammar** (**CDG**) that would be hard to specify and to parse, the usual path is to define such rules, called *semantic* rules, in an informal way, and then to postprocess the syntax tree to check the validity of such rules.

Here, we will call the module that performs such semantic checks `analyzer` (using a semantic checker that verifies some constraints on variables, such as the fact that they must be defined before being used, and the fact that variables cannot be defined more than once), and `calc_analyzer` is the project that adds the module to the parser.

In the next section, we will see the architecture of the `analyzer` module.

Checking the variables of the parsed program

The analyzer starts where the parser finished—with a syntax tree containing strings of identifiers, values of literals, and operators. So, it no longer needs the source code. To accomplish its task, it visits such a tree and, every time it encounters a variable declaration, it must ensure that it has not been declared already, while every time it encounters a variable use, it must ensure it has already been declared.

To perform such tasks without wandering around the syntax tree, another data structure is needed. Such a data structure is a collection of the variables already declared so far, while the syntax tree is visited. When a variable declaration is encountered, the analyzer looks in such a collection for a preceding declaration of the same variable; if it is found, it is a double-declaration error; otherwise, an entry is added to the collection.

Also, when a variable use is encountered, the analyzer looks in such a collection for a preceding declaration of the same variable, though this time, if it is not found, it is a missing-declaration error. For our simple language, such a collection contains only variables, but in more complex languages it will contain any kind of identifiers—constants, functions, namespaces, and so on. An alternative name for the identifier is a **symbol**; so, usually, this collection is named **symbol table**.

To perform variable checking of a `Calc` program, our symbol table just needs to store the names of the variables, although we want our analyzer to perform some other tasks, which will be useful if we want to build an interpreter. An interpreter, when it is running a program, must store the *values* of the identifiers somewhere, not only their name, and as we already have a collection of variables storing the name of each variable, we can reserve space in the entry of a variable for the value of each variable. This will be useful when we build an interpreter for `Calc`.

But that is more than what we can do in the analyzer, in preparation of an interpreter. The interpreter must scan a kind of syntax tree to execute the statements, and when it encounters a variable it must look for its value. The syntax tree generated by the parser contains the identifiers of the variables, not their values, so the interpreter, every time it finds a variable, should search the symbol table for that string.

But we want a fast interpreter, and string lookup is not so fast as using a pointer or an index into an array. So, to prepare for fast interpretation, while the analyzer visits the syntax tree, it replaces every identifier with an index of its position in the symbol table. Well, a string cannot be replaced by a number in Rust, so one possible technique would be to reserve an index field in the syntax tree, and fill that index when the variable is found in the symbol table.

Here, another technique has been chosen. The analyzer, while visiting the syntax tree, constructs a parallel analyzed tree, very similar in structure, but having indexes into the symbol table instead of identifiers. Such a tree, together with the symbol table that reserves space for the values of the variables, will be optimal for interpreting the program.

So, first of all, let's see what is done by this project. Open the `calc_analyzer` folder and type the following: `cargo run data/sum.calc`.

The following output should appear on the console:

```
Symbol table: SymbolTable {
    entries: [
        (
            "a",
            0.0,
        ),
        (
            "b",
            0.0,
        ),
    ],
}
Analyzed program: [
    Declaration(
```

```
        0,
    ),
    Declaration(
        1,
    ),
    InputOperation(
        0,
    ),
    InputOperation(
        1,
    ),
    OutputOperation(
        (
            (
                Identifier(
                    0,
                ),
                [],
            ),
            [
                (
                    Add,
                    (
                        Identifier(
                            1,
                        ),
                        [],
                    ),
                ),
            ],
        ),
    ),
]
```

The preceding code program, as with the one before that, does not have an output for the user. It parses the source code into a syntax tree, and then analyzes that syntax tree, constructing a symbol table and an analyzed program. The output is just the pretty-print of such data structures.

The first structure dumped is the symbol table. It has two entries—the a variable, with 0.0 as its initial value, and the b variable, with 0.0 as its initial value.

Then, there is the analyzed program that is very similar to the parsed program printed by the previous project. The only differences are that all the occurrences of "a" are replaced by 0, and all the occurrences of "b" are replaced by 1. These numbers are the positions of such variables inside the symbol table.

The project extends the preceding project. The `parser.rs` source file is identical, and two other files are added—`symbol_table.rs` and `analyzer.rs`. But let's start with the `main.rs` file first.

Understanding the main.rs file

This file performs all that is done by the preceding project, except the final pretty-print, which is replaced by the following lines:

```
let analyzed_program;
let mut variables = symbol_table::SymbolTable::new();
match analyzer::analyze_program(&mut variables, &parsed_program) {
    Ok(analyzed_tree) => {
        analyzed_program = analyzed_tree;
    }
    Err(err) => {
        eprintln!("Invalid code in '{}': {}", source_path, err);
        return;
    }
}

println!("Symbol table: {:#?}", variables);
println!("Analyzed program: {:#?}", analyzed_program);
```

(handwritten annotations: "symtable" over variables, "sym Tree" over parsed_program)

From the preceding code snippet, the two data structures constructed by the analyzer are first declared—`analyzed_program` is the syntax tree with the indexes to the variables, and `variables` is the symbol table.

All the analysis is performed by the `analyze_program` function. If it succeeds, it will return the analyzed program, and, in the end, the two structures are printed.

Now, let's examine the symbol table (`symbol_table.rs`) implementation.

Looking at the symbol_table.rs file

In the `symbol_table.rs` file, there is an implementation of the `SymbolTable` type, which is a collection of the identifiers found in the source code. Each entry of a symbol table describes a variable. Such an entry must contain at least the name of the variable. In a typed language, it must also contain a representation of the data type of that variable, though `Calc` doesn't need that, as it has only one data type.

If the language supports scoping in blocks, functions, classes, or larger structures (compilation units, modules, namespaces, or packages), there must be several symbol tables or a symbol table that specifies such scoping, though `Calc` doesn't need that, as it has only one scope.

A symbol table is useful primarily for checking identifiers and for translating code into another language, although it can also be used for interpreting code. When an interpreter is evaluating an expression, it needs to get the current value of the variables used in such an expression. A symbol table can be used to store the current value of any variable and provide such values to the interpreter. So, if you want to support an interpreter, your symbol table should also reserve space for the current values of the defined variables.

In the next project, we will create an interpreter, and so, to support it, here, we add to any entry of our symbol table a field where the current value of the variable is stored. The type of each entry of our symbol table will be `(String, f64)`, where the first field is the name of the variable, and the second one is the current value of the variable. This value field will be accessed when interpreting a program.

How can our code access the entries of a symbol table? When analyzing the program, we must search for a string, and so a hash table would offer top performance. However, when interpreting the code, we can replace identifiers with indexes, and so using indexes into a vector would offer top performance. Here, for simplicity, a vector has been chosen, which anyway is good enough if there aren't many variables. So, our definition is given as follows:

```
struct SymbolTable {
    entries: Vec<(String, f64)>,
}
```

For the `SymbolTable` type, three methods are implemented, as shown in the following code snippet:

```
fn new() -> SymbolTable
fn insert_symbol(&mut self, identifier: &str) -> Result<usize, String>
fn find_symbol(&self, identifier: &str) -> Result<usize, String>
```

The `new` method simply creates an empty symbol table.

The `insert_symbol` method tries to insert the specified identifier into a symbol table. If there is no identifier with such a name, an entry is added for that name, with zero as the default value, and the `Ok` result is the index of the new entry. Otherwise, the `Error: Identifier '{}' declared several times.` message is returned in the `Err` result.

The `find_symbol` method tries to find the specified identifier in the symbol table. If it is found, the `Ok` result is the index of the found entry. Otherwise, the `Error: Identifier '{}' used before having been declared.` error message is returned in the `Err` result.

Now, let's see the analyzer source file.

Glancing at the analyzer.rs file

As discussed before, the analysis phase reads the hierarchical structure created by the parsing phase and constructs another hierarchical structure, having the `AnalyzedProgram` type. So, this module must declare such a `type` and all the types it needs, paralleling the `ParsedProgram` type, as follows:

```
type AnalyzedProgram = Vec<AnalyzedStatement>;
```

Any analyzed program is a sequence of analyzed statements, as illustrated in the following code snippet:

```
enum AnalyzedStatement {
    Declaration(usize),
    InputOperation(usize),
    OutputOperation(AnalyzedExpr),
    Assignment(usize, AnalyzedExpr),
}
```

Any analyzed statement is any one of the following:

- A declaration referring a variable by index
- An input operation referring a variable by index
- An output operation containing an analyzed expression
- An assignment referring a variable by index and containing an analyzed expression

Any analyzed expression is a pair of an analyzed term and a sequence of zero or more pairs of an expression operator and an analyzed term, as illustrated in the following code snippet:

```
type AnalyzedExpr = (AnalyzedTerm, Vec<(ExprOperator, AnalyzedTerm)>);
```

Any analyzed term is a pair of an analyzed factor and a sequence of zero or more pairs of a term operator and an analyzed factor, as illustrated in the following code snippet:

```
type AnalyzedTerm = (AnalyzedFactor, Vec<(TermOperator, AnalyzedFactor)>);
```

Any analyzed factor is a literal containing a 64-bit floating-point number, or an identifier referring a variable by index, or a subexpression containing a reference to a heap-allocated analyzed expression, as illustrated in the following code snippet:

```
pub enum AnalyzedFactor {
Literal(f64),
Identifier(usize),
SubExpression(Box<AnalyzedExpr>),
}
```

The entry point of the analyzer is shown in the following code snippet:

```
fn analyze_program(variables: &mut SymbolTable, parsed_program:
&ParsedProgram)                                    table           as tree
    -> Result<AnalyzedProgram, String> {
    let mut analyzed_program = AnalyzedProgram::new();
    for statement in parsed_program {
        analyzed_program.push(analyze_statement(variables, statement)?);
    }
    Ok(analyzed_program)
}
```

The `analyze_program` function, as with all the functions of this module, gets a mutable reference to the symbol table, as they all must, directly or indirectly read and write symbols. In addition, it gets a reference to a parsed program. If the function is successful, it updates the symbol table and it returns an analyzed program; otherwise, it may leave partially updated the symbol table and return an error message.

The body simply creates an empty analyzed program and processes all the parsed statements, by calling `analyze_statement`. Any parsed statement is analyzed, and the resulting analyzed statement is added to the analyzed program. For any failing analysis of a statement, the generated error is returned immediately as an error of this function.

So, we need to know how to analyze statements, which is shown as follows:

```
fn analyze_statement(
    variables: &mut SymbolTable,
    parsed_statement: &ParsedStatement,
) -> Result<AnalyzedStatement, String> {
    match parsed_statement {
        ParsedStatement::Assignment(identifier, expr) => {
            let handle = variables.find_symbol(identifier)?;
```

```
        let analyzed_expr = analyze_expr(variables, expr)?;
        Ok(AnalyzedStatement::Assignment(handle, analyzed_expr))
    }
    ParsedStatement::Declaration(identifier) => {
        let handle = variables.insert_symbol(identifier)?;
        Ok(AnalyzedStatement::Declaration(handle))
    }
    ParsedStatement::InputOperation(identifier) => {
        let handle = variables.find_symbol(identifier)?;
        Ok(AnalyzedStatement::InputOperation(handle))
    }
    ParsedStatement::OutputOperation(expr) => {
        let analyzed_expr = analyze_expr(variables, expr)?;
        Ok(AnalyzedStatement::OutputOperation(analyzed_expr))
    }
  }
}
```

The `analyze_statement` function matches the received parsed statements against the four kinds of statements, extracting the member of the respective variants.

The identifier contained in declarations should never have been defined, and so it should be absent from the symbol table. Therefore, when processing this kind of statement, this identifier is inserted in the symbol table using the `let handle = variables.insert_symbol(identifier)?` Rust statement. If the insertion fails, the error is propagated out of this function. If the insertion succeeds, the position of the symbol is stored in a local variable.

The identifier contained in assignments and in the input operations should have already been defined, and so it should be contained in the symbol table. Therefore, when processing this kind of statement, the identifiers are looked up in the symbol table using the `let handle = variables.find_symbol(identifier)?` Rust statement.

The expressions contained in assignments and in output operations are analyzed by the `let analyzed_expr = analyze_expr(variables, expr)?` Rust statement. If the analysis fails, the error is propagated out of this function. If the analysis succeeds, the resulting analyzed expression is stored in a local variable.

For any of the four `Calc` statement kinds, if no errors have been encountered, the function returns a success result containing the respective analyzed statement variant.

So, we need to know how to analyze expressions, shown as follows:

```
fn analyze_expr(
    variables: &mut SymbolTable,
    parsed_expr: &ParsedExpr,
```

```
) -> Result<AnalyzedExpr, String> {
    let first_term = analyze_term(variables, &parsed_expr.0)?;
    let mut other_terms = Vec::<(ExprOperator, AnalyzedTerm)>::new();
    for term in &parsed_expr.1 {
        other_terms.push((term.0, analyze_term(variables, &term.1)?));
    }
    Ok((first_term, other_terms))
}
```

The received parsed expression is a pair—`&parsed_expr.0` is a parsed term and `&parsed_expr.1` is a vector of pairs of an expression operator and an analyzed term. We want to construct an analyzed expression that has the same structure.

So, first, the first term is analyzed. Then, an empty list of pairs of an expression operator and an analyzed term is created; this is the analyzed vector. Then, for each item of the parsed vector, an item is constructed and added to the analyzed vector. Lastly, the pair of the first analyzed term and the vector of the other analyzed terms are returned.

So, we need to know how to analyze terms, through the following code:

```
fn analyze_term(
    variables: &mut SymbolTable,
    parsed_term: &ParsedTerm,
) -> Result<AnalyzedTerm, String> {
    let first_factor = analyze_factor(variables, &parsed_term.0)?;
    let mut other_factors = Vec::<(TermOperator, AnalyzedFactor)>::new();
    for factor in &parsed_term.1 {
        other_factors.push((factor.0, analyze_factor(variables,
        &factor.1)?));
    }
    Ok((first_factor, other_factors))
}
```

The preceding routine is quite similar to the one before that. The first parsed factor is analyzed to get the first analyzed factor, and the other parsed factors are analyzed to get the other analyzed factors.

So, we need to know how to analyze factors. This is shown as follows:

```
fn analyze_factor(
    variables: &mut SymbolTable,
    parsed_factor: &ParsedFactor,
) -> Result<AnalyzedFactor, String> {
    match parsed_factor {
        ParsedFactor::Literal(value) =>
            Ok(AnalyzedFactor::Literal(*value)),       usize        P253
        ParsedFactor::Identifier(name) => {
```

```
                Ok(AnalyzedFactor::Identifier(variables.find_symbol(name)?))
            }
        ParsedFactor::SubExpression(expr) =>
         Ok(AnalyzedFactor::SubExpression(
            Box::<AnalyzedExpr>::new(analyze_expr(variables, expr)?),
        )),
    }
}
```

The logic of the `analyze_factor` function is this:

- If the parsed factor to analyze is a literal, an analyzed literal is returned, containing the same value.
- If it is an identifier, an analyzed identifier is returned, containing the index into the symbol table where the parsed identifier is found. If it is not found, an error is returned.
- If the parsed factor to analyze is a subexpression, a subexpression is returned, containing a boxed analyzed expression, obtained by analyzing the parsed expression, if successful. If it fails, an error is returned.

So, we have completed the examination of the analyzer module.

In this section, we have seen how the result of the parser created in the previous section can be analyzed, applying a CSG, which is needed to build an interpreter or a compiler. The next project will show us how to use and execute an analyzed program.

The calc_interpreter project

At last, we have reached the project in which we can actually run our `Calc` programs.

To run it, enter the `calc_interpreter` folder, and type `cargo run`. After compilation, the following text will appear on the console:

```
* Calc interactive interpreter *
>
```

The first line is an introduction message, and the second one is a prompt. Now, we type the following as an example:

```
@a >a @b b := a + 2 <b
```

After you press *Enter*, this `Calc` program is executed. The `a` variable is declared, and when the input statement is executed, a question mark will appear on the console. Type 5 and press *Enter*.

The program goes on by declaring the `b` variable, assigning to it the value of the `a` + 2 expression, and then printing 7 as the value of `b`. Then, the program finishes, and the prompt reappears.

So, on the screen, there will be the following:

```
* Calc interactive interpreter *
> @a >a @b b := a + 2 <b
? 5
7
>
```

The interpreter, in addition, has some specific commands to be able to run `Calc` programs. If instead of a command, you type `v` (for *variables*) and then *Enter*, you will see the following:

```
> v
Variables:
  a: 5
  b: 7
>
```

This command has dumped the contents of the symbol table, showing all the variables declared so far, with their current value. Now, you can type other `Calc` commands, using such variables with their current values.

Another interpreter command is `c` (for clear variables), which empties the symbol table. The last one is `q` (for quit), which terminates the interpreter.

And how are `Calc` commands executed? If you have an analyzed program tree, and the associated symbol table containing space for the value of the variables, it is quite easy. It is enough to apply semantics (that is, a behavior) to any analyzed element, and the program will run by itself.

Also, this project extends the previous project. The `parser.rs` and `analyzer.rs` source files are identical; some lines are added to the `symbol_table.rs` file, and one other file is added—`executor.rs`. But let's start with the `main.rs` file.

Learning about the main.rs file

This file contains two functions in addition to the `main` functions—`run_interpreter` and `input_command`.

The `main` function just calls `run_interpreter`, as that is the purpose of an interpreter. This function has the following structure:

```
fn run_interpreter() {
    eprintln!("* Calc interactive interpreter *");
    let mut variables = symbol_table::SymbolTable::new();
    loop {
        let command = input_command();
        if command.len() == 0 {
            break;
        }
        <<process interpreter commands>>
        <<parse, analyze, and execute the commands>>
    }
}
```

After printing an introduction message and creating a symbol table, the function enters an endless loop.

The first statement of the loop is a call to the `input_command` function, which reads a command from the console (or from a file or a pipe, if the standard input is redirected). Then, if EOF has been reached, the loop is exited, and so is the whole program.

Otherwise, the interpreter-specific commands are handled, and if in the input text there is no such command, it is handled like a `Calc` program by parsing it and then analyzing the parsed program, and then executing the analyzed program.

The following code block shows how interpreter commands are implemented:

```
match command.trim() {
    "q" => break,
    "c" => {
        variables = symbol_table::SymbolTable::new();
        eprintln!("Cleared variables.");
    }
    "v" => {
        eprintln!("Variables:");
        for v in variables.iter() {
            eprintln!("  {}: {}", v.0, v.1);
        }
    }
```

A q (quit) command simply breaks out from the loop. A c (clear) command replaces the symbol table with a new one. A v (variables) command iterates the symbol table entries, and prints the name and the current value of each of them.

If the input text is not one of such one-letter commands, it is treated by the following code:

```
trimmed_command => match parser::parse_program(&trimmed_command) {
    Ok((rest, parsed_program)) => {
        if rest.len() > 0 {
            eprintln!("Unparsed input: `{}`.", rest)
        } else {
            match analyzer::analyze_program(&mut variables,
                &parsed_program) {
                Ok(analyzed_program) => {
                    executor::execute_program(&mut variables,
                        &analyzed_program)
                }
                Err(err) => eprintln!("Error: {}", err),
            }
        }
    }
    Err(err) => eprintln!("Error: {:?}", err),
},
```

The parser::parse_program function, if successful, creates a parsed program object. In the case of an error or in the case that some input remains to be parsed, an error message is printed and the command is discarded.

Otherwise, analyzer::analyze_program uses such a parsed program to create, if successful, an analyzed program object. In the case of error, an error message is printed and the command is discarded.

Lastly, the analyzed program is executed by the call to executor::execute_program. Now, let's see what has changed in the symbol_table.rs file.

Glancing at the symbol_table.rs file

Three functions having the following signatures have been added to the implementation of the SymbolTable type:

```
pub fn get_value(&self, handle: usize) -> f64
pub fn set_value(&mut self, handle: usize, value: f64)
pub fn iter(&self) -> std::slice::Iter<(String, f64)>
```

The `get_value` function gets the value of a variable, given its index. The `set_value` function sets the value of a variable, given its index and the value to assign. The `iter` function returns a read-only iterator on the variables stored in the symbol table. For each variable, a pair of the name and the value is returned.

And next, we see the module that implements the core of the interpreter.

Understanding the executor.rs file

This module does not declare types as it uses only the ones declared in the other modules. The entry point is the function capable of executing whole programs, shown as follows:

```
pub fn execute_program(variables: &mut SymbolTable, program:
&AnalyzedProgram) {
    for statement in program {
        execute_statement(variables, statement);
    }
}
```

It receives a mutable reference to a symbol table and a reference to an analyzed program, and simply calls the `execute_statement` function on any statement of that program.

The following code block shows the last function (this is more complex):

```
fn execute_statement(variables: &mut SymbolTable, statement:
&AnalyzedStatement) {
    match statement {
        AnalyzedStatement::Assignment(handle, expr) => {
            variables.set_value(*handle, evaluate_expr(variables, expr));
        }
        AnalyzedStatement::Declaration(handle) => {}
        AnalyzedStatement::InputOperation(handle) => {
            let mut text = String::new();
            eprint!("? ");
            std::io::stdin()
                .read_line(&mut text)
                .expect("Cannot read line.");
            let value = text.trim().parse::<f64>().unwrap_or(0.);
            variables.set_value(*handle, value);
        }
        AnalyzedStatement::OutputOperation(expr) => {
            println!("{}", evaluate_expr(variables, expr));
        }
    }
}
```

According to the kind of statement being used, it performs different actions. For assignments, it calls the `evaluate_expr` function to get the value of the associated expression and uses `set_value` to assign that value to the associated variable.

For declarations, nothing needs to be done, because the insertion of the variable into the symbol table and its initialization has already been done by the analyzer.

For input operations, a question mark is printed as a prompt, and a line is read and parsed to an `f64` number. If the conversion fails, zero is used. The value is then stored into the symbol table as a new value of the variable.

For output operations, the expression is evaluated and the resulting value is printed. The following code shows how to evaluate `Calc` expressions:

```
fn evaluate_expr(variables: &SymbolTable, expr: &AnalyzedExpr) -> f64 {
    let mut result = evaluate_term(variables, &expr.0);
    for term in &expr.1 {
        match term.0 {
            ExprOperator::Add => result += evaluate_term(variables,
                &term.1),
            ExprOperator::Subtract => result -= evaluate_term(variables,
                &term.1),
        }
    }
    result
}
```

First, the first term is evaluated by calling the `evaluate_term` function, and its value is stored as a provisional result.

Then, for every other term, the term is evaluated and the obtained value is added or subtracted to the provisional result, according to the kind of expression operator being used.

The following code block shows how to evaluate `Calc` terms:

```
fn evaluate_term(variables: &SymbolTable, term: &AnalyzedTerm) -> f64 {
    let mut result = evaluate_factor(variables, &term.0);
    for factor in &term.1 {
        match factor.0 {
            TermOperator::Multiply => result *= evaluate_factor(
                variables, &factor.1),
            TermOperator::Divide => result /= evaluate_factor(
                variables, &factor.1),
        }
    }
}
```

```
        result
    }
```

The preceding code block shows a function that is similar to the one before it. It uses the `evaluate_factor` function to evaluate all the factors of the current term, as illustrated in the following code snippet:

```
fn evaluate_factor(variables: &SymbolTable, factor: &AnalyzedFactor) -> f64
{
    match factor {
        AnalyzedFactor::Literal(value) => *value,
        AnalyzedFactor::Identifier(handle) => variables.get_value(*handle),
        AnalyzedFactor::SubExpression(expr) => evaluate_expr(variables,
expr),
    }
}
```

To evaluate a factor, the *kind of factor* is taken into account. The value of `literal` is just the contained value. The value of `identifier` is obtained for the symbol table, by calling `get_value`.

The value of `SubExpression` is obtained by evaluating the expression contained in it. So, we have seen all that is needed to execute a `Calc` program interactively.

In this section, we have seen how the result of the context-sensitive analysis of a `Calc` program can be used to interpret that program. Such an interpretation can be interactive, through a **read-eval-print loop** (REPL) or by processing a file written in the `Calc` language.

In the next project, we will see how to translate a `Calc` program into a Rust program.

The calc_compiler project

Having an analyzed program (and its matching symbol table), it is easy also to create a program that translates it into another language. To avoid introducing a new language, the Rust language has been used here as a target language, but translating to other high-level languages would be no more difficult.

To run it, go into the `calc_compiler` folder and type `cargo run data/sum.calc`. After compiling the project, the program will print the following:

```
Compiled data/sum.calc to data/sum.rs
```

If you go into the `data` subfolder, you will find the new `sum.rs` file, containing the following code:

```
use std::io::Write;

#[allow(dead_code)]
fn input() -> f64 {
    let mut text = String::new();
    eprint!("? ");
    std::io::stderr().flush().unwrap();
    std::io::stdin()
        .read_line(&mut text)
        .expect("Cannot read line.");
    text.trim().parse::<f64>().unwrap_or(0.)
}

fn main() {
    let mut _a = 0.0;
    let mut _b = 0.0;
    _a = input();
    _b = input();
    println!("{}", _a + _b);
}
```

If you like, you can compile it using the `rustc sum.rs` command, and then you can run the executable generated.

This file is always the same for any `Calc` program compiled, up to the line containing `fn main() {`. The `input` routine is the `Calc` runtime library.

The remaining part of the Rust-generated code corresponds to the `Calc` statements. Notice that all variables are mutable and initialized to `0.0`, and so their type is `f64`. The name of the variables begins with an underscore to prevent conflicts with Rust keywords.

Actually, this project also contains the interpreter seen in the preceding project. If you run the project with no command-line argument, an interactive interpreter starts.

Let's see the source code next. Also, this project extends the preceding project. The `parser.rs`, `analyzer.rs`, and `executor.rs` source files are identical; some lines are added to the `symbol_table.rs` file, and one other file is added—`compiler.rs`.

To the `symbol_table.rs` file, only one small function has been added. Its signature is shown as follows:

```
pub fn get_name(&self, handle: usize) -> String
```

It allows the name of an identifier to be obtained, given its index.

But let's start with the `main.rs` file.

Glancing at the main.rs file

The `main` function begins by examining the command-line arguments. If there are no arguments, the `run_interpreter` function is called, identical to that used in the `calc_interpreter` project.

Instead, if there is one argument, the `process_file` function is called on it. This is similar to that used in the `calc_analyzer` project. There are only two differences. One is the insertion of the statement, shown in the following code snippet:

```
let target_path = source_path[0..source_path.len() -
CALC_SUFFIX.len()].to_string() + ".rs";
```

This generates the path of the resulting Rust file. The other is the replacement of the two ending statements, which print the result of the analysis, with the following code:

```
match std::fs::write(
    &target_path,
    compiler::translate_to_rust_program(&variables, &analyzed_program),
) {
    Ok(_) => eprintln!("Compiled {} to {}.", source_path, target_path),
    Err(err) => eprintln!("Failed to write to file {}: ({})", target_path,
err),
}
```

This performs the translation into Rust code, obtaining a multiline string, and writes that string into the target file.

So, we need to examine the `compiler` module, defined in the `compiler.rs` source file.

Understanding the compiler.rs file

This module does not define types, as it uses those defined in the other modules. As with the parser, the analyzer, and the interpreter, it has a function for every language construct, and it performs the translation by visiting the analyzed program tree.

The entry point begins with the following code:

```
pub fn translate_to_rust_program(
    variables: &SymbolTable,
    analyzed_program: &AnalyzedProgram,
) -> String {
    let mut rust_program = String::new();
    rust_program += "use std::io::Write;\n";
    ...
```

This function, as with all the others in this module, gets immutable references to the symbol table and to the analyzed program. It returns a String containing Rust code. An empty string is first created, and then the required lines are appended to it.

The final part of this function is shown in the following code block:

```
    ...
    for statement in analyzed_program {
        rust_program += "    ";
        rust_program += &translate_to_rust_statement(&variables,
         statement);
        rust_program += ";\n";
    }
    rust_program += "}\n";
    rust_program
}
```

For any Calc statement, the translate_to_rust_statement function is called, and the Rust code returned by it is appended to the string.

The body of the function that translates a Calc statement into Rust code is shown as follows:

```
match analyzed_statement {
    AnalyzedStatement::Assignment(handle, expr) => format!(
        "_{} = {}",
        variables.get_name(*handle),
        translate_to_rust_expr(&variables, expr)
    ),
    AnalyzedStatement::Declaration(handle) => {
        format!("let mut _{} = 0.0", variables.get_name(*handle))
    }
    AnalyzedStatement::InputOperation(handle) => {
        format!("_{} = input()", variables.get_name(*handle))
    }
    AnalyzedStatement::OutputOperation(expr) => format!(
        "println!(\"{}\", {})",
        "{}",
```

```
            translate_to_rust_expr(&variables, expr)
        ),
    }
```

To translate an assignment, the name of the variable is obtained from the symbol table by calling the `get_name` function, and the code corresponding to the expression is obtained by calling the `translate_to_rust_expr` function. The same is done for the other statements.

To translate an expression, the following function is used:

```
fn translate_to_rust_expr(variables: &SymbolTable, analyzed_expr:
&AnalyzedExpr) -> String {
    let mut result = translate_to_rust_term(variables, &analyzed_expr.0);
    for term in &analyzed_expr.1 {
        match term.0 {
            ExprOperator::Add => {
                result += " + ";
                result += &translate_to_rust_term(variables, &term.1);
            }
            ExprOperator::Subtract => {
                result += " - ";
                result += &translate_to_rust_term(variables, &term.1);
            }
        }
    }
    result
}
```

The terms are translated by calling the `translate_to_rust_term` function. The additions and subtractions are translated using the " + " and " - " Rust string literals.

The translation of a term is quite similar to that of an expression, but using the term operators and calls to the `translate_to_rust_factor` function instead.

The body of this function is defined as follows:

```
match analyzed_factor {
    AnalyzedFactor::Literal(value) => value.to_string() + "f64",
    AnalyzedFactor::Identifier(handle) => "_".to_string()
    + &variables.get_name(*handle),
    AnalyzedFactor::SubExpression(expr) => {
        "(".to_string() + &translate_to_rust_expr(variables, expr) + ")"
    }
}
```

For translating a literal, it is converted to a string and "f64" is appended to force its type. For translating an identifier, its name is taken from the symbol table. For translating a subexpression, the inner expression is translated, and the result is enclosed in parentheses.

In this section, we have seen how to build a program in Rust that reads a `Calc` program and writes an equivalent Rust program. Such a resulting program can then be compiled using the `rustc` command.

Summary

In this chapter, we have seen some amount of theory of programming languages and the algorithms used to process them.

In particular, we have seen that the syntax of programming languages can be expressed using a formal grammar. There is a useful classification of formal grammars—regular languages, context-free languages, and context-dependent languages.

Programming languages belong to the third category, but usually, they are first parsed as a regular language by a lexer. The result is parsed as a context-free language by a parser and is then analyzed to keep into account the context-dependent features.

We have seen the most popular techniques to process texts written in a formal language, such as a programming language or a markup language—the compiler-compiler and the parser combinator. In particular, we saw how to use the Nom crate, which is a parser combinator library.

We saw many built-in parsers and parser combinators of Nom, and how to use them to create our own parsers, writing many Rust programs that used Nom to parse simple patterns. We defined the grammar of an extremely simple programming language, which we named `Calc`, and we built some tiny programs using it. We built a context-free parser for `Calc` that dumped on the console the data structure resulting from such a parsing (calc_parser).

We built a context-dependent analyzer for `Calc` that dumped on the console the data structure resulting from such an analysis (calc_analyzer). We built an interpreter for `Calc`, using the parser and analyzer described in the preceding projects (calc_interpreter). We built a compiler for `Calc` that could be used to translate a `Calc` program to an equivalent Rust program (calc_compiler).

In the next chapter, we will be seeing another use of Nom and of parsing techniques, for processing binary data.

Questions

1. What are regular languages, context-free languages, and context-dependent languages?
2. What is the Backus-Naur form to specify the grammar of a language?
3. What is a compiler-compiler?
4. What is a parser combinator?
5. Why did Nom have to use only macros before the 2018 edition of Rust?
6. What do the `tuple`, `alt`, and `map` functions of the Nom library do?
7. What are the possible phases of an interpreter of a programming language, without passing through an intermediate language?
8. What are the possible phases of a compiler?
9. What is the purpose of a symbol table, when analyzing the use of variables?
10. What is the purpose of a symbol table, when interpreting a program?

Further reading

The Nom project can be downloaded from `https://github.com/Geal/nom`. This repository also contains some examples.

There are many textbooks about formal languages and about the software that manipulates them. In particular, you may search Wikipedia for the following terms: compiler-compiler, parser combinator, Backus-Naur form, syntax-directed translation.

Creating a Computer Emulator Using Nom

9

In the last chapter, we saw how to parse text files—in particular, how to program source files in a simple programming language. Text files aren't the only thing you could need to parse—several kinds of system software need to parse binary files (such as binary executables, multimedia files, and inter-process communication messages).

In this chapter, we will look at how to cope with the need for parsing binary files and how the nom library can be used to ease this task. First, we will look at how to parse and interpret a very simple machine language without using an external library, and then how the nom library can be used to ease this task.

To do this, we will cover the following topics:

- Introducing a very simple machine language using only 16-bit words
- Writing a couple of programs in this language
- Writing a parser and an interpreter for this language and running it on the previously presented programs
- Defining a byte-addressing machine language derived from the previous one
- Explaining the addressing issue (endianness) that emerges when a byte-addressing machine language must handle words containing several bytes
- Presenting a version in the new machine language of the previously presented machine language program
- Writing a parser and an interpreter for this language using the nom library and running it on the machine language program
- Writing a translator for the C language that converts the machine language program into an equivalent C language program
- Writing a couple of disassemblers—programs that convert machine language programs into assembly language—and applying them to our machine language program

By the end of this chapter, you will have learned the main concepts of CPU architectures, interpretation, and translating machine language.

Technical requirements

For the parts of this chapter referring to the `nom` library, knowledge of the preceding chapter is required.

The complete source code for this chapter is found in the `Chapter09` folder of the repository at https://github.com/PacktPublishing/Creative-Projects-for-Rust-Programmers.

Project overview

In this chapter, first, the general concepts regarding machine languages will be presented. Then, a very simple machine language will be presented. Of course, this will be quite unrealistic to use as no real hardware exists to run it. It will simply be used to demonstrate how to process it.

Then, a very simple algorithm will be written in the machine language—a formatter of integer numbers. A Rust program to interpret this program will be written without using an external library (`word_machine_convert`).

Then, a more complex program will be written in this machine language—the famous algorithms invented by Eratosthenes to find prime numbers (named the **sieve of Eratosthenes**). The previous Rust program will be used to interpret this machine language program (`word_machine_sieve`).

Afterward, a somewhat more realistic machine language will be defined that is capable of addressing single bytes instead of words. The issues raised by this machine language will be explained. A new version of the sieve of Eratosthenes will be written in this updated machine language and an interpreter will be written in Rust to run it. In addition, this Rust program will translate the machine language program into C language. This interpreter and compiler will use the `nom` library, already introduced in the previous chapter, to generate an intermediate version of the program. This intermediate data structure will be both interpreted and compiled to the C language (`nom_byte_machine`).

Finally, a **disassembler** will be built for this machine language (`nom_disassembler`). It will again use the `nom` library and it will show two kinds of disassembling—one meant to aid debugging and the other meant to generate source code for an assembler; that is, a program that translates symbolic code to machine language.

Introducing a very simple machine language

Real machine languages and real computers are way too complex to be covered in a single chapter; therefore, we will use a toy machine language that is easier to process and understand. In fact, two machine languages will be used:

- The first language that we will use is the simpler one. For simplicity, it addresses 16-bit words, instead of memory bytes.
- The second language presented can address single bytes, as most modern computers do.

Therefore, any program of the first language that we will use is just a sequence of 16-bit words, and any program written in it can only manipulate 16-bit words.

Both machine languages use just one memory segment containing both machine code and data. Here, there is no real distinction between code and data; instructions can read or write both code and data and data can wrongly be executed as if it were instructions. Usually, code, and some data as well (the so-called **constants**), is not meant to change, but here, there is no guarantee.

[code, static, heap, stack]

 In most computer architecture, the memory used by any process is composed of several portions, named **segments**. The most common memory segments are machine code (often named text), static data, heaps, and stacks. Some segments can be read-only, while others may be writable. Some segments may have a fixed size and others may be resized. Some segments can be shared with other processes.

Let's look at some reasons why we might need to process machine language software:

- Running a binary program for a computer when that computer is not available (because it is too costly to buy or because it has not yet been built)
- Debugging or analyzing a binary program when its source code is not available and the computer that must run it is so resource-constrained that no debugger can run on it
- Disassembling machine code—that is, translating it into assembly code

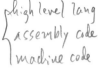

- Translating a binary program into another machine language to run it natively in a much faster way than by interpreting it
- Translating a binary program into a high-level programming language to change it easily and then to recompile it into any machine language

Writing a program directly in machine code is very error-prone, so no one does it. Anyone that needs to write some machine language first writes that code in a symbolic language, named **assembly language**, and then translates it into machine language. This translation can be done manually or by using a specific program, named an **assembler**. Here, we don't have an assembler for our programs, so we will translate the assembly code manually. However, before describing our machine languages, let's look at some concepts relating to machine language.

The most important concepts relating to machine language

In any programming language, you need a way to specify variables and statements. In addition, to document your code, you need a way to insert comments into the program. The following code is a very simple program in assembly language, containing the declaration of some variables, some instructions, and some comments:

```
// data
n
        word 17
m
        word 9
sum
        word 0
// code
        load n
        add m
        store sum
        terminate 0
```

The double backslashes (//) begin the comments. The first comment declares (for humans) where the data section starts. The second comment declares where the code section starts.

> Notice that, apart from comments, some lines are indented and others aren't. Actual declarations and instructions must be indented. Lines written in the first column are **labels** that mark positions in the program.

In the preceding code, there is some data, as shown in the first line. Every data item is a word, and so it is declared using the word keyword. At position n, there is a word whose initial value is 17. At position m, there is another word whose initial value is 9 and at position sum, there is a word whose initial value is 0.

Then, there are four instructions, each on a different line. Each instruction has two parts:

- **Operation Code (opcode)**: This is a command for the processor.
- **Operand**: This is the argument for an opcode command—that is, the data on which the command operates.

All machine language is designed for specific computer architecture. The computer meant to run this program has just two 16-bit CPU registers:

- One to keep the data word to manipulate, named the **accumulator**
- One to keep the address of the next instruction to execute, named the **instruction pointer** (or **program counter**)

The first instruction of the program is load n. This instruction is equivalent to the accumulator = n; Rust statement. It copies the current value of the word that is at the address labeled with n in the accumulator.

The second instruction is add m. This is equivalent to the accumulator += m; Rust statement. It adds the value of the word that is at the address labeled with m to the value currently contained in the accumulator and it stores the result into the accumulator.

The third instruction is store sum. This is equivalent to the sum = accumulator; Rust statement. It copies the current value of the accumulator into the word that is at the address labeled with sum.

The last instruction is terminate 0. This terminates the execution of the program (returning control to the operating system, if there is one) and it returns a value of 0 to the process that launched this program (if there is one).

So, if we follow the effect of the instructions on the data, we find that this program starts with the three data words containing 17, 9, and 0 and ends with them containing 17, 9, and 26.

However, to run this program, we need to translate it into machine language.

Here, a distinction between the words **program** and **process** is needed. A machine language program is the machine code that exists before running it. t is either stored in a storage device or ROM. Instead, a process is found in the RAM area in which the program is loaded and run. This distinction is particularly important in multiprocessing systems, where you may have several processes running on the same program, but it is also important in systems running one process at a time.

Let's assume that our machine requires any program to have the following structure:

Length of the process
First instruction
Second instruction
Third instruction
...
Last instruction
First word of data
Second word of data
Third word of data
...

Code and *Data* braces are drawn to the left grouping the instruction rows and data rows respectively.

This table shows that the first word of the program is meant to be the length of the whole process in words. The words after it are meant to be instructions in machine language. The words that follow the last instruction of the program are meant to be data.

In the preceding program, we have four instructions, and each of them uses one word for the opcode and one for the operand. Therefore, eight words are occupied by four instructions. If we add together the initial word containing the length of the process and the three words occupied by the three variables (one word per variable), we get *1 + 8 + 3 = 12* words. This is the size of the memory space used by this program, measured in words. If we set this number as the initial word of the program, it means that we need exactly that memory in our process.

If we lay out the instructions and data, we get the following array of words for our process:

Position	Contents
0	The length of the process
1	The opcode of the load instruction
2	The n operand
3	The opcode of the add instruction
4	The m operand
5	The opcode of the store instruction

6	The sum operand
7	The opcode of the terminate instruction
8	The 0 operand
9	Data 17
10	Data 9
11	Data 0

The position of any word is its distance from the beginning of the program measured in words. Any position is named the **address** of the word, as this number allows us to access the word in the process.

Machine language does not use labels; it only uses addresses. So, to translate the assembly code into machine language, we must replace the use of labels with memory addresses. The address of the first word is, by definition, 0. The address of the first instruction is 1. Any instruction is two-words long, and so the address of the second instruction is *1 + 2 = 3*. The address after the last instruction—that is, the address of the first data word, labeled by n—is 9. The address of the second data word, labeled m, is 10. The address of the last data word, labeled sum, is 11.

After adding the initial length, moving the instructions before the data, and replacing the labels, our program becomes the following:

```
12
load 9
add 10
store 11
terminate 0
word 17
word 9
word 0
```

Then, we must replace every symbolic code with its corresponding machine language opcode, which is a unique number.

Let's assume the following correspondence between the opcode and symbolic instruction code:

```
0 = terminate
1 = load
2 = store
3 = add
```

The `word` keyword does not actually generate instructions. So, our program becomes the following:

```
12
1: 9
3: 10
2: 11
0: 0
17
9
0
```

Of course, these numbers will be stored as a vector of binary numbers. So, in Rust, it will be the following:

```
let mut program: Vec<u16> = vec![12, 1, 9, 3, 10, 2, 11, 0, 0, 17, 9, 0];
```

So, we have been able to manually translate an assembly language program into a machine language program. However, we used a very small machine language containing only four kinds of instructions—that is, only four different opcodes. To carry out useful work, some more kinds of instructions are needed.

Extending our machine language

The machine language that we saw in the preceding section is only capable of making additions and it has no input/output capabilities. Such a limited language is not very interesting. So, to have a language that can be used to build meaningful programs, let's add some kinds of instruction to our machine language.

Our assembly language (and its corresponding machine language) is defined by the following table:

Opcode	Assembly syntax	Description
0	`terminate operand`	This terminates the program, returning the operand to the caller.
1	`set operand` *immediate*	This copies the operand to the accumulator.
2	`load address`	This copies the value at this address to the accumulator.
3	`store address`	This copies the value of the accumulator to this address.
4	`indirect_load address`	This copies the value whose address is specified at this address to the accumulator.
5	`indirect_store address`	This copies the value of the accumulator to the address specified at this address.

6	input length	This asks the user for console input until the *Enter* key is pressed. Then, at most, the `length` characters of the input line are copied into consecutive memory words. This sequence of memory words begins at the address contained in the accumulator. Each memory word contains exactly one character. If the user types less than length characters, the remaining words are set to binary zero (0). So, in any case, `length` memory words are set by this instruction.
7	output length	This emits to the console the `length` ASCII characters whose codes are in consecutive memory words. This sequence of memory words to output begins at the address contained in the accumulator. Only 7-bit ASCII characters are correctly supported.
8	add address	This adds the value at this address to the value of the accumulator and keeps the result in the accumulator. It uses 16-bit integer arithmetic with a wraparound—that is, in the case of integer overflow, the value modulo of 65,536 is obtained.
9	subtract address	This subtracts the value at this address from the value of the accumulator, using wrap-around arithmetic, and keeps the result in the accumulator.
10	multiply address	This multiplies the value of the accumulator by the value at this address, using wrap-around arithmetic, and keeps the result in the accumulator.
11	divide address	This divides the value of the accumulator by the value at this address using integer arithmetic (truncation) and keeps the result in the accumulator (quotient).
12	remainder address	This divides the value of the accumulator by the value at this address using integer arithmetic (truncation) and keeps the integer remainder in the accumulator.
13	jump address	This proceeds to the execution of the instruction present at address.
14	jump_if_zero address	This proceeds to the execution of the instruction present at address, but only if the value of the accumulator is equal to 0. Otherwise, it proceeds to the next instruction.
15	jump_if_nonzero address	This proceeds to the execution of the instruction present at address if the value of the accumulator is not 0.
16	jump_if_positive address	This proceeds to the execution of the instruction present at address if the value of the accumulator is a positive number.
17	jump_if_negative address	This proceeds to the execution of the instruction present at address if the value of the accumulator is a negative number.

18	`jump_if_nonpositive address`	This proceeds to the execution of the instruction present at `address`, but only if the value of the accumulator is non-positive—that is, if it is a negative number or it is equal to 0.
19	`jump_if_nonnegative address`	This proceeds to the execution of the instruction present at `address` if the value of the accumulator is non-negative—that is, if it is a positive number or it is equal to 0.
–	`word value`	This reserves a word for data. Its initial content is specified by `value`.
–	`array length`	This reserves an array of `length` words. All these words are initialized to 0.

Notice that the `set` instruction type (opcode 1) is quite simple; it assigns the operand to the accumulator. Almost all the other assignment and arithmetic instruction types have one level of indirectness—their operand is the memory address of the data that must be operated on. However, the two instructions—`indirect_load` (opcode 4) and `indirect_store` (opcode 5)—have two levels of indirectness. Their operand is the memory address of a word—that is, the memory address of the data that must be operated on.

Now that we have a powerful enough machine language, we can write a meaningful program using it.

Writing a very simple program

To show you how to use this language, let's write some code with it. We will create a program that, when given a positive integer number in a memory word (in binary format), prints it in decimal notation.

Let's assume that the number to print is hardcoded as `6710`. When we write the algorithm in Rust, it is as shown in the following code snippet:

```rust
fn main() {
    let mut n: u16 = 6710;
    let mut digits: [u16; 5] = [0; 5];
    let mut pos: usize;
    let number_base: u16 = 10;
    let ascii_zero: u16 = 48;
    pos = 5;
    loop {
        pos -= 1;
        digits[pos] = ascii_zero + n % number_base;
```

```
        n /= number_base;
        if n == 0 { break; }
    }
    for pos in pos..5 {
        print!("{}", digits[pos] as u8 as char);
    }
}
```

In the preceding code, the n variable is the unsigned 16-bit number to convert and print. The digits variable is a buffer that will contain the ASCII values of the generated digits. As a 16-bit number can have, at most, five decimal digits, an array of five digits is enough. The pos variable is the position of the current digit in the digits array.

The number_base variable is 10 as we are using decimal notation. The ascii_zero variable contains the ASCII code for the zeroth character (which is 48).

The first loop computes any ASCII decimal digit by computing the remainder of n divided by 10 using the % operator, and by adding it to ascii_zero. Then, n is divided by the number_base variable to remove the least significant decimal digit from it. The second loop prints the five generated digits to the console.

The problem with this program is that it needs to use array indexing. Actually, pos is an index to the digits array. Machine language uses addresses, not indices; so, to mimic machine language, we must replace the type of pos with that of raw pointers, whose dereference operation is unsafe in Rust. Instead of counting up to five, we set an end pointer. When pos reaches this pointer, it will have finished the array.

So, let's translate our Rust program into a format that is more similar to what can be translated into machine language using raw pointers:

```
fn main() {
    let mut n: u16 = 6710;
    let mut digits: [u16; 5] = [0; 5];
    let mut pos: *mut u16;
    let number_base: u16 = 10;
    let ascii_zero: u16 = 48;
    let end = unsafe {
        (&mut digits[0] as *mut u16).offset(digits.len() as isize)
    };
    pos = end;
    loop {
        pos = unsafe { pos.offset(-1) };
        unsafe { *pos = ascii_zero + n % number_base };
        n /= number_base;
        if n == 0 { break; }
```

```
        }
    while pos != end {
        print!("{}", unsafe { *pos } as u8 as char);
        pos = unsafe { pos.offset(1) };
    }
}
```

In the preceding program, the unsafe `offset` method of raw pointers is used. When given a raw pointer, it generates another raw pointer by advancing by the specified number of positions in memory.

To have a program that is even more similar to a machine language program, we should split all the Rust statements into elementary statements that correspond to machine instructions.

However, there is another problem—our accumulator register will sometimes contain numbers and other times addresses. Using Rust, this is inconvenient because numbers and addresses have different types in Rust. Therefore, here, we will use two variables—acc (which represents the accumulator when it is used to store a number) and ptr_acc (which represents the accumulator when it is used to store an address—that is, a memory pointer).

Here is the obtained program, which is quite similar to a machine language program:

```
fn main() {
    let mut ptr_acc: *mut u16; // pointer accumulator
    let mut acc: u16; // accumulator
    let mut n: u16 = 6710;
    let mut digits: [u16; 5] = [0; 5];
    let mut pos: *mut u16;
    let number_base: u16 = 10;
    let ascii_zero: u16 = 48;
    let one: u16 = 1;
    ptr_acc = unsafe {
        (&mut digits[0] as *mut u16).offset(digits.len() as isize)
    };
    pos = ptr_acc;
    loop {
        ptr_acc = pos;
        ptr_acc = unsafe { ptr_acc.offset(-(one as isize)) };
        pos = ptr_acc;
        acc = n;
        acc %= number_base;
        acc += ascii_zero;
        unsafe { *pos = acc };
        acc = n;
```

```
        acc /= number_base;
        n = acc;
        if n == 0 { break; }
    }
    for &digit in &digits {
        print!("{}",
            if digit == 0 { ' ' }
            else { digit as u8 as char}
        );
    }
}
```

Notice that now, the statements after the empty line, except for the final `for` loop, are quite simple. They are only assignments, possibly combined with one operation, such as `%=`, `+=`, or `/=`. In addition, there is one `if` statement used to break the loop when the n variable is 0.

This can be easily translated into our assembly language, as shown:

```
, n
        word 6710
, digits
        array 5
, pos
        word 0
. number_base
        word 10
. ascii_zero
        word 48
. one
        word 1

        set pos
        store pos
before_generating_digits
        load pos
        subtract one
        store pos
        load n
        remainder number_base
        add ascii_zero
        store_indirect pos
        load n
        divide number_base
        store n
        jump_if_nonzero before_generating_digits
        set digits
        output 5
        terminate 0
```

Set operand P288

Set Immediate operand: address over end of digits, adc of pos.

Save to address of pos = + pos = acc

load address

Set immediate operand = address of digits into acc

This assembly language program can be manually translated into machine language.

As there are 5 data words, 1 data array of five words, 16 instructions occupying two words each, and the initial word, we have a total of $5 + 1 * 5 + 16 * 2 + 1 = 43$ words. This number will be the value of the first word of our program.

Then, considering the required layout (the process length, followed by the instruction, followed by the data), we can compute the addresses of the jump destinations and the addresses of the data, obtaining the following code:

```
 0: 43
 1: set 39 // pos
 3: store 39 // pos
 5: before_generating_digits
 5: load 39 // pos
 7: subtract 42 // one
 9: store 39 // pos
11: load 33 // n
13: remainder 40 // number_base
15: add 41 // ascii_zero
17: store_indirect 39 // pos
19: load 33 // n
21: divide 40 // number_base
23: store 33 // n
25: jump_if_nonzero 5 // before_generating_digits
27: set 34 // digits
29: output 5
31: terminate 0
33: n: 6710
34: digits: 0, 0, 0, 0, 0
39: pos: 0
40: number_base: 10
41: ascii_zero: 48
42: one: 1
```

In the preceding code, notice that the symbolic names of the addresses are commented out.

Then, by replacing the symbolic codes with the opcodes and by removing the comments and line addresses, we get the machine language program as a comma-separated list of decimal numbers:

```
43,
1, 39,
3, 39,
2, 39,
9, 42,
3, 39,
```

```
2, 33,
12, 40,
8, 41,
5, 39,
2, 33,
11, 40,
3, 33,
15, 5,
1, 34,
7, 5,
0, 0,
6710,
0, 0, 0, 0, 0,
0,
10,
48,
1
```

For example, we start with the following line:

```
1: set 39 // pos
```

The preceding line becomes the following:

```
1, 39,
```

Because the 1: line address has been removed, the set symbolic code has been replaced by its opcode (1), the // pos comment has been removed, and two commas have been added to separate the numbers.

Now, we can build a Rust program that interprets this program. You can find it in the word_machine_convert project.

If you execute the cargo run command on this project, the program is compiled in a short time because it has no dependencies. The execution will simply print 6710 with a leading space. The name of this project means to convert a number using a machine language that uses word addressing.

The main function of this Rust program just passes the preceding list of numbers to the execute function.

This function begins with the following code:

```
fn execute(program: &[u16]) -> u16 {
    let mut acc: u16 = 0;
    let mut process = vec![0u16; program[0] as usize];
    process[..program.len()].copy_from_slice(program);
```

```
let mut ip = 1;
loop {
    let opcode = process[ip];
    let operand = process[ip + 1];
    //println!("ip: {} opcode: {} operand: {} acc: {}",
    //ip, opcode, operand, acc);
    ip += 2;
```

The previously mentioned function (execute) emulates an extremely simple machine language processor that addresses memory as a slice of 16-bit words. This function, if it returns, returns the operand of the terminate instruction that it may execute.

The acc variable represents the accumulator register. The process variable represents the actual runtime content of memory. Its size, in words, is the number specified by the first word of the program. It makes no sense to have a process shorter than the program that it runs because some data would be lost.

However, it makes sense to have a process larger than the programs that it runs because in doing so, it allocates memory that will be used by code with no need to declare it in the program. In this way, you can have a program with a few words using a memory space of up to 65,536 words, which is 128 **Kibibytes (KiB)**.

The first part of the process variable is initialized with the contents of program, received as an argument of the execute function.

The ip variable is the instruction pointer, which is initialized to 1—that is, it points to the second word, where there is a first instruction to execute.

Then, there is the processing loop. Every instruction has exactly one opcode and one operand, and so they are loaded into the respective variables. Then, there is a debugging statement that is commented out; this can be useful if your program does not do what you hoped.

After executing any instruction, the instruction that follows it will usually be executed, and so the instruction pointer is incremented right away by two words to skip the current instruction. The exceptions are the jump instructions and terminate instructions. The jump instructions, if their condition is satisfied, will change the instruction pointer again and the terminate instruction will jump out of the processing loop, and out of the execute function, too.

The rest of the function is a large `match` statement, which is needed to process the current instruction. Here are its first few lines:

```
match opcode {
    0 => // terminate
        { return operand }
    1 => // set
        { acc = operand }
    2 => // load
        { acc = process[operand as usize] }
```

The behavior of each arm of this kind of a `match` statement is quite simple as it is meant to be executed by hardware. For example, if the current instruction is `terminate`, the function returns the operand; if it is `set`, the operand is assigned to the accumulator; if it is `load`, the memory word whose address is the operand is assigned to the accumulator; and so on.

Here is a pair of arithmetic instructions:

```
 9 => // subtract
        { acc = acc.wrapping_sub(process[operand as usize]) }
10 => // multiply
        { acc = acc.wrapping_mul(process[operand as usize]) }
```

In all modern computers, integer numbers are stored in two complementary formats and they perform their operations accordingly. This has several advantages:

- A single arithmetic operation can work if the operands are both interpreted as signed numbers or unsigned numbers (but not one signed number and the other unsigned).
- If an addition or subtraction causes an integer to overflow and then another operation causes the result to go back into the allowed range, the result is still valid.

In high-level languages, such as Rust, arithmetic overflow is usually not allowed by default. In Rust, the arithmetic of overflow of basic operators causes panic when it shows a message such as `attempt to add with overflow`. To allow two complementary arithmetics, the Rust standard library provides the corresponding wrapping method for any operator, which is the one usually implemented in machine language. To use it, instead of writing a `+ b`, you write `a.wrapping_add(b)`; instead of writing `a - b`, you write `a.wrapping_sub(b)`, and so on for the other operators.

The `jump` instructions are a bit different from other instructions, as shown:

```
15 => // jump_if_nonzero
    { if acc != 0 { ip = operand as usize } }
16 => // jump_if_positive
    { if (acc as i16) > 0 { ip = operand as usize } }
```

In the preceding code, the `jump_if_nonzero` instruction checks the value of the accumulator and sets the instruction pointer to the specified value only if this value is not 0.

The `jump_if_positive` instruction checks whether the value of the accumulator is positive, interpreting it as a signed number. Without the `as i16` clause, the check would always succeed as the `acc` variable is unsigned.

 Notice that in Rust, an unsigned number can be converted into a signed one, even if the result is negative; for example, the expression `40_000_u16 as i16 == -25_536_i16` is true.

The `input` and `output` instructions are unusually complex, and they even interact with the operating system. Of course, they are not real-world machine language instructions. They were added to this pseudo-machine language just to be able to write a complete program with reasonable effort. In practice, in a real-world machine language, I/O is performed using a convoluted sequence of instructions or by calling an operating system service.

So, we have seen how to interpret a machine language program. It was quite a trivial program, however; so, in the next section, we'll look at a more interesting and complex machine language program.

A more complex program – the sieve of Eratosthenes

Now, let's consider a more realistic but challenging problem—implementing an algorithm to print all the prime numbers that are less than a number, *N*, where *N* is typed in by the user at runtime. This is called the **sieve of Eratosthenes** algorithm.

Here is the Rust version of this program:

```
fn main() {
    let limit;
    loop {
        let mut text = String::new();
        std::io::stdin()
```

```
            .read_line(&mut text)
            .expect("Cannot read line.");
        if let Ok(value) = text.trim().parse::<i16>() {
            if value >= 2 {
                limit = value as u16;
                break;
            }
        }
        println!("Invalid number (2..32767). Re-enter:")
    }

    let mut primes = vec![0u8; limit as usize];
    for i in 2..limit {
        if primes[i as usize] == 0 {          0: prime
            let mut j = i + i;
            while j < limit {
                primes[j as usize] = 1; not prime
                j += i;
            }
        }
    }

    for i in 2..limit {
        if primes[i as usize] == 0 {
            print!("{} ", i);
        }
    }
}
```

In the preceding code, the first 14 lines of the `main` function ask the user to type in a number until the typed number is between 2 and 32767.

The next group of statements allocates a vector of bytes to store the numbers that have been detected as non-primes. Initially, it contains all zeros, meaning that every number in the required range could be a prime. Then, all the numbers of the range are scanned in increasing order, and for each of them, if it is still considered a prime number, all of its multiples are marked as non-primes.

The last group of statements again scans all the numbers and prints only those that are still marked as prime numbers.

The difficulty of this program is that it needs to allocate memory to be used by a vector. Our machine language does not allow memory allocation. We can pre-allocate an array with the maximum desired size, say, 400 words.

To pre-allocate such an array, it is enough to specify that the process size is equal to the program size plus 400 words. In doing this, when the process begins its execution, it will allocate the required space and it will initialize it to be a sequence of zeros.

As you can imagine, the corresponding assembly and machine language program is quite complex. It can be found in the `word_machine_sieve` project.

If you run it and then type in a number that isn't larger than 400, all the prime numbers that are smaller than the typed number will be printed to the console. The interpreter is identical to the one used in the preceding projects, but there is another machine language program in the `main` function.

This machine language program is much larger than that of the preceding project, and it is explained by comments. The assembly language is equivalent in any instruction or data item in a comment. Here is the initial part, containing four instructions:

```
600, // 0:
// Let the user input the digits of the limit number.
1, 190, // 1: set digits
6, 5, // 3: input 5
// Initialize digit pointer.
1, 190, // 5: set digits
3, 195, // 7: store pos
```

The process size, `600`, is 400 words, which is larger than the program size by 200 words.

There are some explanatory comments interleaved, such as those in the second and fifth lines.

The third line is a `set` instruction (opcode 1), with operand `190`. The comment explains that this instruction begins at address `1` and corresponds with the `set digits` assembly instruction.

As you can imagine, it is almost impossible to write a machine language program directly without passing through its assembly language version, and it is an error-prone chore to manually translate an assembly language into machine language. Fortunately, it is rather easy to write an assembler program that does this for you. You can do this by using the compiling techniques explained in the preceding chapter.

In the next section, we will look at a more realistic machine language and how to use the `nom` parsing library to ease its interpretation.

Defining a byte-addressing machine language

In the preceding section, we saw a different kind of machine language. However, this kind of machine language is quite unrealistic for several reasons:

- It addresses memory word by word. This was common in the early days of computer technology, until around 1970. Then, it became more and more common to have processors that address single bytes of memory. Today, probably every processor in production can address single bytes of memory.

- It has instructions of the same length. There has probably never been a machine language where all the instructions are of the same length. A very simple instruction, such as a **No-Operation** (**NOP**), can stay in a single byte, while there are processors that have instructions spanning many bytes.

- Any kind of operation operates on a 16-bit word for real-world processors, for any kind of operation—for example, addition. There can be an instruction that operates on single bytes, adding an 8-bit byte to another byte, another instruction that does the same thing but on 16-bit words, adding a word to another word, another instruction for 32-bit double-words, and even instructions that operate on larger bit sequences.

- It has just one processor register—the accumulator. Real-world processors have much more processor registers.

- It has few operations available. Real-world machine languages have more possible operations, such as logical operations, function calls and function return instructions, stack manipulation operations, and increment and decrement operators.

Here, we will change our machine language to introduce the following missing features:

- Byte addressing
- Variable-length instructions
- Instructions to load or store a single byte, in addition to those to load or store words

So, we apply the following changes to our byte-addressing machine language:

- Every address represents the position of a memory byte, not the position of a memory word.

- Every opcode occupies only one byte, instead of the word as was the case in the preceding language.

- While most instruction types still have a one-word operand, three instruction types have a 1-byte operand. They are `terminate operand`, `input length`, and `output length`.
- Four instruction types are added to the language to manipulate a single byte.

To understand this new machine language, it is important to realize that every 16-bit word contains 2 bytes, one containing the eight least significant bits of the number and the other containing the eight most significant bits of the number. The first byte is named the **low byte** and the other is named the **high byte**. When a byte inside a word is manipulated, it is important to know whether it is the low byte or the high byte of that word.

The new instruction types are defined in the following table:

Opcode	Assembly syntax	Description
20	`load_byte address`	This copies the value of the byte at that address to the low byte of the accumulator. The high byte of the accumulator is set to 0.
21	`store_byte address`	This copies the low byte of the value of the accumulator to that address. The high byte of the accumulator is not used.
22	`indirect_load_byte address`	This copies the byte value whose address is specified at that address to the low byte of the accumulator. The high byte of the accumulator is set to 0.
23	`indirect_store_byte address`	This copies the low byte of the value of the accumulator to the address specified at that address. The high byte of the accumulator is not used.

These four instructions are needed because the `load`, `store`, `indirect_load`, and `indirect_store` instruction types still transfer whole words, while we also need to read or write a single byte of memory without reading or writing the byte next to the specified address.

As a result of these changes, in the previous machine language, every instruction occupied four bytes. However, in this new language, the three instruction types—`terminate`, `input`, and `output`—occupy only 2 bytes and all the other instruction types occupy 3 bytes.

Notice that all the other instruction types remain unchanged and the size of the accumulator and the instruction pointer is still 16 bits.

Having byte-addressing capability, together with words spanning several bytes, raises an issue, however. This is the so-called **endianness** issue, described in the next section.

Coping with the endianness issue

Consider a word in the accumulator with a value of 256. The low byte of this word is 0 and the high byte is 1. This word will be stored at the 1000 memory address. Because this address now refers to a single byte, not to a two-byte word, the store instruction must also access another memory byte to store a word. For every computer system, the other byte that is needed is one with the following consecutive address, and so it is at address 1001.

So, our accumulator will be stored in the 2 bytes with addresses 1000 and 1001. However, the low byte of number 256, whose value is 0, could be stored at address 1000 or at address 1001.

In the first case, when the low byte is stored at address 1000, the high byte, whose value is 1, will be stored at address 1001. Here is the memory layout of this case:

Address	Memory content
1000	00000000
1001	00000001

little

In the second case, when the low byte is stored at address 1001, the high byte will be stored at address 1000. Here is the memory layout of this case:

Address	Memory contents
1000	00000001
1001	00000000

This is just a matter of convention.

Unfortunately, some important computer vendors chose one convention and some other important computer vendors chose the other. Some computer hardware can even be programmed to change convention at runtime, and so it is up to the operating system to choose the convention.

The convention where the low byte has a lower memory address is named **little-endian**, which is shown in the first of the previous two tables. The other convention, where the high byte has a lower memory address, is named **big-endian**, and it is shown in the second of the preceding two tables. The issue itself is named the **endianness** issue.

For our machine language, we chose little-endian.

Now that we have defined the new byte-addressing machine language and we have chosen to adopt the little-endian convention for it, we can write an interpreter for this machine language.

The nom_byte_machine project

Now that we have a new machine language, we can write some programs using it and try to build an interpreter for these programs. In addition, it is possible to use the nom library, already seen in Chapter 8, *Using a Parser Combinator for Interpreting and Compiling*, to ease the building of this sort of interpreter.

However, before we start coding, let's consider the possible techniques to execute a machine language program. In fact, there are at least three possible ways to execute a machine language program without having real hardware:

- **Technique 1**: Interpreting it just as the hardware would interpret it. This is the technique used in the previous sections to interpret the sieve of Eratosthenes program in the word_machine_sieve project.
- **Technique 2**: First, parsing it all and transforming it into a high-level data structure, then interpreting this data structure.
- **Technique 3**: Translating it into another programming language, and then using an interpreter or a compiler for this programming language.

Technique 1 is the only one of the three that can obtain the correct result for any possible program. The other two techniques only work if the program is well formed, following these rules:

1. It begins with a little-endian word containing the size of the process in bytes.
2. After the initial word, there is a sequence of valid machine language instructions, with no interleaved spaces or data.
3. The Terminate instruction occurs once—and only once—as the last instruction so that it marks the end of the sequence of instructions. After this, there is only data left.
4. No statement writes on the instructions; only the data can be changed. So, the program is not self-modifying; or, said in another way, the program instructions are the same as the process instructions.

The nom_byte_machine project implements all three techniques and applies them to a well-formed machine language program. This program is a version of the sieve algorithm seen in the preceding section, implemented for the byte-addressing machine language.

First of all, let's try to build and run the project by typing `cargo run` in the `project` folder. The build will take some time because it uses the `nom` library. The execution starts by creating the `prog.c` file, containing a C language version of the machine language program, and printing the following on the console:

```
Compiled to prog.c.
```

Then, the program interprets the program using the first technique described earlier. This causes it to wait until the user types in a number. You should type in a number between 0 and 400 and press *Enter*.

Some prime numbers will be printed using *Technique 1*, and then the program interprets the same program using *Technique 2*, and, therefore, it waits again until the user types in a number. You should type in a number again and press *Enter*.

For example, if you entered 100 the first time and the second time you entered 40, then the console should display this:

```
Compiled to prog.c.
100
    2    3    5    7   11   13   17   19   23   29   31   37   41   43   47
53
   59   61   67   71   73   79   83   89   97
Return code: 0
40
    2    3    5    7   11   13   17   19   23   29   31   37
Return code: 0
```

After executing it, the `prog.c` file will exist in the `project` folder. Using a Unix-like environment, you can compile it with the following command:

```
cc prog.c -o prog.exe
```

This will create the `prog.exe` file. Then, you can run it with the following command:

```
./prog.exe
```

Of course, this program has the same behavior as the previously interpreted program. It first asks for a number, and if, for example, you type in 25, the output is this:

```
25
    2    3    5    7   11   13   17   19   23
```

As this project is somewhat complex, its source code has been split into several source files. They are as follows:

- `main.rs`: This contains the machine language program and the calls to the functions contained in the other source files.
- `instructions.rs`: This contains the definitions of the machine language instructions and the nom parsers to recognize them.
- `emulator.rs`: This is a low-level interpreter of the machine code. Every instruction is first parsed and then executed.
- `parsing_interpreter.rs`: This first parses all the instructions of the machine code, constructing a data structure, and then executes this data structure.
- `translator.rs`: This translates all the instruction of the machine code into C language code and adds some C language lines to create a valid C program.

Let's look at each of the files in the following sections.

Understanding the main.rs source file

The `main.rs` file contains the `main` function, which begins with the following lines:

```
let prog = vec![
    187, 2, // 0: 699
    // Let the user input the digits of the limit number.
    1, 28, 1, // 2, 0: set digits
    6, 5, // 5, 0: input 5
    // Initialize digit pointer.
    1, 28, 1, // 7, 0: set digits
    3, 33, 1, // 10, 0: store pos
```

This machine language program is similar to the one used in the `word_machine_sieve` project. While in those programs the numbers represented words ($u16$), now they represent bytes ($u8$).

First, read the comments, except for the descriptive comments that are on their own in a line. These comments contain the address of the current instruction or data, followed by a colon, followed by an assembly statement.

The first line represents what starts at address 0. In this case, this is number 699, which is the required length of the process. As we said in the previous section, we adopted the little-endian convention to store words, and so this number is stored as the pair of bytes, 187, 2, which means *2 x 256 + 187*.

The second line is a descriptive comment. The third line represents what starts at address 2, which in little-endian notation is 2, 0. The content is the set instruction, with the address of the digits label as its operand. The opcode of the set instruction is 1 and the digits label is at address 284, which in little-endian notation is 28, 1. So, we have, 1, 28, 1 on this line.

$1 \times 256 + 28 = 284$

The fourth line represents what starts at address 5, which is an instruction that in assembly is input 5 and in machine code is 6, 5. The rest of the program is similar.

The last part of the program is the data section. Here is a snippet of it:

```
0, 0, 0, 0, 0, // 28, 1: digits: array 5
0, 0, // 33, 1: pos: word 0
10, 0, // 35, 1: number_base: word 10
```

The first line represents an array of 5 bytes, all of them initialized to 0. Its label is digits and its address is 284, which is represented by the 28, 1 pair.

The second line represents a word initialized to 0 whose label is pos and address is the 33, 1 pair, which is 5 bytes after the digits address.

The third line represents a word initialized to 10 (represented by the 10, 0 pair) whose label is number_base and whose address is the 35, 1 pair, which is two bytes after the pos address.

The main function ends with the following lines:

```
let _ = translator::translate_program_to_c(&prog, "prog.c");

let return_code = emulator::execute_program(&prog).unwrap();
println!("\nReturn code: {}", return_code);

let mut parsed_program =
parsing_interpreter::parse_program(&prog).unwrap();
let return_code = parsing_interpreter::execute_parsed_program(&mut
parsed_program);
println!("\nReturn code: {}", return_code);
```

From the preceding code, the first statement invokes a function that translates the prog machine language program into a C language file with the specified name.

The second statement interprets the program using the first technique instruction by instruction.

The last block of statements first invokes the `parse_program` statement, which translates the program into a data structure and stores it in the `parsed_program` variable, and then the `execute_parsed_program` function is invoked to execute this data structure.

The rest of the Rust program implements these functions and we are going to use the `nom` library for this purpose.

Using the Nom library

The code that will implement what is described in this section can be found in the `instructions.rs` source file.

In the preceding chapters, we saw how to use the `nom` library to parse text, which is string slices. Well, `nom` is not limited to text, however; it can also be used to parse binary data, which is byte slices. In fact, it was created just for that, and the capability to parse strings was added later.

Here, we are going to use the binary parsing capability of `nom` to process our machine language.

Parsing a binary file is no more difficult than parsing a text file. The only difference between them is that when parsing a text file, the parsed text is a reference to a string slice, with an `&str` type, while when parsing a binary file, the parsed text is a reference to a slice of bytes, with an `&[u8]` type.

For example, this is the signature of a parser that recognizes an `add` instruction:

```
fn parse_add(input: &[u8]) -> IResult<&[u8], Instruction> {
```

The `parse_add` function takes a reference to a slice of bytes as input and, of course, its remaining sequence is still a reference to a slice of bytes. We want its return value to fully describe the parsed instruction, and so the custom `Instruction` type is used.

This type can be defined in the following way:

```
#[derive(Debug, Clone, Copy)]
enum Instruction {
    Terminate(u8),
    Set(u16),
    Load(u16),
    Store(u16),
    IndirectLoad(u16),
    IndirectStore(u16),
```

```
    ⎧Input(u8), ₀
    ⎩Output(u8), ₒ
    ⎧Add(u16),
    ⎪Subtract(u16),
    ⎪Multiply(u16),
    ⎨Divide(u16),
    ⎩Remainder(u16),
    ⎧Jump(u16),
    ⎪JumpIfZero(u16),
    ⎪JumpIfNonZero(u16),
    ⎪JumpIfPositive(u16),
    ⎪JumpIfNegative(u16),
    ⎪JumpIfNonPositive(u16),
    ⎩JumpIfNonNegative(u16),
    ⎧LoadByte(u16),
    ⎩StoreByte(u16),
    ⎧IndirectLoadByte(u16),
    ⎩IndirectStoreByte(u16),
    -Byte(u8),
}
```

From the preceding code snippet, every instruction type is a variant of the Instruction enum, and these variants have a parameter to store the value of the operator. The Terminate, Input, and Output variants have a u8 parameter, while the other instruction types have a u16 parameter. Notice that the last variant is not an instruction; it is Byte(u8), which represents a data byte contained in the process.

Using a Rust enum, it is quite easy to encapsulate the operands of the instructions in a variant, even if there are more than one, as is typical of real-world machine languages. The operands are always rather small objects, and so it is efficient to derive the Copy trait for the Instruction enum.

The body of the parse_add function is as follows:

```
preceded(tag("\x08"), map(le_u16, Instruction::Add))(input)
```

The preceded parser combinator, already seen in preceding chapters, gets two parsers, applies them in sequence, discards the result of the first one, and returns the result of the second one.

Its first parser is tag("\x08"). In the preceding chapters, we already saw the tag function used as a parser that can recognize a literal string slice. In fact, it can also recognize a literal sequence of bytes, specified as a literal string. To specify a byte using a number instead of an ASCII character, a hexadecimal escape sequence is appropriate. So, this parser recognizes a byte as having a value of 8, which is the opcode of the add instruction.

The second parser processed by `preceded` must recognize a little-endian 2-byte operand. So, the `le_u16` parser is used for this. Its name means little-endian u16. There is also a corresponding `be_u16` to recognize a word using the big-endian byte order.

The `le_u16` parser just returns a u16 value. However, we want an `Instruction::Add` object to encapsulate this value. So, the `map` function is used to create an `Add` object containing the parsed word.

So, the body of the `parse_add` function first checks whether there are 8 bytes, then discards them; then, it reads a pair of bytes to build a 16-bit number according to the little-endian byte order, then returns an `Add` object containing this word.

For all the instructions with a word operand, a similar parser can be created. However, for the instructions with a byte operand, a different operand parser must be used. When parsing a single byte, there is no endianness issue; however, for terminological consistency, the `le_u8` parser will be used, even if the `be_u8` parser could have been used just as well as it is identical to it.

So, here the parser is used to recognize a `terminate` instruction, with opcode 0:

```
fn parse_terminate(input: &[u8]) -> IResult<&[u8], Instruction> {
    preceded(tag("\x00"), map(le_u8, Instruction::Terminate))(input)
}
```

We invoke `parse_add` when we want to recognize an `add` instruction and `parse_terminate` when we want to recognize a `terminate` instruction; however, when we want to recognize any possible instruction, we must combine all the parsers for all the instructions as alternatives using the `alt` parser combinator, already seen in the preceding chapters.

This parser combinator has a limitation, however—it cannot combine more than 20 parsers. Actually, we have 24 instruction types, and so 24 parsers to combine. This issue can easily be overcome by nesting the use of `alt`. Here is the resulting function:

```
fn parse_instruction(input: &[u8]) -> IResult<&[u8], Instruction> {
    alt((
        alt((
            parse_terminate,
            parse_set,
            parse_load,
            parse_store,
            parse_indirect_load,
            parse_indirect_store,
            parse_input,
            parse_output,
```

```
                parse_add,
                parse_subtract,
                parse_multiply,
                parse_divide,
                parse_remainder,
                parse_jump,
                parse_jump_if_zero,
                parse_jump_if_nonzero,
                parse_jump_if_positive,
                parse_jump_if_negative,
                parse_jump_if_nonpositive,
                parse_jump_if_nonnegative,
            )),
            alt((
                parse_load_byte,
                parse_store_byte,
                parse_indirect_load_byte,
                parse_indirect_store_byte,
            )),
        ))(input)
    }
```

From the preceding code, the `parse_instruction` function uses `alt` to combine just two parsers; the first one uses `alt` to combine the parsers for 20 instructions and the other one uses `alt` to combine the parsers for the remaining 4 instructions. When a byte slice is passed to this function, it returns the only instruction that can be parsed from it or an error if no instruction is recognized.

The `Instruction` enum implements the `len` method, which is useful to find out the length of the instruction. It is given as follows:

```
impl Instruction {
    pub fn len(self) -> usize {
        use Instruction::*;
        match self {
            Byte(_) => 1,
            Terminate(_) | Input(_) | Output(_) => 2,
            _ => 3,
        }
    }
}
```

In the preceding code, `Byte` occupies 1 byte, the `Terminate`, `Input`, and `Output` instructions occupy 2 bytes, and the other instructions occupy 3 bytes.

The `get_process_size` function is useful for reading the length of the process from the first two bytes of the program. Notice that all the parsers (of this module) are private, except for `parse_instruction`, so that we can parse machine code instructions.

Now that we have a parser for the instructions, we can build a low-level interpreter (that is, an emulator) using it.

The emulator.rs source file

This emulator is implemented in the `emulator.rs` source file. The entry point of the interpreter is the following function:

```
pub fn execute_program(program: &[u8]) -> Result<u8, ()> {
    let process_size_parsed: u16 = match get_process_size(program) {
        Ok(ok) => ok,
        Err(_) => return Err(()),
    };
    let mut process = vec![0u8; process_size_parsed as usize];
    process[0..program.len()].copy_from_slice(&program);
    let mut registers = RegisterSet { ip: 2, acc: 0 };
    loop {
        let instruction = match parse_instruction(&process[registers.ip as
usize..]) {
            Ok(instruction) => instruction.1,
            Err(_) => return Err(()),
        };
        if let Some(return_code) = execute_instruction(&mut process, &mut
registers, instruction) {
            return Ok(return_code);
        }
    }
}
```

The preceding function receives a program as an argument and executes it by parsing and executing one instruction at a time. If any parse error occurs because of a malformed instruction, the function returns that parse error. If no parse error occurs, the program goes on until a `Terminate` instruction is encountered. Then, the program returns the operand of the `Terminate` instruction.

The first statement gets the required size of the process. Then, a `process` variable is created as a vector of bytes, with the specified length. The content of the program is copied into the first part of the process, then the rest of the process is initialized to zeros.

Then, at the eighth line of the preceding code, the `registers` variable is declared with a `RegisterSet` type, declared as follows:

```
pub struct RegisterSet {
    ip: u16,
    acc: u16,
}
```

In this simple machine architecture, there is no big gain in encapsulating the instruction pointer and the accumulator in a struct, but with more complex processors with many registers, it would be convenient.

At last, there is the interpretation loop. It consists of two steps:

1. The call to `parse_instruction` parses the process from the current position of the instruction pointer and returns `Instruction`.
2. The call to `execute_instruction` executes the instruction generated by the preceding step, taking into account the whole process and the register set.

The `execute_instruction` function is just a large `match` statement that begins with the following:

```
match instruction {
    Terminate(operand) => {
        r.ip += 2;
        return Some(operand);
    }
    Set(operand) => {
        r.acc = operand;
        r.ip += 3;
    }
    Load(address) => {
        r.acc = get_le_word(process, address);
        r.ip += 3;
    }
    Store(address) => {
        set_le_word(process, address, r.acc);
        r.ip += 3;
    }
```

For each instruction type, the appropriate action is taken. Notice the following:

- The `Terminate` instruction causes the function to return `Some`, while for any other instruction, `None` is returned. This allows the caller to terminate the execution loop.
- The `Set` instruction sets the accumulator (`r.acc`) to the operand value.

- The `Load` instruction uses the `get_le_word` function to read a little-endian word from the `address` position of `process` and assigns it to the accumulator.
- The `Store` instruction uses the `set_le_word` function to assign a little-endian word taken from the accumulator to the `address` position of `process`.
- All the instructions increment the instruction pointer (`r.ip`) by the length of the instruction itself.

Let's see the auxiliary functions used every time an instruction needs to read or to write a word in memory, respectively:

```
fn get_le_word(slice: &[u8], address: u16) -> u16 {
    (u16::from(slice[address as usize]) + (u16::from(slice[address as usize
+ 1]) << 8)
}

fn set_le_word(slice: &mut [u8], address: u16, value: u16) {
    slice[address as usize] = value as u8;
    slice[address as usize + 1] = (value >> 8) as u8;
}
```

In the preceding code, the `get_le_word` function gets a byte at `address` and another byte at the next position. The second one is the most significant in little-endian notation, and so its value is shifted to the left by 8 bits before adding it to the other byte.

`set_le_word` saves a byte, along with the address position, and another one at the next position. The first one is obtained by converting the word into a `u8` type, and the second one is obtained by shifting the word to the right by 8 bits.

Of course, the `jump` instructions are different. For example, look at the following code snippet:

```
JumpIfPositive(address) => {
    if (r.acc as i16) > 0 {
        r.ip = address;
    } else {
        r.ip += 3;
    }
}
```

Consider the `JumpIfPositive` instruction's operand as a signed number. If this value is positive, the instruction pointer is set to the operand. Otherwise, the usual increment is performed.

As another example, let's see how to indirectly load a byte:

```
IndirectLoadByte(address) => {
    r.acc = get_byte(process, get_le_word(process, address));
    r.ip += 3;
}
```

Using the `get_le_word` function, the 16-bit value at the `address` position is read from `process`. This value is an address of a byte, and so the `get_byte` function is used to read this byte to assign it to the accumulator.

So, in this section, we have seen the first execution technique—the one that parses and executes one instruction at a time.

The parsing_interpreter.rs source file

Now, we can look at the other execution technique—the one that first parses the whole program and then executes the result of the parsing.

The `parsing_interpreter` module has two entry points:

1. `parse_program`
2. `execute_parsed_program`

The first one calls `get_process_size` once to get the process size from the first two bytes, then it parses the program instructions using the following loop:

```
let mut parsed_program = vec![Instruction::Byte(0); process_size_parsed];
let mut ip = 2;
loop {
    match parse_instruction(&program[ip..]) {
        Ok(instruction) => {
            parsed_program[ip] = instruction.1;
            ip += instruction.1.len();
            if let Instruction::Terminate(_) = instruction.1 {
                break;
            }
        }
        Err(_) => return Err(()),
    };
}
```

In the following code, the data structure that we are going to build is the `parsed_program` variable. That variable is a vector of instructions or byte data. It is initialized by single data bytes with zero value, but then some of these bytes are replaced with instructions.

Starting at position 2, the program is repeatedly parsed using the `parse_instruction` function. This function returns an instruction that is stored in the vector at the position corresponding to its position in the program. When the `Terminate` instruction is parsed, the loop ends.

The `parse_instruction` function is the same as the one we saw in the `instructions` module.

After this loop, we need to set the data values into the vector. This is done by using the following loop:

```
for ip in ip..program.len() {
    parsed_program[ip] = Instruction::Byte(program[ip]);
}
```

This replaces any byte of the vector with another byte whose value is taken from the program. The `execute_parsed_program` function has the following body:

```
let mut registers = ParsedRegisterSet { ip: 2, acc: 0 };
loop {
    if let Some(return_code) = execute_parsed_instruction(parsed_program,
&mut registers) {
        return return_code;
    };
}
```

The preceding code defines a register set and then calls `execute_parsed_instruction` repeatedly until it returns `Some`. This function is very similar to the `execute_instruction` functions of the `emulator` module.

The main differences are in the use of the `get_parsed_le_word`, `set_parsed_le_word`, `get_parsed_byte`, and `set_parsed_byte` functions, instead of `get_le_word`, `set_le_word`, `get_byte`, and `set_byte`.

These functions, instead of getting or setting the u8 values in a slice of u8 objects, get or set the `Instruction::Byte` values in a slice of the `Instruction` objects. This slice is the parsed program.

We will now move on to the last technique.

The translator.rs source file

Now, we can look at the last execution technique—the one that translates the program into a C language program so that it can be compiled with any C compiler.

The `translator.rs` module has just one entry point:

```
pub fn translate_program_to_c(program: &[u8], target_path: &str) ->
Result<()> {
```

This function gets the machine language program to translate the program and the path of the file to create and return a result that indicates its success or failure.

Its body creates a text file and writes into it using statements such as this one:

```
writeln!(file, "#include <stdio.h>")?;
```

std::fs::write
P276

It writes a string into the `file` stream. Notice that the `writeln` macro, in a similar way to the `println` macro, supports string interpolation through pairs of braces:

```
writeln!(file, " addr_{}: acc = {};", *ip, operand)?;
```

Therefore, any real brace must be doubled:

```
writeln!(file, "unsigned char memory[] = {{")?;
```

The translation algorithm is quite simple. First, the declaration of a global byte array is emitted:

C code

```
unsigned char memory[];
```

Then, we have the definitions of two utility functions. Their signatures are as follows:

```
unsigned short bytes_to_u16_le(unsigned int address)
void u16_to_bytes_le(unsigned int address, unsigned short operand)
```

read
write

The first one reads the two bytes in the `memory` array at two positions—`address` and `address + 1`—and, interpreting them as a little-endian 16-bit number, returns the number. The second one generates the two bytes that comprise the `operand` value and writes them in memory as a little-endian 16-bit number at the `address` and `address + 1` positions.

Then, the `main` C function is emitted. It begins by declaring the `acc` variable, which will be used as an accumulator register.

It may be surprising that there is no need for a variable containing the instruction pointer. This means that during the execution of the C program, the current C language statement corresponds to the current machine language instruction.

The machine language jumps are implemented using the infamous `goto` statement. To be able to jump to any instruction, the instructions that are the destination of a jump must be preceded by a C language unique label. For simplicity, when translating any instruction, a different label is generated, even if most of them will never be used by a `goto` statement.

As an example, let's consider the `store pos` assembly language instruction, corresponding to the `3, 33, 1` machine language instruction, where `3` is the opcode of the `store` instruction and `33, 1` represents `289` in little-endian notation. Assume that this instruction starts at position `10` of the program. For this instruction, the following C language statement will be generated:

```
addr_10: u16_to_bytes_le(289, acc);
```

First, there is the label as a target of a possible `jump` instruction. Labels are created, concatenating the position of the instruction to the `addr_` constant. Then, there is a function call that copies the value of the `acc` variable to the bytes at positions `289` and `230` of the `memory` array in little-endian notation.

To create these statements, a loop is performed that parses an instruction at a time using the `parse_instruction` function, and then generates the corresponding C language statement using the `translate_instruction_to_c` function.

This function contains a large `match` statement, with a branch for every instruction type. For example, the branch that translates the `Store` instructions is as follows:

```
Store(address) => {
    writeln!(file, " addr_{}: u16_to_bytes_le({}, acc);", *ip, address)?;
    *ip += 3;
}
```

After the `Terminate` statement has been processed by the loop, the `main` C function is closed and the `memory` array, which was only just declared, is now defined and initialized using the entire content of the machine language program.

In fact, the machine language instructions could be omitted from this array as they are not used by the C language code, but this way is simpler.

So, we have seen how to generate an equivalent C language program from a machine language program, assuming it is well formed. This technique could be used to generate programs in other programming languages, as long as there is a `goto` statement.

Now that we have seen several ways to execute machine language programs, we can look at another use of a machine language parser.

The nom_disassembler project

We have seen that usually, machine language programs are written in assembly language and are then translated into machine language. So, if we want to understand or debug a machine language program written by our company, we should look at the assembly language program used to generate it.

However, if this program wasn't written by our company and we don't have its assembly language source code available, it is useful to have a tool that tries its best to translate machine language programs into the corresponding assembly language programs. This tool, named a disassembler, cannot create an excellent assembly language program for the following reasons:

- No meaningful comments can be inserted into the code.
- Data variables have no symbolic name to make sense of them. They are just bytes of memory positions where some data is placed, and so they are referenced by their address.
- The destinations of jumps have no symbolic names to make sense of them. They are just memory positions where some instruction begins, and so they are referenced by their address.

Regarding 16-bit words, sometimes it is useful to see them as single numbers and sometimes as pairs of bytes. If you are disassembling a program to apply some changes to it and then submit the changed assembly program to an assembler (to obtain a changed machine language program), it is better to only generate a single number for every 16-bit number (in little-endian notation, for our kind of processor).

Instead, if you are disassembling a program just to understand it deeply, it is better to generate both a single number notation and a pair of its bytes for every 16-bit number.

Typical disassemblers use hexadecimal notation. A 16-bit number is represented by four hexadecimal digits, where two digits represent one byte and the other two digits represent the other byte.

Instead, to continue with decimal notation, the `nom_disassembler` project generates two outputs from the same machine language program:

- A `FOR DEBUG` output, where every 16-bit number is shown both as a single number and as a pair of bytes
- A `FOR ASSEMBLING` output, where every 16-bit number is shown only as a single number

We will now learn how to run the project in the next subsection.

Running the project

If you type in `cargo run` for this project, you'll see a long output that begins with the following:

```
FOR DEBUG
Program size: 299
Process size: 699
     2: Set(284: 28, 1)
     5: Input(5)
     7: Set(284: 28, 1)
    10: Store(289: 33, 1)
    13: IndirectLoadByte(289: 33, 1)
```

After a few lines, you'll find the following:

```
   297: Byte(2)
   298: Byte(0)
```

```
FOR ASSEMBLING
process size 699
     2: set 284
     5: input 5
     7: set 284
    10: store 289
    13: indirect load byte 289
```

At the end, you'll find the following:

```
   297: data byte 2
   298: data byte 0
```

The first part of the output is the FOR DEBUG disassembly. After showing the size of the program and the process, the disassembled instructions begin. The first one is a Set instruction, whose 16-bit operand is number 284, which is composed of the 28 and 1 bytes in little-endian order. The second instruction is Input, which has an 8-bit operand.

Any instruction is preceded by the address of the first byte of the instruction. So, Set is preceded by 2 (it is the third byte of the program), and Input is preceded by 5 (it is the sixth byte of the program).

The program ends with a sequence of bytes. As machine language has no concept of word data, the data is just a sequence of bytes.

The second part of the output is the FOR ASSEMBLING disassembly. This differs from the first kind of disassembling technique by the following aspects:

- There is no program size. Any assembler program can compute the size of the corresponding machine language program. There is no need to specify it in the source for the assembler.
- Instructions' symbolic names only contain lowercase letters and they can be composed of several words, separated by spaces. In this way, they are easier to read and to write. Instead, the FOR DEBUG output uses just the names of the variants of the instruction enum.
- The operands are a single number.

We will now take a look at the source code to help us understand it further.

Examining the source code

Now, let's see how this project obtained this output by examining the source code, which is all in the main.rs file. This function, after defining the prog variable as in the preceding project, contains just these statements:

```
println!("FOR DEBUG");
let _ = disassembly_program_for_debug(&prog);
println!();
println!("FOR ASSEMBLING");
let _ = disassembly_program(&prog);
```

The disassembly_program_for_debug function produces the first kind of output and the disassembly_program function produces the second kind of output. Let's see what these functions do.

Generating disassembly code that is useful for debugging

The interesting part of the `disassembly_program_for_debug` function is the following code snippet:

```
loop {
    let instruction = parse_instruction(rest)?;
    println!("{:5}: {:?}", offset, instruction.1);
    offset += instruction.1.len();
    rest = instruction.0;
    if let Terminate(_) = instruction.1 {
        break;
    }
}
for byte in rest {
    let instr = Byte(*byte);
    println!("{:5}: {:?}", offset, instr);
    offset += instr.len();
}
```

In the preceding code, there is first a loop that parses each instruction using the `parse_instruction` function, and then there is a loop that scans each data byte. For every parsed instruction, the obtained instruction is printed by `println` and its size is added to the current position inside the program, named `offset`.

This loop ends when the `Terminate` instruction is found. For the data bytes, a `Byte` variant is built and it is printed in a similar way. This raises the question of how an object of the `Instruction` type can be printed.

To be printed using the `{:?}` placeholder of `println`, the `Debug` trait must be implemented. However, if you print an `Instruction` object such as those defined in the preceding chapters, we don't get the output we want. For example, if you execute the `print!("{:?}", Instruction::Set(284))` statement, you will get the following output:

```
Set(284)
```

But instead, we want the following output:

```
Set(284: 28, 1)
```

To obtain the desired formatting, a new type must be defined in the following way:

```
#[derive(Copy, Clone)]
struct Word(u16);
```

The `Word` type encapsulates all the `u16` arguments of the variants of `Instruction` in the following way:

```
#[derive(Debug, Copy, Clone)]
enum Instruction {
    Terminate(u8),
    Set(Word),
    Load(Word),
    ...
```

Of course, this causes any construction of an `Instruction` object to construct a `Word` object inside of it, and every trait implemented by `Instruction` must be implemented also by `Word`. The `Copy` and `Clone` traits are implemented using default derivations.

Instead, the `Debug` trait is implemented in the following way:

```
impl std::fmt::Debug for Word {
    fn fmt(&self, f: &mut std::fmt::Formatter) -> std::fmt::Result {
        write!(f, "{}: {}, {}", self.0, self.0 as u8, self.0 >> 8)
    }
}
```

The body of the `fmt` function writes three numbers—the whole argument (`self.0`), its low byte (`self.0 as u8`), and its high byte (`self.0 >> 8`). In this way, we get the desired formatting.

`Instruction` objects are created by the instruction parsers. So, these parsers must be changed, with respect to the project, `nom_byte_machine`. In that project, we saw that some parsers accept 16-bit numbers, such as this one:

```
fn parse_set(input: &[u8]) -> IResult<&[u8], Instruction> {
    preceded(tag("\x01"), map(le_u16, Instruction::Set))(input)
}
```

For all of these parsers, the use of the `le_u16` parser must be replaced with the use of the `le_word` parser, obtaining the following:

```
fn parse_set(input: &[u8]) -> IResult<&[u8], Instruction> {
    preceded(tag("\x01"), map(le_word, Instruction::Set))(input)
}
```

This parser is defined as follows:

```
fn le_word(input: &[u8]) -> IResult<&[u8], Word> {
    le_u16(input).map(|(input, output)| (input, Word(output)))
}
```

It still calls the `le_u16` parser, but then it gets the generated `(input, output)` pair and encapsulates the `output` item in a `Word` object, obtaining an `(input, Word(output))` pair.

We have seen how to convert a machine language program into a kind of assembly code. That disassembled code is useful for debugging purposes, but it is not easy to change and reassemble it to generate a new machine language program. In the next section, we will look at another kind of disassembly code that is useful for assembling it again.

Generating disassembly code that is useful for reassembling

Regarding the other kind of output, FOR ASSEMBLING, we must examine the `disassembly_program` function, which is quite similar to the corresponding part of the `disassembly_program_for_debug` function. The only differences are the following:

- The program size is not emitted.
- The format strings of the two `println` statements are `"{:5}: {}"`, instead of `"{:5}: {:?}"`.

For this kind of format placeholder, the `Display` trait must be implemented by the `Instruction` type:

```
impl std::fmt::Display for Instruction {
    fn fmt(&self, f: &mut std::fmt::Formatter) -> std::fmt::Result {
        use Instruction::*;
        match self {
            Terminate(byte) => write!(f, "terminate {}", byte),
            Set(word) => write!(f, "set {}", word),
            Load(word) => write!(f, "load {}", word),
            ...
            Byte(byte) => write!(f, "data byte {}", byte),
        }
    }
}
```

For any variant, the `write` macro is used to emit the symbolic name of the instruction, followed by the formatted value of the byte or word. This formatting also requires the implementation of the `Display` trait for the arguments. Bytes are of the `u8` type, which already implements the `Display` trait. Instead, for words, the following declaration is required:

```
impl std::fmt::Display for Word {
    fn fmt(&self, f: &mut std::fmt::Formatter) -> std::fmt::Result {
        write!(f, "{}", self.0)
    }
}
```

This simply produces the numeric value encapsulated in a `Word` object. So, we have seen how to transform a machine language program into two possible formats of disassembled text.

We have also seen another kind of disassembling. As an exercise, you should write an assembler for this machine language, run it on the code generated by this disassembler, and check that the resulting machine code is identical to the original one.

Summary

In this chapter, we first defined an extremely simple toy machine language, and then a slightly more complex one to experiment with techniques of machine language manipulation.

The first machine language defined assumes that memory is just a sequence of 16-bit words and that any instruction is composed of two parts of one word each—an opcode and an operand. The second machine language assumes that memory is a sequence of bytes and some instructions can manipulate single bytes, while other instructions can manipulate whole words.

This introduced the endianness issue, which concerns how to interpret two consecutive bytes as a word. As an example, the sieve of Eratosthenes algorithm was first written in Rust and then translated into both machine languages.

For the first machine language, an interpreter was written without using any external library. It was used to first interpret a small number conversion program (`word_machine_convert`) and then the more complex sieve algorithm (`word_machine_sieve`).

For the second machine language, three procedures were written in a single project (`nom_byte_machine`). All of these procedures used the `nom` parsing library. The first procedure was an instruction-by-instruction interpreter. The second procedure first parsed the whole program and then interpreted the parsed program. The third procedure translated the program into C language.

For the second machine language, two kinds of disassemblers were built using the `nom` library (`nom_disassembler`)—one disassembler emitted output useful for debugging and the other emitted output useful for reassembling it after editing.

So, after reading this chapter, you should now understand what a machine language is, what its corresponding assembly language is, how to translate assembly language into machine language and vice versa, how to translate machine language into C language, how to interpret machine language, and how to use the `nom` parsing library to carry out these tasks.

In the next chapter, we will learn how to create a Linux kernel module.

Questions

1. How can a machine language emulator be useful?
2. What is the accumulator of a processor?
3. What is the instruction pointer of a processor?
4. Why is it very difficult to write directly in machine language and, therefore, better to use an assembler?
5. How can a Rust enum represent a machine language instruction?
6. What is little-endian notation and what is big-endian notation?
7. What is the difference between a `nom` parser that accepts text and one that accepts binary data?
8. Which rules must be respected by a machine language program to be able to parse it all or to be able to translate it into another programming language?
9. Why might different kinds of output, or a hexadecimal output format, be preferred for a disassembler?
10. How can a single number be printed in different ways?

Creating a Linux Kernel Module

10

Any decent operating system can be extended by loadable modules. This is required to support hardware that is not specifically supported by the organization that created the operating system, and so these loadable modules are often named **device drivers**.

However, this extensibility of operating systems can also be exploited for other purposes. For example, a specific filesystem or network protocol can be supported by the kernel itself through loadable modules without changing and recompiling the actual kernel.

In this chapter, we will look at how to build a kernel-loadable module, specifically for the Linux operating system and the x86_64 CPU architecture. The concepts and commands that are described here are also applicable to other CPU architectures.

The following topics will be covered in this chapter:

- Preparing the environment
- Creating a boilerplate module
- Using the global variable
- Allocating memory
- Creating a driver for a character device

By the end of this chapter, you will have learned some general concepts regarding operating system-extension modules and, in particular, how to create, manage, and debug Linux kernel modules.

Technical requirements

To understand this chapter, some concepts of the Linux operating system should be known. In particular, you need to know the following:

- How to use the Linux command interpreter (that is, the **shell**)
- How to understand C language source code
- How to use the GCC compiler or the Clang compiler

If you don't have this knowledge, you can refer to the following web resources:

- There are many tutorials that teach you how to use the Linux command interpreter. One that is suitable for beginners of the Ubuntu Linux distribution can be found at `https://ubuntu.com/tutorials/command-line-for-beginners#1-overview`. A more advanced and complete free book can be found at `https://wiki.lib.sun.ac.za/images/c/ca/TLCL-13.07.pdf`.
- There are many tutorials that teach you about the C programming language. One of them is `https://www.tutorialspoint.com/cprogramming/index.htm`.
- A reference for the Clang compiler can be found at `https://clang.llvm.org/docs/ClangCommandLineReference.html`.

The code examples in this chapter have only been developed and tested on a specific version of Linux—a Linux Mint distribution with the 4.15.0-72-generic kernel version—and so they are only guaranteed to work with this version. The Mint distribution is derived from the Debian distribution and so it shares most of Debian's commands. The desktop environment is irrelevant.

To run the examples in this chapter, you should have access as a superuser (root) to a system running the preceding distribution based on a CPU with the x86_64 architecture.

To build a kernel module, a lot of boilerplate code needs to be written. This work has already been done for you in an open source project available on GitHub at `https://github.com/lizhuohua/linux-kernel-module-rust`. Parts of this GitHub project have been copied into a framework to write Linux kernel modules, which will be used in this chapter. This can be found in the `linux-fw` folder of the repository associated with this chapter.

Also, for simplicity, no cross-compilation will be done—that is, the kernel module will be built in the same operating system in which it will be used. This is a bit unusual as often, loadable modules are developed for operating systems or architectures that are not suitable for software development; in some cases, the target system is too constrained to run a convenient development environment, such as a micro-controller.

In other cases, the opposite applies—the target system is too costly to be used by a single developer, such as a supercomputer.

The complete source code for this chapter can be found in the `Chapter10` folder of the repository at `https://github.com/PacktPublishing/Creative-Projects-for-Rust-Programmers`.

Project overview

In this chapter, we'll look at four projects that will show you how to build increasingly complex Linux kernel modules:

- `boilerplate`: An extremely simple kernel module that shows the minimal requirements to build your own module
- `state`: A module that keeps some global static variables—that is, a **static** state
- `allocating`: A module that allocates heap memory—that is, a **dynamic** state
- `dots`: A module that implements a read-only character device that can be associated with a filesystem pathname, and then it can be read as a file

Understanding kernel modules

Kernel modules must satisfy certain requirements imposed by the operating system, and so it is quite unreasonable to try to write a kernel module in an application-oriented programming language, such as Java or JavaScript. Usually, kernel modules are only written in assembly language or in C, and sometimes in C++. However, Rust is designed to be a system programming language, and so it is actually possible to write kernel-loadable modules in Rust.

While Rust is usually a portable programming language—the same source code can be recompiled for different CPU architectures and for different operating systems—this is not the case for kernel modules. A specific kernel module must be designed and implemented for a specific operating system. In addition, a specific machine architecture must usually be targeted, although the core logic can be architecture-independent. So, the examples in this chapter will only target the Linux operating system and the x86_64 CPU architecture.

Preparing the environment

Some of the installation work must be performed with superuser privileges. So, you should prefix the `sudo` command before any command that installs a system-wide package or that changes something in the kernel. Alternatively, you should routinely work as a superuser. Needless to say, this is dangerous as you can jeopardize the whole system with a wrong command. To work as a superuser, type the following command into a terminal:

```
su root
```

Then, type in your superuser password.

The Linux operating system expects its modules to only be written in C. If you want to write a kernel module in Rust, a glue software must be used to interface your Rust code to the C language of Linux.

So, a C compiler must be used to build this glue software. Here the `clang` compiler will be used. This is part of the **Low-Level Virtual Machine (LLVM)** project.

 The Rust compiler also uses libraries of the LLVM project to generate machine code.

You can install the `clang` compiler in your Linux system by typing the following commands:

```
sudo apt update
sudo apt install llvm clang
```

Notice that the `apt` command is typical of Debian-derived distributions and is not available on many Linux distributions, nor on other operating systems.

Then, you need to ensure that the C language headers of your current operating system are installed. You can discover what the version of your current operating system is by typing the `uname -r` command. This will print something similar to `4.15.0-72-generic`. You can install the headers for the specific version of the kernel by using a command similar to the following:

```
sudo apt install linux-headers-4.15.0-72-generic
```

You can combine the two commands by typing the following command:

```
sudo apt install linux-headers-"$(uname -r)"
```

This will generate the correct command for your system.

At the time of writing, Linux kernel modules can only be created using the `nightly` version of the Rust compiler. To install the latest version of this compiler, type the following:

```
rustup toolchain install nightly
```

Also, the source code of the Rust compiler and the tool to format Rust source code are needed. You can ensure they are installed by typing the following command:

```
rustup component add --toolchain=nightly rust-src rustfmt
```

To ensure that the `nightly` toolchain of Rust for the x86_64 architecture and Linux will be used by default, run this command:

```
rustup default nightly-x86_64-unknown-linux-gnu
```

This can be shortened to `rustup default nightly` if there are no other target platforms installed on your system.

We know that the `cargo` utility has several subcommands, such as `new`, `build`, and `run`. For this project, an additional `cargo` subcommand will be needed—the `xbuild` subcommand. This name stands for **cross-build**, which means to compile for another platform. Actually, it is used to generate machine code for a platform different from the one running the compiler. In this case, it means that while the compiler we are running is a standard executable that is running in user space, the code we are generating will run in kernel space, and so it will need a different standard library. You can install that subcommand by typing this line:

```
cargo install cargo-xbuild
```

Then, after you have downloaded the source code associated with this chapter from GitHub, you are ready to run the examples.

Notice that in the downloaded source code, there is a folder for every project, plus a folder named `linux-fw`. This contains the framework to develop Linux kernel modules, and the examples assume that it is located in this position.

A boilerplate module

The first project is the minimal, loadable kernel module, and so it is called **boilerplate**. It will just print a message when the module is loaded and another message when it is unloaded.

In the `boilerplate` folder, there are the following source files:

- `Cargo.toml`: The build directives for the Rust project
- `src/lib.rs`: The Rust source code
- `Makefile`: The build directives to generate and compile the C language glue code and to link the generated object code into a kernel module
- `bd`: A shell script to build a debug configuration of the kernel module
- `br`: A shell script to build a released configuration of the kernel module

Let's start with building the kernel module.

Building and running the kernel module

To build the kernel module for debugging purposes, open the `boilerplate` folder and type in this command:

```
./bd
```

Of course, this file must have executable permissions. However, it should already have them when it is installed from the GitHub repository.

The first time you run this script, it will build the framework itself, and so it will take quite a while. After that, it will build the `boilerplate` project in a couple of minutes.

After the completion of the `build` command, several files should appear in the current folder. Among them is one named `boilerplate.ko`, where `ko` (short for **kernel object**) is the kernel module we want to install. Its size is huge because it contains a lot of debugging information.

A Linux command that gives information about a Linux module file is `modinfo`. You can use it by typing the following command:

```
modinfo boilerplate.ko
```

This should print some information about the specified file. To load the module into the kernel, type the following command:

```
sudo insmod boilerplate.ko
```

The `insmod` (insert module) command loads a Linux module from the specified file and adds it to the running kernel. Of course, this is a privileged operation that can jeopardize the safety and security of the whole computer system, and so only a superuser can run it. This explains the need to use the `sudo` command. If the command is successful; nothing is printed to the terminal.

The `lsmod` (list module) command prints a list of all the currently loaded modules. To select the one you are interested in, you can filter the output using the `grep` utility. So, you can type the following command:

```
lsmod | grep -w boilerplate
```

If `boilerplate` is loaded, you will get a line similar to the following:

```
boilerplate            1634304  0
```

This line contains the name of the module, the memory used by it in bytes, and the number of current uses of these modules.

To unload the loaded module, you can type the following command:

```
sudo rmmod boilerplate
```

The `rmmod` (remove module) command unloads the specified module from the running Linux kernel. If the module is not currently loaded, this command prints an error message and does nothing.

Now, let's look at the behavior of this module. Linux has a memory-only log area called the **kernel buffer**. Kernel modules can append lines of text to this buffer. When the `boilerplate` module is loaded, it appends the `boilerplate: Loaded` text to the kernel buffer. When the `boilerplate` module is unloaded, it appends the `boilerplate: Unloaded` text. Only the kernel and its modules can write to it, but everyone can read it using the `dmesg` (short for **display messages**) utility.

If you type `dmesg` into the terminal, the whole content of the kernel buffer will be printed to the terminal. Typically, there are thousands of messages in the kernel buffer, written by several modules since the last reboot of the system, but the last two lines should be those appended by the `boilerplate` module. To view just the last 10 lines while keeping their colors, type the following:

```
dmesg --color=always | tail
```

The last two lines should look something like the following:

```
[166961.483086] boilerplate: Loaded
[167311.490511] boilerplate: Unloaded
```

The first part of any line, enclosed in brackets, is a **timestamp** written by the kernel. This is the time in seconds and microseconds since the start of the kernel. The rest of the line is written by the module code.

Now, we can see how the `bd` script built this kernel module.

The build commands

The `bd` script has the following content:

```
#!/bin/sh
cur_dir=$(pwd)
cd ../linux-fw
cargo build
cd $cur_dir
RUST_TARGET_PATH=$(pwd)/../linux-fw cargo xbuild --target x86_64-linux-
kernel-module && make
```

Let's see what happened in the code:

- The first line declares that this is a shell script, and so the Bourne shell program will be used to run it.
- The second line saves the path of the current folder in a temporary variable.
- The third, fourth, and fifth lines enter the framework folder, build the framework for a debug configuration, and return back to the original folder.

- The last line builds the module itself. Notice that it ends with `&& make`. This means that after having successfully run the command in the first part of the line, the command in the second part (the `make` command) must be run. Instead, if the command in the first part fails, the second command will not be run. The line begins with the `RUST_TARGET_PATH=$(pwd)/../linux-fw` clause. It creates an environment variable named `RUST_TARGET_PATH`, which is only valid for the rest of the command line. It contains the absolute pathname of the `framework` folder. Then, the `cargo` tool is invoked, with an `xbuild --target x86_64-linux-kernel-module` argument. This is an `xbuild` subcommand to compile for a different platform than the current one, and the rest of the command specifies that the target is `x86_64-linux-kernel-module`. This target is specific to the framework we are using. To explain how this target is used, it is necessary to examine the `Cargo.toml` file, which consists of the following code:

```
[package]
name = "boilerplate"
version = "0.1.0"
authors = []
edition = "2018"

[lib]
crate-type = ["staticlib"]

[dependencies]
linux-kernel-module = { path = "../linux-fw" }

[profile.release]
panic = "abort"
lto = true

[profile.dev]
panic = "abort"
```

The `package` section is the usual one. The `crate-type` item of the `lib` section specifies that the target of the compilation is a static-link library.

The `linux-kernel-module` module of the `dependencies` section specifies the relative path of the folder containing the framework. If you prefer to install the `framework` folder in another position relative to this project or with another name, you should change this path, as well as the `RUST_TARGET_PATH` environment variable.

Thanks to this directive, it is possible to use the target specified in the `cargo` command line.

The remaining sections specify that in case of panic, an immediate abort should be done (with no output) and that in the release configuration, **Link-Time Optimization (LTO)** should be activated.

After completing this `cargo` command, the `target/x86_64-linux-kernel-module/debug/libboilerplate.a` static-link library should have been created. As with any other Linux static-link library, its name starts with `lib` and ends with `.a`.

The last part of the command line runs the `make` utility, which is a `build` tool used mainly when developing in C. Just as the `cargo` tool uses the `Cargo.toml` file to know what to do, the `make` tool uses the `Makefile` file for the same purposes.

Here, we don't examine `Makefile`, but we just say that it reads the static library generated by `cargo` and encapsulates it with some C language glue code to generate the `boilerplate.ko` file, which is the kernel module.

In addition to the `bd` file, there is a `br` file, which is similar but runs both `cargo` and `make` with a `release` option, and so it generates an optimized kernel module. You can run it by typing the following:

```
./br
```

The generated module will overwrite the `boilerplate.ko` file, which was created by `bd`. You can see that the new file is much smaller on disk and, using the `lsmod` utility, you can see that it is also much smaller in memory.

The source code of the boilerplate module

Now, let's examine the Rust source code of this project. It is contained in the `src/lib.rs` file. The first line is as follows:

```
#![no_std]
```

This is a directive to avoid loading the Rust standard library in this project. Actually, many routines of the standard library assume to be run as application code—in user-space, not inside a kernel—and so they cannot be used in this project. Of course, after this directive, many Rust functions that we are accustomed to using are no longer automatically available.

In particular, no heap memory allocator is included by default and so, by default, vectors and strings that need heap memory allocation are not allowed. If you try to use `Vec` or the `String` type, you will get a `use of undeclared type or module` error message.

The next lines are as follows:

```
use linux_kernel_module::c_types;
use linux_kernel_module::println;
```

These lines import some names into the current source file. These names are defined in the framework.

The first line imports the declarations of some data types corresponding to the C language data types. They are needed to interface with the kernel, which expects that modules are written in C. After this declaration, you can use, for example, the `c_types::c_int` expression, which corresponds to the C language `int` data type.

The second line imports a macro named `println`, just like that of the standard library, which is no longer available. Actually, it can be used in the same way, but instead of printing on the terminal, it appends a line to the kernel buffer, prefixed by a timestamp.

Then, there are two entry points of the module—the `init_module` function, which is invoked by the kernel when the module is loaded, and the `cleanup_module` function, which is invoked by the kernel when the module is unloaded. They are defined by the following code:

```
#[no_mangle]
pub extern "C" fn init_module() -> c_types::c_int {
    println!("boilerplate: Loaded");
    0
}

#[no_mangle]
pub extern "C" fn cleanup_module() {
    println!("boilerplate: Unloaded");
}
```

Their `no_mangle` attribute is a directive to the linker to keep this exact function name so that the kernel can find this function by its name. Its `extern "C"` clause specifies that the *function-calling* convention must be the one normally used by C.

These functions get no arguments, but the first one returns a value that indicates the outcome of the initialization. A `0` result represents success and a `1` result represents failure. It is specified by Linux that the type of this value is the C language `int` variable and the `c_types::c_int` type of the framework represents just that binary type.

Both functions print the messages that we saw in the previous section to the kernel buffer. Also, both functions are optional, but if the `init_module` function is absent, a warning is emitted by the linker.

The last two lines of the file are as follows:

```
#[link_section = ".modinfo"]
pub static MODINFO: [u8; 12] = *b"license=GPL\0";
```

They define a string resource for the linker to insert into the resulting executable. The name of that string resource is .modinfo and its value is licence=GPL. That value must be a null-terminated ASCII string because that is the string type normally used in C. This section is not required, but if it is absent, a warning is emitted by the linker.

Using global variables

The module boilerplate of the preceding project just printed some static text. However, it is quite typical for a module to have some variables that must be accessed during the lifetime of the module. Usually, Rust does not use mutable global variables because they are not safe and just defines them in the main function and passes them as arguments to the functions called by main. However, kernel modules do not have a main function. They have entry points called by the kernel and so, to keep shared mutable variables, some unsafe code must be used.

The State project shows you how to define and use shared mutable variables. To run it, enter the state folder and type ./bd. Then, type the following four commands:

```
sudo insmod state.ko
lsmod | grep -w state
sudo rmmod state
dmesg --color=always | tail
```

Let's see what we did there:

- The first command will load the module into the kernel with no output to the console.
- The second command will show that the module is loaded by fetching all the loaded modules and filtering the one called state.
- The third command will unload the module from the kernel with no output to the console.
- The last command will show the two lines added by this module to the kernel buffer. They will look like this:

```
[123456.789012] state: Loaded
[123463.987654] state: Unloaded 1001
```

Apart from the timestamps, they differ from the `boilerplate` example due to the name of the module and the addition of the number `1001` to the second line.

Let's see the source code of this project, showing the differences compared with the boilerplate source code. The `lib.rs` file contains the following additional lines:

```
struct GlobalData { n: u16 }

static mut GLOBAL: GlobalData = GlobalData { n: 1000 };
```

The first line defines a data structure type, named `GlobalData`, containing only a 16-bit unsigned number. The second line defines and initializes a static mutable variable of this type, named `GLOBAL`.

Then, the `init_module` function contains the following additional statement:

```
unsafe { GLOBAL.n += 1; }
```

This increments the global variable. As it was initialized to `1000`, after the module is loaded, the value of this variable is `1001`.

Finally, the statement in the `cleanup_module` function is replaced by the following:

```
println!("state: Unloaded {}", unsafe { GLOBAL.n });
```

This formats and prints the value of the global variable. Notice that both reading and writing a global variable is an *unsafe operation* as it provides access to a mutable static object.

The `bd` and `br` files are identical to those in the `boilerplate` project. The `Cargo.toml` and `Makefile` files differ from those in the `boilerplate` project due to the replacement of the `boilerplate` string with the `state` string.

Allocating memory

The preceding project defined a global variable, but it did not carry out memory allocation. Even in kernel modules, it is possible to allocate memory, as shown in the `allocating` project.

To run this project, open the `allocating` folder and type in `./bd`. Then, type the following four commands:

```
sudo insmod allocating.ko
lsmod | grep -w allocating
sudo rmmod allocating
dmesg --color=always | tail
```

These commands have a behavior quite similar to the corresponding commands for the preceding project, but the last one will print a line that, after the timestamp, will contain the following text:

```
allocating: Unloaded 1001 abcd 500000
```

Let's examine the source code of this project and see its differences compared with the `boilerplate` source code. The `lib.rs` file contains the following additional lines:

```
extern crate alloc;
use crate::alloc::string::String;
use crate::alloc::vec::Vec;
```

The first line explicitly declares that a memory allocator is needed. Otherwise, as the standard library is not used, no memory allocator will be linked to the executable module.

The second and third lines are required to include the `String` and `Vec` types in the source code, respectively. Otherwise, they will not be available to the source code. Then, there are the following global declarations:

```
struct GlobalData {
    n: u16,
    msg: String,
    values: Vec<i32>,
}

static mut GLOBAL: GlobalData = GlobalData {
    n: 1000,
    msg: String::new(),
    values: Vec::new(),
};
```

Now, the data structure contains three fields. Two of them, `msg` and `values`, use heap memory when they are not empty, and the `GLOBAL` variable initializes all of them. Here, no memory allocation is allowed, and so these dynamic fields must be empty.

In the `init_module` function, as in other entry points, allocations are allowed, and so the following code is valid:

```
unsafe {
    GLOBAL.n += 1;
    GLOBAL.msg += "abcd";
    GLOBAL.values.push(500_000);
}
```

This changes all the fields of the global variable, allocating memory for both the `msg` string and the `values` vector. Finally, the global variable is accessed to print its values by using the following statement in the `cleanup_module` function:

```
unsafe {
    println!("allocating: Unloaded {} {} {}",
        GLOBAL.n,
        GLOBAL.msg,
        GLOBAL.values[0]
    );
}
```

The rest of the code is unchanged.

A character device

Unix-like systems are famous for their feature that maps I/O devices to the filesystem. In addition to the predefined I/O devices, it is possible to define your own devices as kernel modules. A kernel device can be attached to real hardware or it can be **virtual**. In this project, we will build a virtual device.

In Unix-like systems, there are two kinds of I/O devices: **block devices** and **character devices**. The former handle packets of bytes in a single operation (that is, they are buffered), while the latter can handle only one byte at a time, with no buffering.

In general, a device can be read, written, or both. Our device will be a read-only device. So, we are going to build a filesystem-mapped, virtual, read-only character device.

Building the character device

Here, we are going to build a character device driver (or **character device** for short). A character device is a device driver that can handle only one byte at a time with no buffering. The behavior of our device will be quite simple— for every byte read from it, it will return a dot character, but for every 10 characters, an asterisk will be returned instead of a dot.

To build it, open the `dots` folder and type in `./bd`. Several files will be created in the current folder, including the `dots.ko` file, which is our kernel module.

To install it and check whether it is loading, type the following:

```
sudo insmod dots.ko
lsmod | grep -w dots
```

Now, the kernel module is loaded as a character device, but it is not yet mapped to a special file. However, you can find it among the loaded devices by using the following command:

```
grep -w dots /proc/devices
```

The `/proc/devices` virtual file contains a list of all the loaded device modules. Among them, in the `Character devices` section, there should be a line like this:

```
236 dots
```

This means that there is a loaded character device driver named `dots` whose internal identifier is `236`. This internal identifier is also named a **major number** because it is the first number of a pair of numbers that actually identifies the device. The other number, known as a **minor number**, is not used but can be set to `0`.

The major number may vary from system to system and from loading to loading because it is assigned by the kernel when the module is loaded. Anyway, it is a small, positive integer number.

Now, we must associate these device drivers with a special file, which is an entry point in the filesystem, that can be used as a file, but is actually a handle to a device driver. This operation is performed by the following command, in which you should replace `236` with the major number you found in the `/proc/devices` file:

```
sudo mknod /dev/dots1 c 236 0
```

The `mknod` Linux command creates a special device file. The preceding command creates a special file named `dots1` in the `dev` folder.

This is a privileged command for two reasons:

- Only a superuser can create special files.
- Only a superuser can create a file in the `dev` folder.

The `c` character means that the created device will be a character device. The following two numbers—`236` and `0`—are the major and minor numbers of the new virtual device.

Notice that the name of the special file (`dots1`) can be different from the name of the device (`dots`) because the association between the special file and the device driver is performed through the major number.

After creating the special file, you can read some bytes from it. The `head` command reads the first lines or bytes of a text file. So, type the following:

```
head -c42 /dev/dots1
```

This will print the following text to the console:

```
.........*.........*.........*.........*..
```

This command reads the first 42 bytes from the specified file.

When asked for the first byte, the module returns a dot. When asked for the second byte, the module returns another dot, and so on for the first nine bytes. However, when asked for the 10th byte, the module returns an asterisk. Then, this behavior is repeated—after nine dots, an asterisk is returned over and over again. In fact, only 42 characters are returned because the `head` command requested 42 characters from our device.

In other words, if the character generated by the module has an ordinal number that is a multiple of 10, then it is an asterisk; otherwise, it is a dot.

You can create other special files based on the `dots` module. For example, type the following:

```
sudo mknod /dev/dots2 c 236 0
```

Then, type the following command:

```
head -c12 /dev/dots2
```

This will print the following text to the console:

```
.......*....
```

Notice that 12 characters are printed, as requested by the head command, but this time, the asterisk is at the 8th character, instead of the 10th. This happens because both the dots1 and dots2 special files are associated with the same kernel module, with an identifier (236, 0) and the name dots. This module remembers it has already generated 42 characters, and so after it has generated seven dots, it has to generate its 50th character, which must be an asterisk as it is a multiple of 10.

You can try to type the whole file, but these operations will never end spontaneously because the module will continue to generate characters, as if it were an infinite file. Try to type the following command, and then stop it by pressing *Ctrl + C*:

```
cat /dev/dots1
```

A fast stream of characters will be printed until you stop it.

You can remove the special files by typing the following command:

```
sudo rm /dev/dots1 /dev/dots2
```

You can unload the module by typing the following:

```
sudo rmmod dots
```

If you unload the module without removing the special files, they will be invalid. If you then try to use one of them, such as by typing head -c4 /dev/dots1, you will get the following error message:

```
head: cannot open '/dev/dots1' for reading: No such device or address
```

Now, let's see what has been appended to the kernel buffer by typing the following:

```
dmesg --color=always | tail
```

You will see that the last two lines that are printed will be similar to the following:

```
[123456.789012] dots: Loaded with major device number 236
[123463.987654] dots: Unloaded 54
```

The first line, printed at module loading, also shows the major number of the module. The last line, printed at module unloading, also shows the total number of bytes generated by the module (*42 + 12 = 54*, if you didn't run the cat command). Now, let's see the implementation of this module.

The source code of the dots module

The only relevant differences that you will find from the other projects are in the src/lib.rs file.

First, the src/lib.rs file declares the use of the Box generic type, which is not included by default, similar to String and Vec in the preceding project. Then, it declares some other bindings to the kernel:

```
use linux_kernel_module::bindings::{
    __register_chrdev, __unregister_chrdev, _copy_to_user, file,
file_operations, loff_t,
};
```

Their meanings are as follows:

- __register_chrdev: The function to register a character device in the kernel.
- __unregister_chrdev: The function to unregister a character device from the kernel.
- _copy_to_user: The function to copy a sequence of bytes from kernel space to user space.
- file: The data type representing a file. This is not really used in this project.
- file_operations: The data type containing the implemented operation on files. Only the read operation is implemented by this module. Consider this to be the perspective of the user code. When the user code *reads*, the kernel module *writes*.
- loff_t: The data type representing a long memory offset, as used by the kernel. This is not really used in this project.

The global information

The global information is kept in the following data type:

```
struct CharDeviceGlobalData {
    major: c_types::c_uint,
    name: &'static str,
    fops: Option<Box<file_operations>>,
    count: u64,
}
```

Let's understand the preceding code:

- The first field (`major`) is the major number of the device.
- The second field (`name`) is the name of the module.
- The third field (`fops`, short for **file operations**) is the set of references to the functions that implement the required file operations. This set of references will be allocated to the heap, and so it is encapsulated in a `Box` object. Any `Box` object must encapsulate a valid value since its creation, but the set of references to file operations referenced by the `fops` field can only be created when the kernel initializes the module; so, this field is encapsulated in an `Option` object, which will be initialized as `None` by Rust and will receive a `Box` object when the kernel initializes the module.
- The last field (`count`) is the counter of generated bytes.

As anticipated, the following is the declaration and initialization of the global object:

```
static mut GLOBAL: CharDeviceGlobalData = CharDeviceGlobalData {
    major: 0,
    name: "dots\0",
    fops: None,
    count: 0,
};
```

The module contains only three functions: `init_module`, `cleanup_module`, and `read_dot`. The first two functions are the ones invoked by the kernel when the module is loaded and unloaded, respectively. The third function is called by the kernel every time some user code tries to read a byte from this module.

While the `init_module` and `cleanup_module` functions are linked using their name (so they must have exactly these names) and must be preceded by the `#[no_mangle]` directive to avoid that their name is changed by Rust, the `read_dot` function will be passed to the kernel through its address, and not its name. Therefore, it can have any name you like, and the `#[no_mangle]` directive is not required for it.

The initialization call

Let's see the first part of the body of the `init_module` function:

```
let mut fops = Box::new(file_operations::default());
fops.read = Some(read_dot);
let major = unsafe {
    __register_chrdev(
```

```
            0,
            0,
            256,
            GLOBAL.name.as_bytes().as_ptr() as *const i8,
            &*fops,
        )
    };
```

In the first statement, a file_operations structure, containing the references to the file operations, is created with default values and put into a Box object.

The default value of any file operation is None, meaning that nothing is performed when this kind of operation is required. We will use just the read file operation and we will need this operation to call the read_dot function. Therefore, in the second statement, this function is assigned to the read field of the newly created structure.

The third statement calls the __register_chrdev kernel function, which registers a character device. This function is officially documented on a web page, available at https://www.kernel.org/doc/html/latest/core-api/kernel-api.html?highlight=__register_chrdev#c.__register_chrdev. The five arguments of this function have the following purposes:

- The first argument is the required major number of the device. However, if it is 0, as in our case, a major number will be generated by the kernel and returned by the function.
- The second argument is the value to start from in order to generate the minor number. We will start from 0.
- The third argument is the number of minor numbers that we request to allocate. We will allocate 256 minor numbers, from 0 to 255.
- The fourth argument is the name of the range of devices we are registering. The kernel expects a null-terminated ASCII string. Therefore, the name field has been declared with an ending binary of 0, and here, a rather complex expression just changes the data type of this name. The as_bytes() call converts the string slice into a byte slice. The as_ptr() call gets the address of the first byte of this slice. The as *const i8 clause converts this Rust pointer into a raw pointer to bytes.
- The fifth argument is the address of the file operation structure. Only its read field will be used by the kernel when a read operation is performed.

Now, let's see the rest of the body of the `init_module` function:

```
if major < 0 {
    return 1;
}
unsafe {
    GLOBAL.major = major as c_types::c_uint;
}
println!("dots: Loaded with major device number {}", major);
unsafe {
    GLOBAL.fops = Some(fops);
}
0
```

The major number returned by the call to `__register_chrdev` should be a non-negative number generated by the kernel. It is only a negative number in the case of an error. As we want to fail the loading of the module in case of a registration fail, we return 1—in this case, meaning there has been a failure in the loading of the module.

In case of success, the major number is stored in the `major` field of our global structure. Then, a success message is added to the kernel buffer, containing the generated major number.

Finally, the `fops` file operation structure is stored in the global structure.

Notice that after the registration call, the kernel keeps the address of the `fops` structure, and so this address should never be changed while the function is registered. This holds, however, because this structure is allocated by the `Box::new` call and the assignment of `fops` moves just the `Box` object, which is the pointer to the heap object, not the heap object itself. This explains why a `Box` object has been used.

The cleanup call

Now, let's look at the body of the `cleanup_module` function:

```
unsafe {
    println!("dots: Unloaded {}", GLOBAL.count);
    __unregister_chrdev(
        GLOBAL.major,
        0,
        256,
        GLOBAL.name.as_bytes().as_ptr() as *const i8,
    )
}
```

The first statement prints the unloading message to the kernel buffer, including the total count of bytes read from this module since its loading.

The second statement calls the __unregister_chrdev kernel function, which unregisters a previously registered character device. This function is officially documented on a web page, available at https://www.kernel.org/doc/html/latest/core-api/kernel-api. html?highlight=__unregister_chrdev#c.__unregister_chrdev.

Its arguments are quite similar to the first four arguments of the function used to register the device. They must be identical to the corresponding registered values. However, while, in the registering function, we specified 0 as the major number, here we must specify the actual major number.

The reading function

Finally, let's see the definition of the function that will be invoked by the kernel every time some user code tries to read a byte from this module:

```
extern "C" fn read_dot(
    _arg1: *mut file,
    arg2: *mut c_types::c_char,
    _arg3: usize,
    _arg4: *mut loff_t,
) -> isize {
    unsafe {
        GLOBAL.count += 1;
        _copy_to_user(
            arg2 as *mut c_types::c_void,
            if GLOBAL.count % 10 == 0 { "*" } else { "." }.as_ptr() as
*const c_types::c_void,
            1,
        );
        1
    }
}
```

Also, this function must be decorated by the extern "C" clause to ensure that its calling convection is the same as the one used by the kernel, which is the one used by the system's C language compiler.

This function has four arguments, but we will only use the second one. This argument is a pointer to a structure in user-space where the generated character must be written. The body of the function contains only three statements.

The first statement increments the total count of bytes read by the user code (which is written by the kernel module).

The second statement is a call to the `_copy_to_user` kernel function. This is the function to use when you want to copy one or more bytes from a memory area controlled by kernel code to a memory area controlled by the user code because a simple assignment is not allowed for this operation. This function is officially documented at `https://www.kernel.org/doc/htmldocs/kernel-api/API---copy-to-user.html`

Its first argument is the destination address, which is the memory position where we want to write our byte. In our case, this is simply the second argument of the `read_dot` function, converted into the proper data type.

The second argument is the source address, which is the memory position where we put the byte we want to return to the user. In our case, we want to return an asterisk after every nine dots. So, we check whether the total number of read characters is a multiple of `10`. For this case, we use a static string slice containing only an asterisk: otherwise, we have a string slice containing a dot. The call to `as_ptr()` gets the address of the first byte of the string slice and the `as *const c_types::c_void` clause converts it into the expected data type that corresponds to the `const void *` C language data type.

The third argument is the number of bytes to copy. Of course, in our case, this is `1`.

That's all that is needed to emit dots and asterisks.

Summary

In this chapter, we looked at the tools and techniques that can be used to create loadable modules for the kernel of the Linux operating system using Rust, instead of the typical C programming language.

In particular, we saw the sequence of commands that can be used in a Mint distribution on an x86_64 architecture to configure the appropriate environment to build and test loadable kernel modules. We also looked at the `modinfo`, `lsmod`, `insmod`, `rmmod`, `dmesg`, and `mknod` command-line tools.

We saw that to create a kernel module, it is useful to have a framework of code that implements a target framework for the Rust compiler. The Rust source code is compiled to a Linux static library using this target. Then, this library is linked with some C language glue code into a loadable kernel module.

We created four projects of increasing complexity—boilerplate, state, allocating, and dots. In particular, the dots project created a module that can be mapped to a special file using the mknod command; after this mapping, when this special file is read, a stream of dots and asterisks is generated.

In the next and final chapter, we'll consider the advancements of the Rust ecosystem over the next few years—the language, the standard library, the standard tooling, and the freely available libraries and tools. A description of the newly supported asynchronous programming is also included.

Questions

1. What is a Linux loadable kernel module?
2. What is the programming language expected to be used by the Linux kernel for its modules?
3. What is the kernel buffer and what is the first part of every line in it?
4. What is the purpose of the modinfo, lsmod, insmod, and rmmod Linux commands?
5. Why, by default, are the String, Vec, and Box data types not available to Rust code for building kernel modules?
6. What is the purpose of the #[no_mangle] Rust directive?
7. What is the purpose of the extern "C" Rust clause?
8. What is the purpose of the init_module and cleanup_module functions?
9. What is the purpose of the __register_chrdev and __unregister_chrdev functions?
10. Which function should be used to copy a sequence of bytes from kernel space memory to user-space memory?

Further reading

The framework used for the projects in this chapter is a modification of the open source repository that can be found at `https://github.com/lizhuohua/linux-kernel-module-rust`. This repository contains further examples and documentation pertaining to this topic.

The documentation for the Linux kernel can be found at `https://www.kernel.org/doc/html/latest/`.

11
The Future of Rust

The buzzword of the 2015 edition of Rust was *stability* because version 1.0 promised to be compatible with the versions that followed.

The buzzword of the 2018 edition of Rust was *productivity* because version 1.31 offered a mature ecosystem of tools that allowed command-line developers for desktop operating systems (Linux, Windows, macOS) to be more productive.

There is an intent to have a new Rust edition in the coming years, but for this edition, neither its release date, nor its features, nor its buzzword is defined yet.

However, after the release of the 2018 edition, several needs of Rust developers are being targeted by Rust ecosystem developers around the world. It is probable that the new buzzword will come out of one of these development lines.

The most interesting lines of development are as follows:

- **Integrated Development Environments (IDEs)** and interactive programming
- Crate maturity
- Asynchronous programming
- Optimization
- Embedded systems

By the end of this chapter, we will see the most probable developments of the Rust ecosystem: the language, the tooling, and the available libraries. You will learn what to expect in the next few years.

Two of the most exciting new features of the Rust language are the *asynchronous programming* paradigm and the *const generics* language feature. At the end of 2019, the former was already added to the language, while the latter was still under development. This will be explained in this chapter using code examples, and so you will get a working knowledge about them.

IDEs and interactive programming

A lot of developers prefer to work inside a graphical application that contains or orchestrates all the development tools, instead of using terminal command lines. Such graphical applications are usually named **Development Environments**—or **DEs** for short.

At present, the most popular IDEs are probably the following ones:

- **Eclipse**: This is used mainly for development in the Java language.
- **Visual Studio**: This is used mainly for development in the C# and Visual Basic languages.
- **Visual Studio Code**: This is used mainly for development in the JavaScript language.

In the 20th century, it was typical to create an IDE from scratch for a single programming language. That was a major task, though. Therefore, in the last decades, it has become more typical to create customizable IDEs, and then to add extensions (or plugins) to support specific programming languages. For most programming languages, there is at least one mature extension for a popular IDE. However, in 2018, Rust had very limited IDE support, meaning that there were some extensions to use Rust in a pair of IDEs but they offered few features, bad performance, and were also rather buggy.

In addition, many programmers prefer an interactive development style. When creating a new feature of a software system, they do not like to write a lot of software and then compile and test all of it. Instead, they prefer to write a single line or a bunch of few lines and test such snippets of code right away. After testing that snippet of code successfully, they integrate it into the rest of the system. This is typical of developers using interpreted languages such as JavaScript or Python.

The tools that are able to run snippets of code are **language interpreters** or **fast in-memory compilers**. Such interpreters read a command from the user, evaluate it, print the result, and go back to the first step. Therefore, they are usually named **read-eval-print loop**, or **REPL** for short. For all interpreted programming languages, and for some compiled languages, there are mature REPLs. In 2018, the Rust ecosystem was missing a mature REPL.

Here, the IDE issue and the REPL issue are presented together because they share the following common problem. The main feature of modern IDEs is to analyze source code as it is edited, with the following goals:

- To highlight the code containing invalid syntax, and to display a compilation error message in a popup window that appears near the invalid code
- To suggest the completion of identifiers, to be chosen among the already declared identifiers
- To show the synopsis documentation of an identifier selected in the editor
- To jump in the editor from the definition of an identifier to its uses, or vice versa
- In a debugging session, to evaluate an expression inside the current context, or to change the memory contents owned by a variable

Such operations require very fast parsing of Rust code, and this is also what is required by a Rust REPL. An attempt to address such issues is a project named the **Rust Language Server** (`https://github.com/rust-lang/rls`) that is developed by the Rust language team. Another attempt is the project named **Rust Analyzer** (`https://github.com/rust-analyzer/rust-analyzer`) that is developed by the Ferrous Systems company, supported by several partners. Hopefully, before the next Rust edition, there will be a fast and powerful Rust language analyzer to support smart programmers' editors, source-level debuggers, and REPL tools, just as many other programming languages have.

Crate maturity

A crate becomes mature when it reaches *version 1.0*. That milestone means that the following versions 1.x will be compatible with it. Instead, for versions 0.x, there is no such guarantee, and any version can have an **application programming interface (API)** that's quite different from the previous one.

Having a mature version is important for several reasons, listed as follows:

- When you upgrade your dependency to a newer version of a crate (to use new features of that library), you are guaranteed that your existing code won't get broken—that is, it will continue to behave in a previous way, or in a better way. Without such a guarantee, you typically need to review all your code using that crate and fix all the incompatibilities.
- Your investment in know-how is preserved. You need to neither retrain yourself nor your coworkers and not even update your documentation.

- Typically, software quality is improved. If a version of an API remains unchanged for a long time, and many people use it in different corner cases, untested bugs and real-world performance issues can emerge and be fixed. Instead, a quickly changing version is usually bug-ridden and inefficient in many application cases.

Of course, there is an advantage to iterating through several improvement steps of the API, and APIs created in a few weeks are usually badly designed. Although there are still many crates that have been in a 0.x version for several years, the time is coming to stabilize them.

This is a reinterpretation of the buzzword *stability*. In 2015, it meant *the stability of the language and of the standard library*. Now, the rest of the mature ecosystem must stabilize to be accepted in real-world projects.

Asynchronous programming

A major innovation was introduced in stable Rust in November 2019—with release 1.39—it is the `async-await` syntax, to support asynchronous programming.

Asynchronous programming is a programming paradigm that is very useful in many application areas, mainly in multiuser servers, so that many programming languages—such as JavaScript, C#, Go, and Erlang—support it in the language. Other languages, such as C++ and Java, support asynchronous programming through the standard library.

Around 2016, it was very hard to do asynchronous programming in Rust because neither the language nor the available crates supported it in an easy and stable way. Then, some crates supporting asynchronous programming were developed, such as `futures`, `mio`, and `tokio`, though they were not much easier to use, and remained at a version before 1, meaning instability of their API.

After having seen the difficulty of creating convenient support for asynchronous programming using only libraries, it appeared clear that a language extension was needed.

The new syntax, similar to that of C#, includes the new `async` and `await` language keywords. The stabilization of this syntax means that the previous asynchronous crates should now be considered obsolete until they migrate to use the new syntax.

The new syntax—announced on the `https://blog.rust-lang.org/2019/11/07/Async-await-stable.html` web page—is described on the `https://rust-lang.github.io/async-book/` web page.

For those who never felt the need for asynchronous programming, here is a quick example of it. Create a new Cargo project, with the following dependencies:

```
async-std = "1.5"
futures = "0.3"
```

Prepare in the root folder of that project a file named `file.txt` that contains only five `Hello` characters. Using a Unix-like command-line, you can do this using the following command:

```
echo -n "Hello" >file.txt
```

Put the following content into the `src/main.rs` file:

```
use async_std::fs::File;
use async_std::prelude::*;
use futures::executor::block_on;
use futures::try_join;

fn main() {
    block_on(parallel_read_file()).unwrap();
}

async fn parallel_read_file() -> std::io::Result<()> {
    print_file(1).await?;
    println!();
    print_file(2).await?;
    println!();
    print_file(3).await?;
    println!();
    try_join!(print_file(1), print_file(2), print_file(3))?;
    println!();
    Ok(())
}

async fn print_file(instance: u32) -> std::io::Result<()> {
    let mut file = File::open("file.txt").await?;
    let mut byte = [0u8];
    while file.read(&mut byte).await? > 0 {
        print!("{}:{} ", instance, byte[0] as char);
    }
    Ok(())
}
```

If you run this project, the output is not quite deterministic. The possible output is the following one:

```
1:H 1:e 1:l 1:l 1:o
2:H 2:e 2:l 2:l 2:o
3:H 3:e 3:l 3:l 3:o
1:H 2:H 3:H 1:e 2:e 3:e 1:l 1:l 3:l 1:o 2:l 3:l 2:l 3:o 2:o
```

The first three lines are deterministic. Instead, the last line can be shuffled a bit.

In a first reading, pretend it is synchronous code, ignoring the words `async`, `await`, `block_on`, and `join!`. With this simplification, the flow is easy to follow.

The `main` function calls the `parallel_read_file` function. The first six lines of the `parallel_read_file` function call the `print_file` function three times, with the arguments 1, 2, and 3, in different lines, each followed by a call to `println!`. The seventh line of the `parallel_read_file` function again calls the `print_file` function three times, with the same three arguments.

The `print_file` function uses the `File::open` function call to open a file, and then uses the `file.read` function call to read a byte at a time from that file. Any byte read is printed, preceded by the argument of the function (`instance`).

So, we obtain the information that the first call to `print_file` prints `1:H 1:e 1:l 1:l 1:o`. They are the five characters read from the file, preceded by the number 1, received as an argument.

The fourth line prints the same contents of the first three lines, mixing the characters. First, the three `H` characters are printed, then the three `e` characters, then the three `l` characters, and then something weird happens: an `o` is printed before all the `l` characters have been printed.

What is happening is that the first three lines are printed by three sequential invocations of the `print_file` function, while the last line is printed by three parallel invocations of the same function. In any parallel invocation, all the letters printed by one invocation are in the correct order, but the other invocations may interleave their output.

If you think that this is similar to multithreading, you are not far from the truth. There is an important difference, though. Using threads, the operating system may interrupt the threads and pass control to another thread at any time, with the effect that the output may be broken at undesirable points.

To avoid such interruptions, critical regions or other synchronization mechanisms must be used. Instead, with asynchronous programming, functions are never interrupted except when a specific asynchronous operation is performed. Typically, such operations are an invocation of external services, such as accessing the filesystem, which could cause a wait. Instead of waiting, another asynchronous operation is activated.

Now, let's see the code from the beginning, implementing asynchronous operations. It uses the `async_std` crate. It is an asynchronous version of the standard library. The standard library is still available, but its functions are synchronous. The code can be seen in the following snippet:

```
use async_std::fs::File;
use async_std::prelude::*;
```

To have an asynchronous behavior, the functions of this crate must be used. In particular, we will use the functions of the `File` data type. In addition, some features of the not-yet-stabilized `futures` crate are used. The code can be seen in the following snippet:

```
use futures::executor::block_on;
use futures::try_join;
```

Then, there is the `main` function, whose body contains only the following line:

```
block_on(parallel_read_file()).unwrap();
```

Here, the `parallel_read_file` function is called first.

This is an asynchronous function. When you call an asynchronous function using the normal function-call syntax, as in the `parallel_read_file()` expression, the body of that function is not actually executed, as a normal and synchronous function would be. Instead, such a call just returns an object, called a **future**. A future is similar to a closure, as it encapsulates a function and the arguments used to invoke such a function. The function encapsulated in the returned future is the body of the function we were calling.

To actually run the function encapsulated in the future, a particular kind of function is needed, called an **executor**. The `block_on` function is an executor. When an executor is invoked, passing a future to it, the body of the function encapsulated in that future is run, and the value returned by such a function is then returned by the executor itself.

So, when the `block_on` function is called, the body of `parallel_read_file` is run, and when it terminates, `block_on` also terminates, returning the same value returned by `parallel_read_file`. As this last function has a `Result` value type, it should be unwrapped.

Then, a function is defined whose signature is as follows:

```
async fn parallel_read_file() -> std::io::Result<()>
```

The `async` keyword marks that function as asynchronous. It is also fallible, and so a `Result` value is returned.

Asynchronous functions can be invoked only by other asynchronous functions or by executors, such as `block_on` and `try_join`. The `main` function is not asynchronous, and so there, we needed an executor.

The first line of the body of the function is added in the following code snippet. It is an invocation of the `print_file` function, passing the value 1 to it. As the `print_file` function is asynchronous too, to invoke it from inside an asynchronous function, the `.await` clause must be used. Such a function is fallible, and so a `?` operator is added, like this:

```
print_file(1).await?;
```

When an asynchronous function is invoked using `.await`, the execution of the body of that function starts right away, but as soon as it yields control because it executes a blocking function, such as an operating system call, another ready asynchronous function may proceed. However, the flow of control does not proceed beyond the `.await` clause until the body of the called function is complete.

The second line of the body of the function is an invocation of a synchronous function, and so `.await` is neither needed nor allowed, as can be seen in the following code snippet:

```
println!();
```

We can be sure that it is run after the previous statement because that statement ended with a `.await` clause.

This pattern is repeated three times, and then the seventh line consists of a set of three invocations in parallel with the same asynchronous function, as illustrated in the following code snippet:

```
try_join!(print_file(1), print_file(2), print_file(3))?;
```

Even the `try_join!` macro is an executor. It runs all the three futures generated by the three calls to `print_file`. Only one thread is used by asynchronous programming, and so, in fact, one of the three futures is run first. If it never has to wait, it ends before the other futures have the opportunity to start.

Instead, as this function will have to wait, at any wait the context is switched to another running future, starting from the statement that had put it on wait. So, the executions of the three futures are interleaved.

Now, let's see the definition of such an invoked function. Its signature is shown in the following code snippet:

```
async fn print_file(instance: u32) -> std::io::Result<()> {
```

It is an asynchronous function, receiving an integer argument and returning an empty `Result` value.

The first line of its body opens a file using the `File` data type of the asynchronous standard library, as illustrated in the following code snippet:

```
let mut file = File::open("file.txt").await?;
```

As such, the `open` function is asynchronous too, and it must be followed by `.await`, as illustrated in the following code snippet:

```
let mut byte = [0u8];
while file.read(&mut byte).await? > 0 {
    print!("{}:{} ", instance, byte[0] as char);
}
```

The asynchronous `read` function is used to read bytes to fill the `byte` buffer. This buffer has length 1, and so just one byte at a time is read. The `read` function is fallible, and if it is successful, it returns the numbers of bytes read. This means that it returns 1 if a byte is read and 0 if the file is ended. If the call reads a byte, the loop continues.

The body of the loop is a synchronous output statement. It prints the identifier of the current instance of the file stream, and the byte just read.

So, the sequence of steps is as follows.

First, the `print_file(1)` future is started. When it executes the `File::open` call that is blocking, this future is put on hold, and a ready-to-run future is looked for. There are two ready futures: `print_file(2)` and `print_file(3)`. The first one is chosen, and it is started. Also, it reaches the `File::open` call, and so it is put on hold, and the third future is started. When it reaches the `File::open` call, it is put on hold and a ready future is looked for. If there is no ready-to-run future, the thread itself waits for the first ready future.

The first future to complete the `File::open` call is the first one, which resumes its execution just after that call and starts to read a byte from the file. Even this one is a blocking operation, and so this future is put on hold, and control is moved to the second future, which starts to read one byte.

There is always a queue of ready futures. When a future has to wait for an operation, it yields control to the executor, which passes control to the first future in the queue of ready futures. When the blocking operation is complete, the waiting future is appended to the queue of ready futures and can be yielded control if no other future is running.

When all the bytes of a file have been read, the `print_file` function ends. When all the three calls to `print_file` are ended, the `try_join!` executor ends, and the `parallel_read_file` function can proceed. When it reaches its end, the `block_on` executor ends and, with it, the whole program.

As blocking operations take a variable amount of time, the sequence of steps is non-deterministic. Indeed, the last line of output of the example program seen before can be slightly different in different runs, swapping some portions of it.

As we have seen, asynchronous programming is similar to multithreaded programming but it is more efficient, saving both context-switch time and memory usage. It is appropriate primarily for **input/output (I/O)**-bound tasks as only one thread is used, and the flow of control is interrupted only when an I/O operation is performed. Instead, multithreading can allocate a different thread on any core, and so it is more appropriate for **central processing unit (CPU)**-bound operations.

After the addition of the `async`/`await` syntax extension, what is still needed is the development and stabilization of crates using and supporting such syntax.

Optimization

Usually, system programmers are quite interested in efficiency. In this regard, Rust shines as one of the most efficient languages, though there are still some issues with performance, as follows:

- A full build—in particular, an optimized release build—is quite slow, even more so if link-time optimization is enabled. For large projects, this can be quite a nuisance. At present, the Rust compiler is just a frontend that generates **Low-Level Virtual Machine (LLVM) intermediate representation** (IR) code and passes such code to the LLVM machine code generator. However, the Rust compiler generates a disproportionate amount of LLVM IR code, and so the LLVM backend must take a long time to optimize it. An improved Rust compiler would pass to LLVM a much more compact sequence of instructions. A refactoring of the compiler is in progress, and this could lead to a faster compiler.

- Since version 1.37, the Rust compiler supports **profile-guided optimization** (**PGO**), which can enhance performance for the typical processor workflows. However, such a feature is rather cumbersome to use. A graphical frontend or an IDE integration would make it easier to use.

- A development underway is an addition to the language of the **const generics** feature, described in the next section.

- In LLVM IR, any function argument of a pointer type can be tagged with the `noalias` attribute, meaning that the memory reference by this pointer will not be changed inside this function, except through this pointer. Using this information, LLVM can generate faster machine code. This attribute is similar to the `restrict` keyword in the C language. Yet in Rust, for *every* mutable reference (`&mut`), the `noalias` property is guaranteed by language ownership rules. Therefore, faster programs could be obtained that always generate LLVM IR code with the `noalias` attribute for every mutable reference. This has been done in versions 1.0 through 1.7 and in versions 1.28 and 1.29, although, because of bugs in the LLVM backend compiler, the resulting code was bugged. Therefore, until a correct LLVM implementation is released, the `noalias` optimization hint will not be used.

The const generics feature

At present, generic data types are parameterized only by types or lifetimes. It is useful to be able to also parameterize a generic data type by a constant expression. In a way, this feature is already available, but only for one kind of generic type: the arrays. You can have the `[u32; 7]` type that is an array parameterized by the `u32` type and by the `7` constant, though you cannot define your own generic type parameterized by a constant.

This feature, already available in C++ language, is in development in the nightly build. It would allow variables to be replaced with constants in generic code, and this would surely improve performance. Here is an example program that uses as dependencies the `num` crate:

```
#![feature(const_generics)]
#![allow(incomplete_features)]

use num::Float;

struct Array2<T: Float, const WIDTH: usize, const HEIGHT: usize> {
    data: [[T; WIDTH]; HEIGHT],
}

impl<T: Float, const WIDTH: usize, const HEIGHT: usize>
Array2<T, WIDTH, HEIGHT> {
    fn new() -> Self {
        Self { data: [[T::zero(); WIDTH]; HEIGHT] }
    }
    fn width(&self) -> usize { WIDTH }
    fn height(&self) -> usize { HEIGHT }
}

fn main() {
    let matrix = Array2::<f64, 4, 3>::new();
    print!("{} {}", matrix.width(), matrix.height());
}
```

This program, to be compiled only using a nightly version of the compiler, creates a data type implementing a bidimensional array of floating-point numbers. Notice that the parameterization is as follows: `T: Float, const WIDTH: usize, const HEIGHT: usize`. The first parameter is the type of array items. The second and third parameters are the sizes of the array.

Having constant values instead of variables allows important code optimizations.

Embedded systems

Rust has been developed since when Mozilla started to sponsor it in 2009, with a specific goal: to create a web browser. Even after 2018, the core team of developers works for Mozilla Foundation, whose main business is to build client-side web applications. Such software is multiplatform, but oriented exclusively toward the following requirements:

- **Random-access memory (RAM)**: At least 1 GB
- **Supported CPUs**: Initially only x86 and x86_64; later, also ARM and ARM64.
- **Supported operating systems**: Linux, Windows, macOS

These requirements excluded most microcontrollers as the Mozilla Foundation was not interested in such platforms, though the features of Rust appear to be a good match with the requirements of many embedded systems with more constrained requirements. Therefore, thanks to a worldwide group of volunteers, in 2018, the Embedded Working Group was created to develop the ecosystem needed to use Rust on embedded systems—that is, on bare-metal or on stripped-down operating systems, and with severe resource limitations.

Progress in this application area has been rather slow and directed mainly at a few architectures, but the future is promising, at least for 32-bit or 64-bit architectures, because any architecture supported by the LLVM backend is easily targetable by the Rust compiler.

Some specific improvements to the language, which ease the use of Rust for embedded systems, are listed as follows:

- The standard-library `Pin` generic class avoids moving objects in memory. This is needed when some external device is accessing a memory location.
- The `cfg` and `cfg_attr` attributes, which allow conditional compilation, have been extended. This feature is needed because trying to compile code for a wrong platform can create unacceptable code bloat, or even cause compilation errors.
- The `allocator` API has been made more customizable.
- The applicability of `const fn` has been extended. This construct allows a code base that is maintainable as normal algorithmic code, but as efficient as a wired constant.

Summary

In this chapter, we have seen the most probable development lines of the Rust ecosystem in the next few years—support for IDEs and for interactive programming; the maturity of the most popular crates; widespread support of the new asynchronous programming paradigm and its keywords (`async` and `await`); further optimization of both the compiler and the generated machine code; and widespread support of embedded systems programming.

We have learned how to write asynchronous code and a possible way to define and use const generics (still unstable at the time of writing).

We have seen that there are quite a lot of application areas where Rust could really shine. Of course, if you are going to use it only for fun, the sky is the limit, but for real-world applications, the ecosystem of libraries and tools can really decide the viability of a programming system. Now, at last, the critical mass of high-quality libraries and tools is about to be reached.

Assessments

Chapter 1

1. Yes, it is *The Rust Programming Language* by Steve Klabnik and Carol Nichols.
2. In 2015, it was long 64 bits (or 8 bytes). At the end of 2018, it was long 128 bits (or 16 bytes).
3. They are networking, command-line applications, WebAssembly, and embedded software.
4. It checks for non-idiomatic syntax and suggests changes to code for better maintainability.
5. It converts a 2015 edition project to a 2018 edition project.
6. Add this dependency to the `Cargo.toml` file:

   ```
   rand = "0.6"
   ```

   Then, add this code to the `main.rs` file:

   ```
   use rand::prelude::*;
   fn main() {
       let mut rng = thread_rng();
       let mut numbers = vec![];
       for _ in 0..10 {
           numbers.push(rng.gen_range(100_f32, 400_f32));
       }
       println!("{:?} ", numbers)
   }
   ```

7. With the dependency used in the previous question, add this code to the `main.rs` file:

   ```
   use rand::prelude::*;
   fn main() {
       let mut rng = thread_rng();
       let mut numbers = vec![];
       for _ in 0..10 {
           numbers.push(rng.gen_range(100_i32, 401_i32));
       }
       println!("{:?} ", numbers)
   }
   ```

8. Add this dependency to the `Cargo.toml` file:

```
lazy_static = "1.2"
```

Then, insert this code into the `main.rs` file:

```
use lazy_static::lazy_static;
lazy_static! {
    static ref SQUARES_FROM_1_TO_200: Vec<u32> = {
        let mut v = vec![];
        for i in 1.. {
            let ii = i * i;
            if ii > 200 { break; }
            v.push(ii);
        }
        v
    };
}
fn main() {
    println!("{:?}", *SQUARES_FROM_1_TO_200);
}
```

9. First, add this dependency to the `Cargo.toml` file:

```
log = "0.4"
env_logger = "0.6"
```

Then, insert this code into the `main.rs` file and execute RUST_LOG=warn cargo run:

```
#[macro_use]
extern crate log;
fn main() {
    env_logger::init();
    warn!("Warning message");
    info!("Information message");
}
```

10. Add this dependency to the `Cargo.toml` file:

```
structopt = "0.2"
```

Then, add this code to the `main.rs` file:

```
use structopt::StructOpt;
#[derive(StructOpt, Debug)]
struct Opt {
    #[structopt(short = "l", long = "level")]
```

```
        level: u32,
    }

    fn main() {
        let options = Opt::from_args();
        if options.level < 1 || options.level > 20 {
            println!("Invalid level (1 to 20 is expected): {}",
    options.level);
        } else {
            println!("Level is {}", options.level);
        }
    }
```

Chapter 2

1. Because changes applied by software lose all the comments inserted by the user and sort the items in alphabetical order.
2. Dynamically typed parsing is better when you are not sure which fields will be present in the file and you want to allow some missing fields. Statically typed parsing is better when you want to discard files that do not respect the expected format.
3. A derive from `Serialize` is needed when you want to send (write) a data structure out of your software. A derive from `Deserialize` is needed when you want to receive (read) a data structure.
4. This is a format in which fields are indented to show the structure of the data visually.
5. Because it minimizes the use of memory by loading data into memory a little at a time.
6. SQLite is better when you want to save disk space, memory space, start up time, and sometimes also throughput. PostgreSQL is better when you have complex security needs, or when your data must be accessible for several users at a time.
7. This is a reference to a slice of references to objects that can be converted to `ToSql`.
8. This replaces the parameters in a SQL `SELECT` statement and then creates and returns an iterator on the rows selected by that statement.
9. The `get` function reads a value; the `set` function writes a value.
10. Let's use a local instance of Redis, already containing the association *aKey => a string*. Add this dependency to the `Cargo.toml` file:

```
redis = "0.16"
```

Then, add this code to the `main.rs` file:

```
use redis::Commands;

fn main() -> redis::RedisResult<()> {
    let id = std::env::args().nth(1).unwrap();

    let client = redis::Client::open("redis://localhost/")?;
    let mut conn = client.get_connection()?;

    if let Ok(value) = conn.get::<_, String>(&id) {
        println!("Value of '{}' is '{}'.", id, value);
    } else {
        println!("Id '{}' not found.", id);
    }
    Ok(())
}
```

Chapter 3

1. `GET` requests a resource to be downloaded; `PUT` sends some data to replace existing data; `POST` sends some data that the server should consider as new; `DELETE` requests the removal of a resource.
2. The Curl utility.
3. The handler declares an argument, such as `info: Path<(String,)>`, and then the value of the `&info.0` expression is a reference to the first URI parameter.
4. By using the `content_type` method of the `HttpResponse` type – for example, `HttpResponse::Ok().content_type("application/json")`.
5. Using a pseudo-random number generator, you generate a large integer number, format it as a string, and append that string to a prefix. Then, you try to create a new file having that name. If such creation fails because another file exists with that name, you try to generate another filename, until you find an unused combination.
6. To cache information that can be obtained again using any request, but for which it would be costly to do so.
7. Because the state is shared by all requests, and Actix web uses several threads to handle the requests, and so the state must be thread-safe. The typical way of declaring a thread-safe object in Rust is to encapsulate it in a Mutex object.

8. Because the server may have to wait for the arrival of data from a database, the filesystem, or another process. During such a wait, it can serve other requests. Multithreading is another possible solution, but that yields an inferior performance.

9. It chains another future to the current one. The second closure will be executed asynchronously after the first one has finished.

10. `serde`, to serialize anything; `serde_derive`, to automatically implement serialization for some data types; and `serde_json` to automatically implement serialization for JSON data.

Chapter 4

1. The possible strategies for creating HTML code containing variable parts are as follows:

   - **Code only**: You have a programming language source file that contains a lot of statements that print strings to create the desired HTML page.
   - **HTML with tags**: You write an HTML file containing the desired constant HTML elements and the desired constant text, but it also contains some statements enclosed in specific markers.
   - **HTML templates**: You write HTML templates containing tags and application code that fills those tags.

2. Double braces are used – for example, `{{id}}`.

3. The `{%` and `%}` markers are used, as shown here:

```
{%if person%}Id: {{person.id}}\
{%else%}No person\
{%endif%}
```

4. First, an object of the `tera::Context` type is created, and then, the necessary name-value associations are added to such an object, using its `insert` method. Finally, that context is passed as an argument to the `render` method of the Tera engine.

5. At an architectural level, a request can be thought of as a data manipulation command, or as a request to get a document to display in the browser. Traditionally, the two kinds of requests were merged in a data manipulation command whose response is the new content of the current page.

6. Because some parts (the metadata, the scripts, the styles, and possibly the page header and footer) do not change during the session or change rarely. Other parts (usually the central part, or a smaller part) change with any click from the user. By reloading only the part that changes, the app has better performance and usability.

7. The loading of all template files happens at runtime, and so the template's subtree must be deployed.

8. The built-in JavaScript `XMLHttpRequest` class can be instantiated, and such instances have methods to send HTTP requests.

9. It should be stored in a global JavaScript variable inside the current web page in the web browser.

10. A handler can have an argument of the `BasicAuth` type that encapsulates the authorization header of the HTTP request. Such an object has the `user_id` and `password` methods.

Chapter 5

1. It is a standard machine language-like programming language, accepted by all major web browsers. It can be more efficient than JavaScript, but is more portable than other machine language-like programming languages.

2. It is an architectural pattern for interactive software. It uses the concepts of *model*, meaning the data structure that contains the state of the application; *view*, meaning the code that uses the current value of the model to display the contents of a window or a portion of a window; and *controller*, meaning the code that is activated by user actions on the window, updating the value of the model and activating the view refresh.

3. The specific version of the MVC implementation used by Yew and the Elm language is based on a collection of programmer-defined possible events, named *messages*. When the view detects such a possible event, the controller is notified by a message that's associated with the kind of event.

4. The Yew components are the instances of an MVC pattern. Every triple model-view-controller is a component.

5. The Yew properties are the data that any parent component passes to its child component when it creates them. They are needed to share data in a hierarchy of components.

6. You create two Yew components – one that handles the inner section and one that handles the header and footer – and that one contains the other component as its child.

7. Callbacks are callable objects that a component passes as properties to one of its child components to let it access features of the parent component.

8. You pass it as a property, encapsulating it into an object of the `std::rc::Rc<std::cell::RefCell>` type.

9. Because if you keep it only in a local variable, it is destroyed when the function in which it is created ends. To ensure it survives until the arrival of the response from the server, this object must be kept in a structure that lives longer.

10. In your model, you declare an object of the `DialogService` type, and you use its `alert` and `confirm` methods.

11. It is left to the reader. I've created an example in the book's GitHub repo.

Chapter 6

1. It is an architecture of interactive software, used mainly in games. At periodic intervals, the framework checks the status of input devices, modifies the model accordingly, and then invokes the draw routine. Its advantage is that it better corresponds to a situation in which input devices have continuous input, such as a key being pressed for some time, or screen output changing continuously, even if the user does nothing.

2. When input events are discrete, such as a mouse click on a button or text typed into a box, and when output happens only because of a user action.

3. Continuous simulation software, industrial machine monitoring software, or multimedia software.

4. To draw a shape, you call the `draw_ex` method of the current window. The first argument of that method describes the shape to draw; it may be an instance of the `Triangle`, `Rectangle`, or `Circle` type.

5. In the `update` function, you can check the state of any key of the keyboard. For example, the `window.keyboard()[Key::Right].is_down()` expression returns `true` if the right-arrow key is pressed.

6. The model must implement the `State` trait. In that trait, the `update` method is the controller, and the `draw` method is the view.

7. Quicksilver has two rates, one for the `update` method and one for the `draw` method. They have default values, but if you want to change them, set the `update_rate` and `draw_rate` fields of the `Settings` structure passed to the `run` function that starts the application.

8. You start to load a font by calling the `Font::load(filename)` function, you start to load a sound by calling the `Sound::load(filename)` function, and so on. Such calls return a future waiting for the actual asset to load. Then, you call the `Asset::new` function, specifying the future as its argument. The first time it is used, it will wait for the complete loading of the asset. The assets must be in a folder named `static` at the root of the project.

9. After having loaded a recorded sound asset in a variable, you may call the `play_sound` function, and pass that asset as an argument.

10. After having loaded a font asset in a variable, in the `draw` method, you may call the `execute` method of that asset, which waits for the complete loading of the font, and then you call the `render` method of the loaded asset to draw the text in an image. Then, you can draw that image on the window by calling the `draw` method of the window.

Chapter 7

1. A vector is an entity that can be added to another vector and can be multiplied by a number. It is senseless to add two points or to multiply a point by a number.

2. In geometry, a vector is a translation or displacement; a point is a position.

3. Because some events are discrete. For example, when I click on a button, I am not interested in how many milliseconds the mouse is pressed; I just want to get one click event. If I type a word, I want to get just one character input for every key pressed.

4. Because assets are usually loaded only at application startup, or when a level is entered or exited.

5. The optional `key_down_event`, `key_up_event`, `mouse_button_down_event`, and `mouse_button_up_event` methods can be defined for the `EventHandler` trait. Such methods register in the model that they have been called (that is, that the corresponding events have happened in the time frame). Then, the `update` method checks and resets such settings in the model.

6. It is a set of shapes to draw. To draw a shape, first, you build a new `Mesh` instance, then you add shapes to it (rectangles, triangles, and so on), and then you can draw that mesh on the screen.

7. The general way is to create a `MeshBuilder` instance by using `MeshBuilder::new()`; add shapes to that builder, with its methods (`rectangle`, `polygon`, and so on); and then call the `build` method, which returns a `Mesh` instance. But there are shorter ways, such as the `Mesh::new_circle` function, which returns a `Mesh` instance containing a single circle.

8. The `update` method is always called at top speed, but it checks the internal timer repeatedly to execute its body only the desired number of times.

9. The `draw` function uses as arguments the context to receive the drawing, the mesh to draw, and a `DrawParam` structure. This structure can contain the geometric transformation to apply to the mesh while drawing it.

10. The `audio::Source` objects have several methods, including the `play` and `play_detached` methods. The first one automatically stops the previous sound before playing the specified one; the second one overlaps its sound with existing ones.

Chapter 8

1. Regular languages are ones that can be defined by a regular expression, which is a combination of three operators: concatenation, alternation, and repetition. Context-free languages are ones that can contain regular operators, plus matching symbols (such as parentheses). Context-dependent languages are those in which the validity of any expression may depend on any other expression defined previously.

2. It is a set of rules in which the program is a symbol, and every symbol is defined as the concatenation or alternation of symbols or characters.

3. It is a program that gets as input a formal definition of a programming language and generates as output a compiler, which is a program that parses (or even compiles to machine language) programs written in the language specified by that formal definition.

4. It is a function that takes as input one or more parsers and returns a parser that combines the input parsers in some way.

5. Because, before the 2018 edition of Rust, the Rust language did not allow functions that returned functions without encapsulating them in an allocated object. The feature that allows a function to be returned with no allocation is named `impl Trait`.

6. The `tuple` parser combinator gets a fixed sequence of parsers and returns a parser that applies them in sequence. The `alt` parser combinator gets a fixed sequence of parsers and returns a parser that applies them alternatively. The `map` parser combinator gets a parser and a closure and returns a parser that applies that parser and then uses the closure to transform its output.

7. Lexical analysis, syntax analysis, semantic analysis, and interpretation.

8. Lexical analysis, syntax analysis, semantic analysis, generation of intermediate code, optimization of intermediate code, generation of relocatable machine code, and linking.

9. When an identifier is defined, the symbol table is needed to check that such a name has not been defined yet in the current scope, if the language does not allow the shadowing of an identifier. When an identifier is used, the symbol table is needed to check that such a name has already been defined and that it has a type compatible with the usage.

10. When an identifier is defined, the symbol table is needed to store the initial value of the identifier. When an identifier is used, the symbol table is needed to get or set the value associated with such an identifier.

Chapter 9

1. Possible uses:

   - To run a binary program for a computer when that computer is not available
   - To debug or analyze a binary program when its source code is not available
   - To disassemble machine code
   - To translate a binary program into another machine language
   - To translate a binary program into a high-level programming language

2. It is the main data register. It is the default source and destination of any instruction.

3. It is the main address register. It contains the address of the next instruction that will be fetched and executed.

4. One reason is that the use of numbers is more error-prone than the use of names. The other is that when an instruction or a variable is added or removed, the addresses of all the following instructions or variables change, and so a lot of addresses in code must be incremented or decremented.

5. Defining a variant for every instruction type. The name of the variant is the symbolic name of the instruction, and its parameters are the types of the operands of the instruction.

6. Little-endian notation is where the low byte of a word has a lower memory address, and big-endian notation is where the high byte has a lower memory address.

7. For a parser that accepts text, the input is a reference to a string slice, with an `&str` type, while for a parser that accepts binary data, the input is a reference to a slice of bytes, with an `&[u8]` type.

8. The rules to be respected are as follows:

   - It begins with a little-endian word containing the size of the process in bytes.
   - After the initial word, there is a sequence of valid machine language instructions, with no interleaved spaces or data.
   - The `Terminate` instruction occurs once—and only once—as the last instruction so that it marks the end of the sequence of instructions. After this, there is only data left.
   - No statement writes on the instructions; only the data can be changed. So, the program is not self-modifying; put differently, the program instructions are the same as the process instructions.

9. Because a 16-bit number can be usefully regarded sometimes as a pair of bytes and sometimes as a single number. Hexadecimal format satisfies both requirements because every pair of hexadecimal digits is a byte, and the whole four-digit sequence is a 16-bit number.

10. By encapsulating it in a new type and then implementing the `Debug` trait for the type.

Chapter 10

1. It is an extension of the Linux operating system kernel that can be added or removed at runtime.

2. The C programming language, with GCC extensions.

3. It is a memory-only log area to which every kernel module can write. When a kernel module writes to it, a bracket-enclosed timestamp is added at the beginning of every line; this is the number of seconds and microseconds since the start of the kernel.

4. `ModInfo` prints some information about a Linux module file; `LsMod` prints the list of all the currently loaded modules; `InsMod` loads a Linux module from the specified file and adds it to the running kernel; and `RmMod` unloads the specified module from the running Linux kernel.

5. Because the `#![no_std]` directive prevents the use of the standard heap allocator and of all the standard types that use it. This directive is required as any kernel module needs a custom allocator.

6. It is a directive to the linker to keep the exact name of the following function so that the kernel can find that function by name.

7. It specifies that the function-calling convention must be the one normally used by the C language.

8. They are two entry points of the module: the `init_module` function is invoked by the kernel when the module is loaded, and the `cleanup_module` function is invoked by the kernel when the module is unloaded.

9. `__register_chrdev` is used to register a character device in the kernel; `__unregister_chrdev` is used to deregister it.

10. The `_copy_to_user` function.

Other Books You May Enjoy

If you enjoyed this book, you may be interested in these other books by Packt:

Rust Programming Cookbook
Claus Matzinger

ISBN: 978-1-78953-066-7

- Understand how Rust provides unique solutions to solve system programming language problems
- Grasp the core concepts of Rust to develop fast and safe applications
- Explore the possibility of integrating Rust units into existing applications for improved efficiency
- Discover how to achieve better parallelism and security with Rust
- Write Python extensions in Rust
- Compile external assembly files and use the Foreign Function Interface (FFI)
- Build web applications and services using Rust for high performance

Hands-On Microservices with Rust

Denis Kolodin

ISBN: 978-1-78934-275-8

- Get acquainted with leveraging Rust web programming
- Get to grips with various Rust crates, such as hyper, Tokio, and Actix
- Explore RESTful microservices with Rust
- Understand how to pack Rust code to a container using Docker
- Familiarize yourself with Reactive microservices
- Deploy your microservices to modern cloud platforms such as AWS

Leave a review - let other readers know what you think

Please share your thoughts on this book with others by leaving a review on the site that you bought it from. If you purchased the book from Amazon, please leave us an honest review on this book's Amazon page. This is vital so that other potential readers can see and use your unbiased opinion to make purchasing decisions, we can understand what our customers think about our products, and our authors can see your feedback on the title that they have worked with Packt to create. It will only take a few minutes of your time, but is valuable to other potential customers, our authors, and Packt. Thank you!

Index

X

Y

Made in the USA
Coppell, TX
03 December 2020